BLACK BOOMERANG

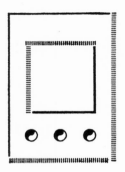

Black
Boomerang

SEFTON DELMER

The Viking Press · New York

44.583
February, 1963

Published in 1962 by The Viking Press, Inc.
625 Madison Avenue, New York 22, N.Y.

Library of Congress catalog card number: 62-17938
Printed in the U.S.A. by Vail-Ballou Press, Inc., Binghamton, N.Y.

*I dedicate this book to my fellow "black" men—
British, American, and German. May they enjoy this
account of our operation against our common enemy.*

Publisher's Foreword

It would be difficult to imagine a combination of circumstances better calculated to fit a man for an important task than that which preceded Sefton Delmer's appointment as director of Britain's "black radio" program during World War II. That operation not only contributed to the breakdown of German civilian and military morale, but it also helped to build up the myth of the good anti-Nazi Wehrmacht—a myth which has been used to cover the return to power in Germany of men who were the pillars of Hitler's Third Reich. That, at any rate, is Delmer's chagrined belief.

Born in Berlin in 1904, the son of an Australian father who was a lecturer in English and English literature at Berlin University, "Tom" Sefton Delmer (all his life he has been known to his friends and family as "Tom") learned to speak German almost before he could speak English, went to German schools, and took part in German life as naturally as the son of a Berliner of several generations.

As the debacle of 1914 approached, the elder Delmer, who was held by strong ties of friendship to his German colleagues, hesitated so long about making a decision to join the stream of French and British who were leaving the country that the outbreak of war found him and his family still in Berlin, where the Delmer family spent the following three years. During most of this period Tom's father was in an internment camp, for some time under suspicion of being a British spy.

Now the ten-year-old Tom had the unusual experience of being an enemy schoolboy at a German "gymnasium" called *Verräter* (traitor) when he showed pleasure at the news that the Australian cruiser *Sydney* had sunk the *Emden,* and forced to fight a larger boy (whom, incidentally, he whipped) as a result.

But what impressed itself on his memory even more deeply than his own difficulties was the strange pattern of conflict between the friendly concern and good sense of the Delmer family's friends, and the frenetic enthusiasm for the war and the sadistic hatred of the enemy expressed by the people as a whole.

There were, for instance, the Delmers' landlord, who materially reduced the rent when the elder Delmer was interned; the wealthy family who secretly diverted some of their food supplies to Tom and his mother while the populace raged against the treacherous British; and Dr. Lange, headmaster of Sefton's school, who in his private and public utterances seemed to exhibit the ambivalence which was a salient facet of the German character. In a private talk with Tom and his mother the benevolent doctor expressed his deepest sympathy and his conviction that neither the German nor the British people—nor for that matter, the British government—wanted the war.

Yet a week later, sitting in assembly at his school, the boy
listened in amazement while the same kindly, liberal Dr.
Lange delivered a tirade against the "wretched pedlar
people," the British, who had long plotted to encircle
"peace-loving" Germany, and now had started this war
in which they would be destroyed by the Fatherland fighting for the right.

So did the young Sefton Delmer during the impression-
able years of his childhood gain an intimate first-hand
acquaintance with the complex character of the German
people—the beginning of a deeper understanding which
was to serve him, his country, and the free world well in
the important assignment of which he writes in *Black
Boomerang*.

As he grew into manhood that acquaintance and understanding were furthered by almost constant contact with
between-the-wars Germany. With his father and mother
he left Germany for England in 1917. In 1921, when
Tom was still a schoolboy in England, the elder Delmer
returned to Berlin as a member of the Interallied Commission of Control, and the boy often visited him there.
Now he heard the pious German declaration *"Nie wieder
Krieg!"* ("Never again war!") mixed with declarations of
hatred against Poland—then in control of Posen, Upper
Silesia, and West Prussia—and eagerness to march against
the Poles, and he saw the inexorable rise of militaristic
chauvinism in Bavaria, the citadel of Germany's secret
and sometimes open nationalist and revanchist movement.

In 1927, after being graduated from Oxford, young Delmer joined his parents in Berlin as a teacher of English
and a free-lance correspondent for British newspapers.
The following year he was in charge of Beaverbrook's
Daily Express Berlin office.

Now he had a ringside seat from which to watch the accelerating march of German militarism, the subterfuges by which military training was carried on in open defiance of the peace treaty, the rise of the Nazi Party, the growing strength of Hitler, and the increasing manifestations of anti-Semitism. As the representative of an influential British newspaper Delmer had access to the leaders of the National Socialist Party, and became acquainted with Göring, Goebbels, Himmler, and Hitler. He well remembers his first meeting with Der Führer and Hitler's passionate declaration of friendship for England, and his assertion that the interests of Britain and Germany were similar, a sentiment he was to hear repeated often by Hitler as their acquaintance ripened.

On tour with Der Führer in the election campaign of 1932 the young British correspondent became acquainted at first hand with Hitler's alternating moods of deep depression and exaltation, his authoritarianism, his unwillingness to make awkward decisions, his almost hypnotic ability to sway audiences with his impassioned harangues, and the fanatic devotion and obedience which he inspired in his subordinates. In moments of depression Hitler sought knowledge from Delmer of the true attitude of the British toward the Nazi movement, probing deeply in an attempt to assuage his fears that England might be an enemy when he put into effect his plan for the conquest of Europe.

After the outbreak of World War II Delmer was a war correspondent in Europe until the fall of Paris. It is not surprising that the Germans, remembering his close association with the leaders of the Nazi Party, should have suspected that he was a British spy, or that the British, with the same knowledge and memory of his German background, should have suspected him of being a German agent. But with the British suspicion cleared away he was obviously the man to head Britain's "black radio" operation, producing programs broadcast from England, but purporting to originate in undercover stations within the Reich, operated by members of the "good" Wehrmacht, loyal Germans all, dedicated to the Fatherland but disturbed by the fanatical authoritarianism and corruption of the Nazi Party.

"It was a job," Delmer himself reports, "for which my whole life, from my first-war schooling in Berlin to my travels with Hitler and my work as a reporter around Europe had been the almost ideal preparation." *

How successful the operation was *Black Boomerang* reveals. Indeed, from one point of view, its influence lived beyond the war and has, contrary to all intention, played its dangerous part in the contemporary threat to world peace. His desire to counteract this influence is responsible for the present book. Here, as he himself writes, he is trying to banish from the new Germany "the legend of the good generals and the good Wehrmacht who were always against Hitler," by showing that it *is* a legend, a myth which he himself did so much to create and encourage by his skillful propaganda.

Thus he hopes to help counteract the influence in Germany of the men, now disguised as anti-Nazis, who actually sponsored Hitler and supported his evil ambitions for conquest.

---

* *Trail Sinister*, Vol. I of an autobiography. By Sefton Delmer. London, Secker and Warburg, 1961.

Author's Preface

I cannot conceive of a more appropriate spot from which to launch this American edition of *Black Boomerang* than Fort Bragg, the Special Warfare Center of the United States Army. Here I have spent the last few days meeting the world's most modern soldiers, picked men trained to be experts in guerrilla warfare and subversion against the enemies of the Free World.

It fills me with pride that they, the past masters of unconventional warfare, should have invited me to talk to them about some of the unconventional operations of the war against Hitler described in this book.

Among the many encouraging experiences and pieces of information that came my way during this visit to Fort Bragg and the Special Forces there is one in particular that fills me with confidence for the future. I know now that, should the present Cold War ever turn into a hot one, it will not be necessary—as it was for my wartime colleagues and me—to convert the military men to the usefulness of Psychological Warfare as an ancillary form of attack. Not only do the Special Forces trained here at Fort Bragg include Psychological Warfare Battalions equipped with the most up-to-date apparatus and staffed with skilled operators, but all their officers and men, from their commander, Major General William P. Yarborough, to the sergeants leading the guerrilla detachments in the field, are highly conscious of how the Sykewar units can help them and how they can help Sykewar. For those of us who had to struggle in the early days of World War II, without advice from the fighting services, without operational requests, without intelligence, this seems indeed the dawn of a new age in Psychological Warfare.

D. S. D.

Fort Bragg, North Carolina, U.S.A.
June 15, 1962

BLACK BOOMERANG

Some of the names of persons mentioned in this volume have been camouflaged, for reasons that will be obvious.

D. S. D.

This is Frankfort on the Main, November 1960. I am taking a look at the 9 P.M. performance in a little suburban cinema.

The seats are hard and uncomfortable. My knees are crammed painfully against the wall of what the woman in the ticket office calls the "box." From under the door cold gusts of mist blow into the hall.

Those two lovers clamped together in the corner of my "box." They are devouring each other with the cannibalistic salivation of mating frogs. And their moans!

But I stay on.

On the screen is a thriller drama about the last war. It

is all booming guns, marching steel helmets, Secret Service, and bombs. Yes, this is Frankfort, November 1960. And this, presumably, is what the German public wants—or what the film producers think it wants.

The German Wehrmacht, it seems, was fighting two enemies during the last war, the Allies and the Nazi Party. Brave young heroes from the Army, the Kriegsmarine, and the Luftwaffe are constantly shooting it out with the Gestapo and the S.S. It is just like listening to one of those speeches of old man Adenauer when he is talking about the Eichmann affair. The Germans were all against Hitler —all except a small Nazi minority. The rest were victims of Hitler and Himmler, just like the Jews and the Poles.

Aha! Here at last is what I have come to see. The hero, a young naval officer who had been denounced by his Nazi concierge to the Gestapo, has fled to Britain. And here now he is being led blindfolded up the broad steps of a lovely old Palladian country mansion—near London they say it is—to see the boss of the British Secret Service outfit who has invited him to come and help fight Hitler. The boss is a pot-bellied fellow with a beery-looking ginger moustache, lots of fluffy ginger hair, and protuberant hyperthyroid eyes. He is a terrible cynic. As he talks to the German hero—who is, of course an idealist, though a bitter and somewhat disillusioned one—the British boss contemptuously twirls a huge globe. He explains to the hero some of the dirty things that he will have to do now that he is irrevocably committed as a traitor.

The hero has met the boss before. He knew him as a British newspaper reporter in Berlin. The secret operation the boss is directing is the "German Soldiers' Radio Calais," *Soldatensender Calais,* which, as we have been told at the outset, was neither a soldiers' radio, nor German, nor situated in Calais, but a British counterfeit which had the unique purpose of causing confusion among the Germans and giving instructions to foreign Resistance groups.

The boss is a slick operator, and has his agents everywhere. During R.A.F. bombing raids dark-skinned, Oriental-looking creatures in raincoats pop up among the ruins of Essen, switch on secret transmitters, which they carry around in attaché cases, and flash him a quick signal reporting what has been hit. While a Nazi Party leader is having a knockdown quarrel with heroes of the Luftwaffe on an airfield near Paris, one of the French workers who are looking on breaks open a loaf of bread, takes a transmitter out of it, and taps out a quick message about the quarrel to the maestro.

The boss even has his men inside the Gestapo. And that is how he gets a chance to show that under that cynical surface a human heart is beating after all. (This picture, of course, is all in favour of "forgive and forget," "Anglo-German friendship," and "European unity.")

When he learns that during the impending evacuation of Paris the Gestapo and S.S. men mean to murder all their hostages, old pot-belly is terribly shocked. He calls for volunteers. Leading his rabble from the country mansion—our German Resistance hero in the vanguard—he parachutes into Paris and descends on the Gestapo jail, only to find that the good chaps of the Wehrmacht have had the same idea and got there first.

Tableau: The two parties stand facing each other with their guns. Among the good Germans of the Wehrmacht —they have freed the prisoners—is the hero's own brother, whom the wicked boss has been suborning the hero to kidnap. Now the fat British boss gives in and cheerfully lets the good anti-Nazi Germans of the Wehrmacht withdraw in their lorries under a white flag of truce.

By rights I should sue the producers for libel. That ludicrous last scene with me letting those Wehrmacht fellows get away in their lorries—I should have been court-martialled, if I had really done anything like that. Well, prosecuted anyhow. For I was the boss of the Soldatensender Calais.

The Soldatensender was a real-life operation, not a piece of German film fiction. I was the fat man in the mansion. And there are quite a few people in Germany, Britain, and America who know this, even though it is supposed to be an official secret.

I did, of course, have German anti-Nazis working with me, but they were not a miserable obsequious rabble like this lot in the picture. Wehrmacht men, too, were in my team. They were prisoners of war. But there was nothing going on like the nonsense that goes on in this film. Real life at the Soldatensender was remote from this uncouth fantasy.

But how ironic is this legend of the good upright patriotic Germans of the Wehrmacht being the bitter enemies of the Nazi Party and the Gestapo! How ironic that this legend should now be the justification for all those things I hoped would not happen—for the Germans forgetting that they were responsible for Hitler, for their re-armament, for the return of Hitler's judges and civil servants to key posts in the new Germany, and for the revival of German ambitions of territorial conquest. ("Restoration of Germany's lost territories" is what they call it today.) Ironic, because the propagation of that legend was the work of my unit and my men, of *Der Chef* and of the Soldaten-sender Calais. We bolstered and built up the legend to help in the overthrow of Hitler, and now, in this flourishing, rebuilt, reinvigorated Germany, it is being used to summon back his ghost.

Odd—I have seen myself tonight being played by an actor in what is called a screen drama. It should have been a flattering experience, a piece of massage for my ego, like getting my name into *Who's Who* for the first time, or being mentioned in a history book. But I feel no elation. For today this legend is dangerous, and the truth that it hides is so different, both about the war-time Germans, and about me, and about the Soldatensender.

The reader, if he has persistence, will see this for himself. But first I must tell the story of how I ever got to the point of having to do with secret things. For a long time I thought I never would.

The aged P. & O. liner *Madura,* which had picked us up in Bordeaux after the fall of France in June 1940, took five days to zig-zag home to England across the grey, U-boat-haunted Atlantic seas. On her decks camped the refugees. Indian Army colonels and their wives, scared out of their retreats on the Riviera, swapped escape stories with businessmen who had also been forced to flee. Long-legged girl dancers from the Paris night-spots bewailed the loss of their make-up kits to mannish, uniformed women from the volunteer welfare services. Brooding dis-approvingly over them all sat the original passengers of the *Madura,* bitterly resenting our intrusion.

"Disgusting rabble," said one matron from Mombasa as she stumbled over my feet.

In the deck chair next to mine—I had managed to obtain a pair of them in the first assault for my wife and myself—sat an elderly man with a wooden leg who talked of the rabbit-skin business and the felt factory he had left behind in France.

"How many skins a year do you think I used to buy? It ran into millions. Made them into felt in my own works and exported it to Britain—for the hat-making industry, you know. Never see my factory or my home again, I don't suppose. The Germans'll get it all."

Anna McLaren, a beautiful blue-eyed Irish girl from a volunteer Transport Corps called the S.S.A.—"Sans Sex Appeal" she said the letters meant—teased him with more and more questions about rabbits and hats. But I hardly listened to them. I listened to the talk of my war-correspondent colleagues. Throughout the five days they talked of little but how they were going to join the fighting services as soon as they landed. George Millar, the ablest writer of us all and the youngest, had a commission waiting for him in the Rifle Brigade. Geoffrey Cox, a bright and energetic little New Zealander, was going to join the New Zealand Army.

I envied them. For I had no plans to reveal. Sitting there on the deck in my nest of sleeping bags and luggage, I felt miserable and useless. What I had seen during those weeks that had followed the German breakthrough had made me fiercely determined to abandon my work as a reporter and get myself a job more directly connected with the conduct of the war than writing articles about it. But what was I going to do? At the age of thirty-six and with a weight of two hundred and forty-five pounds to drag around, I did not feel that I would be of much use as a soldier.

Of course, with my special qualifications and experience there ought to be something I could do in the field of intelligence work, if the powers that be would have me. Perhaps I could become a spy? After all, I did speak German like a German. Or I might be able to help in the interpretation and evaluation of intelligence. Surely there must be some job on the secret side of the war, in which my qualifications would come in useful. But would the mysterious "they" give me the chance to do a secret job?

Ever since the war had begun, I had been suggesting to those of my friends whom I knew to be connected with the Secret Departments that they should find me some work in which my experience would be of service. But, although my friends did their best to get me in, every time they were close to succeeding the shadow of suspicion had intervened to balk me. The very fact of my having been born in Berlin militated against me. My acquaintance with the Nazis was held to be not a qualification but a ground for distrust. Stool-pigeons had been sent to test me. I remembered how on my return to London from Poland in October 1939 a young stranger had contacted me and sounded me out on the best way of getting in touch with the Fascists. Colleagues had been instigated to watch and report on my "secret Nazi activities." Officers from the "spy-catcher" department, M.I.5, got into oh-so-casual conversation with me on leave trains, and tried to catch me out as a German agent.

The whole thing had been as idiotic and as wounding to my pride as the same suspicions had been to that of my father twenty-three years earlier, when he and we, his family, much to our and everyone else's surprise had been allowed to leave Germany and return to Britain in May 1917. But I welcomed the investigations, stupid as they were, because I believed that sooner or later I would be cleared, and that then I would at last be able to play the part for which I was fitted.

All through those five days on the Atlantic I had kept asking myself, was I clear now? Would "they" be ready to make use of me at last? Then, shortly after reaching England on a drizzly July afternoon in 1940, a message reached me in our flat in London's ancient Lincoln's Inn which suggested to me that the answer was going to be yes.

The message was from Duff Cooper, the new Minister of Information. Duff wanted me to help "improve" the B.B.C. German broadcasts, as he flatteringly put it, by doing one or two talks a week myself. "Don't drop your reporting for the *Daily Express*," he said. "That is valuable war work. But if you could fit in the occasional German broadcast on the B.B.C. we shall all be most grateful."

I could not have felt more exhilarated if I had been given a knighthood. Here at last, I believed, was a first auspicious raising of the barrier, even if it was only by an inch. I immediately rushed to the office to obtain the permission of Arthur Christiansen, my editor.

Chris, I think, must have guessed a bit of what it meant to me. He looked almost as pleased as I did. "Go ahead, Tom," he said. "It is a fine idea, I'll print some of your talks. Some of them may even be news."

And news they were, too, though not in the sense he or I had intended. For, without meaning to do so, I stumbled into the headlines with my very first talk. In my inexperience I got myself into trouble with the pacifist critics of Churchill in the House of Commons.

The German-speaking news commentators of the B.B.C., of whom I was now one, had worked out a rota for themselves. Lindley Frazer, the fuzzy-haired Aberdeen professor who had been a contemporary of mine at Oxford, spoke one day; R. H. S. Crossman, the future Socialist M.P., the next; F. A. Voigt, the former Berlin correspondent of the *Manchester Guardian*, the day after that; and so on. I was assigned the Friday-evening pitch. And on my very first Friday—I had never spoken on the radio before, not even in English, let alone in German—I had the task of replying to Hitler himself. For Hitler had chosen my first day—Friday July 19, 1940—to make his triumphal Reichstag oration in celebration of his victory over France. More important still, he had chosen it as the occasion for his "final peace appeal" to Britain.

"It almost causes me pain," I heard him piously intone as I listened in at the B.B.C. studio, "to think that I should have been selected by providence to deal the final blow to the edifice which these men have already set tottering. . . . Mr. Churchill ought for once to believe me, when I prophesy that a great empire will be destroyed which it was never my intention to destroy or even to harm. . . . In this hour I feel it my duty before my conscience to appeal once more to reason and common sense in Britain. . . . *I can see no reason why this war must go on!*"

Within an hour of Hitler's speech I was on the air with my reply. My colleagues at the B.B.C. had approved of what I meant to say, and that was enough authority for me.

"Herr Hitler," I said in my smoothest and most deferential German, "you have on occasion in the past consulted me as to the mood of the British public. So permit me to render your excellency this little service once again tonight. Let me tell you what we here in Britain think of this appeal of yours to what you are pleased to call our reason and common sense. *Herr Führer* and *Reichskanzler,* we hurl it right back at you, right in your evil-smelling teeth. . . ."

It was not diplomatic language or very elegant. But I reckoned a little earthy vulgarity in answer to the Führer's cant would be just the thing to shock my German listeners out of their complacency, especially as I then followed it up with some orthodox moralizing about British reason permitting no compromise with murder and aggression. I even ventured to make a prophecy. I told Hitler that though things might look quite bright for him at the moment, the tide would inevitably turn, and he, like the Kaiser before him, would find that he had been "conquering himself to death." It was a phrase I well remembered from my first-war school days in Berlin, and it soon became a stock slogan of the second-war B.B.C.

My quick reply to Hitler had resonant reverberations. Everywhere in the non-Hitler world newspapers printed long excerpts from it right alongside Hitler's speech. In Germany too it had its echo. William L. Shirer, who was in Berlin at the time, describes in his book *The Rise and Fall of the Third Reich* the consternation among the officials at the German radio when my broadcast came through:

I drove directly to the Rundfunk to make a broadcast report of [Hitler's] speech to the United States. I had hardly arrived at Broadcasting House when I picked up a B.B.C. broadcast in German from London. It was giving the British answer to Hitler already—within the hour. It was a determined No!

Junior Officers from the High Command and Officials from

various ministries were sitting around with rapt attention. Their faces fell. They could not believe their ears. "Can you make it out?" one of them shouted to me. He seemed dazed. "Can you understand those British fools?" he continued to bellow. "To turn down peace now? They're crazy!"

Mussolini's son-in-law Count Ciano was also in Berlin for the speech. He too describes the effect of the B.B.C. turn-down in his diary. "Late in the evening when the first British re-actions to the speech arrived," he wrote, "a sense of ill-concealed disappointment spread among the Germans."

This however, was exactly where I got in trouble. My off-the-cuff rejection—Churchill in his book *Their Finest Hour* says with characteristic understatement that this immediate and brusque rejection of Hitler's peace offer was made by the B.B.C. "without any prompting from H.M. Government"—aroused the anger of the Socialist pacifists, who would have liked to take it up.

But my most outspoken critic was certainly no pacifist. This was Richard Stokes, the Socialist M.P. for Ipswich. He now attacked me in the House of Commons for my presumption in turning Hitler down without first obtaining the authority of Parliament.

Bitterly Stokes demanded of the government how they had come to allow Sefton Delmer, "a person of no importance [flattering cries of "Oh!" from the Tory benches] to deliver an answer to Hitler less than two hours after the Chancellor had spoken.

"I think it entirely wrong," he said, "that a speech broadcast in Germany at six o'clock should not first have had better consideration from responsible people. Surely the responsible authority in this country to make a reply to a speech of that kind is the Prime Minister, or the Secretary of State for Foreign Affairs, if possible after consultation with this House."

Duff Cooper rallied to my support with all his suave authority. He assured the House that my talk had the Cabinet's full approval. And when the Foreign Secretary Lord Halifax replied to Hitler a couple of days after me, the sense of what he said was the same, although he used rather more restrained language.

But there was still another sequel to my unauthorized rejection of Hitler's offer. At least I like to think of it as a sequel. In these days of July 1940 the special commando of Himmler's Security Service, which was intended to take charge of occupied Britain in the wake of the Wehrmacht's invasion, was putting the finishing touches to a list of personalities who were to be immediately arrested and handed over to the Gestapo. The list—*Sonderfahndungsliste G.B.** was its official title—was among the many secret documents captured by the Allies in Germany in 1945. Number 33 on the list was a certain Sefton Delmer, Paris representative of the *Daily Express*. He was to be handed over, said the list, to Dept. IV B.4 of the Central Reich Security Office.

Maybe I would have been on that list in any case, for other well-known journalists were also included. But, as I have said, I like to think it was my maiden broadcast that put me there.

---

* The only copy of the list now in existence is in the possession of The Hoover Institution, Stanford University, California, which most obligingly let me have a photostat of page 42, on which number 33 appears.

3

On July 16, three days before his "peace offer," Hitler had given orders for the invasion of England to be prepared. The Battle of Britain was the result. I reported that battle in my new dual capacity as a war correspondent and a psychological warrior.

Between scanning the coast of France from the cliffs above Dover for the departure of Hitler's invasion armada, watching German fighters shoot down the harbour's barrage balloon "Sefton"—so named by the R.A.F. men because they claimed there was a resemblance between us—and chasing after downed German aircraft in the hope of interviewing the pilots, I raced back to London two or three times a week to talk for the German service of the B.B.C. Cheerful little talks they were, full of teasing and derision for the would-be invaders across the water, to show them that we in Britain were a long way from having our tails down. I watched our colliers and merchantmen as they struggled through the Channel being bombed and machine-gunned by the Luftwaffe and bombarded by the coastal batteries from France. I travelled with one convoy myself in order to experience the ordeal of these British merchant seamen and write about it. But contrary to all my expectations we sailed safely through the Channel and made our way from Gravesend to Portsmouth without the loss of a single ship. So I went on the air in the B.B.C. studio and did a little more teasing. I pretended to have a telephone conversation with my old friend Göring, told the story of my smooth and uneventful voyage, and taunted him with his inefficiency.

A few days later I followed this up by broadcasting an English lesson for would-be invaders.

"We English, as you know, are notoriously bad at languages," said I, talking my most impeccable German, "and so it will be best, meine Herren Engellandfahrer, if you learn a few useful English phrases before visiting us.

"For your first lesson we will take: *Die Kanalüberfahrt* . . . the Channel crossing, the Chan-nel cros-sing."

"Now just repeat after me: *Das Boot sinkt* . . . the boat is sinking, the boat is sink-ing."

"*Das Wasser ist kalt* . . . the water is cold. *Sehr kalt* . . . very cold."

"Now, I will give you a verb that should come in useful. Again please repeat after me: *Ich brenne* . . . I burn. *Du brennst* . . . you burn. *Er brennt* . . . he burns. *Wir brennen* . . . we burn. *Ihr brennt* . . . you are burning.

—Yes, meine Herren, in English, a rather practical language, we use the same word 'you' for both the singular and the plural—*Ihr brennt* . . . you are burning. *Sie brennen* . . . they burn. And if I may be allowed to suggest a phrase: *Der S.S. Sturmführer brennt auch ganz schön* . . . the S.S. captain is also burning quite nicely, the S.S. captain is al-so burn-ing quite nice-ly!"

Crude stuff, but excellent in one important respect. The line about burning in the Channel fitted in perfectly, as of course it was intended to, with the information which our deception services had planted on Admiral Canaris, the head of Hitler's espionage. Our rumour agencies, too, had been busy spreading it everywhere. The mean, murderous British, it said, had apparatus in readiness with which they were going to set the Channel and the beaches on fire whenever Hitler launched his boats.

This was a lie. But it went over so well that it is believed by many Germans to this day.

Leonard Ingrams was among the select few of my friends whom I knew to have something to do with the cloak-and-dagger side of the war, and he looked the part of the mysterious Mr. X to perfection. He was tall and athletic (he had won a Half-Blue at Oxford for the broad jump immediately after the first war), and his eyes and mouth had just the right expression of drawling sardonic pity for the world around him. Victoria, his wife, a member of the influential Baring family, was his devoted slave. So too were her brothers, and so for that matter was I. Leonard had been one of my special friends in Berlin, where he was known as "the flying banker" because of his habit of piloting himself around Europe in his private

Puss Moth plane on his business trips for the Chemical
Bank of New York.

Hitherto, he had ignored all my requests to be allowed
to do something more actively connected with the war
than reporting defeats and retreats for the *Daily Express*.
But now, at last, in September 1940, with the bombs
dropping all around us, Leonard was relenting. He had a
job for me.

"How would it be," he said, "if you resigned from the
Express and came in full-time on this racket of broadcasting to the Germans? It really is in urgent need of being
improved, and you have impressed everyone with these
talks of yours." He grinned and added, "The money, of
course, is bad. Nothing like as good as the *Express*."

It was like Leonard to end his invitation with a sneer
like that. But I told him that I would do anything he suggested, and I meant it. So Leonard got moving. Not with
the B.B.C., but with the Secret Department that "gave
advice" to the B.B.C. Leonard arranged for me to meet
Valentine Williams, the Secret Department's deputy director at Boodles. Valentine Williams, a former "golden-
haired boy" of Lord Northcliffe, was the successful author
of such novels of suspense as *Clubfoot*. Leonard saw to it
that ours was the most hush-hush meeting ever—just like
a scene from one of Valentine's own thrillers. Stealthily
the three of us crept upstairs to a card-room, assured ourselves that it was empty, and sat down in comfortable
chairs by the fire.

Valentine Williams was a neat, compact man with thick
black curly hair, a humorous crinkly red face, and laughing blue eyes. But there was no laughter in him now. He
lowered his voice almost to a whisper and started to ask

me questions. At the end of the questioning he said he would like me to join his outfit. I said I would be delighted, and I was. For I believed I was to enter the secret war at last.

"It will take a little time," Valentine whispered when I had filled in the forms. "You have to be vetted, you know. You must be patient. I'll let you know when it's all fixed."

I did not mind the melodrama. For I thought I was in at last. But I waited and waited, and nothing happened.

And then I learned from hints which Leonard gave me that, much to his and Valentine Williams' disgust, the Security people had turned me down once again.

The real irony of this Security bar against me was that while one branch of M.I.5 was telling Leonard Ingrams and his friends that it would be unwise to have me join the Psychological Warfare Department, a red-haired young Oxford man from another branch of the same service was inviting me to help him catch German spies who were masquerading as American reporters covering the Battle of Britain.

The red-haired young man called on me one morning at my flat and, with remarkably little preliminary skirmishing, revealed himself as an officer in Field Security. He asked me whether I would help him in his work. Needless to say, I assented with alacrity. As we lunched at Scott's and Christopher Catamole explained to me in greater detail what he wanted me to do, I once more thrilled to the hope that the real war was beginning to come my way after all.

"If you have to break the law while you are working

for us," he said, "do so without hesitation. We shall be behind you. If you are arrested, you will be released immediately. There will be no prosecution. All you have to do is to get the police to call this number, and ask for this extension. That will be enough." And he presented me with a card with two numbers on it. It sounded almost too romantic to be true.

But when I came to work on that first assignment, the whole thing petered out most prosaically. What little I did manage to discover did not fit in with any theory of espionage activities. That, however, did not upset "Kitkat" —a most scholarly young man he was, with an enviable first in Greats, and a praiseworthy thirst for the objective truth. He thanked me effusively for what I had done, and asked me to go on helping him.

When, at the end of October the *Express* ordered me to fly to Lisbon, Christopher Catamole asked me whether I would be prepared to lend his people a hand while I was there.

"Of course," he said, when I had accepted, "I don't know whether they will in fact require your services for anything. But if they should, they will contact you. There is nothing you need do about finding them."

The *Express* wanted me in Lisbon because Hitler and Franco had just met at Hendaye, and reports were coming through which spoke of German and Spanish preparations for an assault on Gibraltar. The *Express* wanted me to be on hand if it took place.

My expedition provided little in the way of headlines for the *Express*, for Hitler abandoned his Gibraltar project just as he had previously abandoned the invasion of Britain. Nevertheless, looking back on them now, I see the weeks I spent in Lisbon as one of the most important assignments of my life—in the first place because it finally persuaded the Security men to lift the barrier against me, and secondly because it gave me a fresh and intimate contact with German Jews who, in return for a fat payment to the S.D. or the Gestapo, had been allowed to bypass the gas chambers of Auschwitz, and go instead to Lisbon in order, later, to join relatives in North or South America. My Lisbon refresher course in German affairs proved of vital importance to me when, a few months later, I began to forge the new weapon of psychological warfare which twenty years later was to become the subject of that German thriller film.

With two friends whom I had engaged to help me—one of them, amazingly, was Albrecht Ernst, a German left-wing journalist whom I had first met during the Spanish civil war, when he was the deputy chief of staff of the Communist General Kleber in besieged Madrid—I surreptitiously contacted the Jews as they arrived, and questioned them about life in Germany.

Not all of them were old and decrepit by any means. A surprisingly large number were young and strong, and many had been working in German armaments factories. From them I picked up a great deal of interesting information and colourful gossip, all of which I carefully noted down, meaning to use it for a series of articles on "Inside Germany."

I learned the names and foibles of the foremen, engineers, and Nazi Party officials in the munition workshops where the refugees had been working. I learned what they had been manufacturing, and I also learned many of the new German war-time expressions. But above all I got the feel of life in Hitler's war-time Reich.

Before very long Christopher Catamole's "friends" had contacted me, and I began to pass them useful titbits garnered from the refugees. My Lisbon Secret Service boss was quite enthusiastic about this new source of information about Germany. And I was frankly amazed, myself, that the Gestapo should have allowed men and women to go abroad who could give so much information about such important electronic firms as Askania and Lorenz, to mention but two of them.

4

I was just beginning to build an interesting new contact with an Italian Travel Agency, which regularly sent couriers across Hitler-occupied Europe to Spain and Portugal, when a telegram arrived for me from Leonard Ingrams.

"Suggest you return earliest possible, and resign from *Express*," it said. "Important job awaits you."

This time it was no false alarm. The Security officials had been persuaded at last to waive their objection to me. Presumably my brief employment by S.I.S. (the Secret Intelligence Service) had done the trick.

Within ten days of receiving the cable, I had flown back to London, obtained my release from the *Express,* and was proudly riding around London in a huge black Rolls Royce with the magic letters O.H.M.S. ("On His Majesty's Service") on the windscreen. And I was rather proud too, of the fact that I had signed up with my new bosses for a salary which was less than a third of what I had been earning as a newspaper reporter.

Not that there was any real need for this financial sacrifice. I could have been much better off during the four years of my absence from Fleet Street that now began, had it not been for my lack of tact and my almost idolatrous respect for official regulations. It prompted me into one of the most absurd gaffes of my life.

Full of curiosity about my new work and my new surroundings, I had been driven down to the secret "Country Headquarters" in a vast Daimler, which, apart from myself, contained a German-Jewish woman economist from the Bank of England, a goatee-bearded Harrow schoolmaster who was the expert on Spain, a portrait painter in R.A.F. uniform, and a couple of girl typists. Not even once the car was on its way would any of them tell me where "C.H.Q.," as they called it, was situated. That was a secret, they said. But at last we drove into the village of Woburn and turned right, and a few minutes later I found myself at the gates of Woburn Abbey, the centuries-old residence of the Dukes of Bedford.

A police sergeant came to the door of the car and inspected our passes. "I am afraid you'll have to get out, Mr. Delmer, sir," he said politely. "You'll have to come into the guard house to sign the Official Secrets Act. Everyone has to the first time."

So out I got and inspected an imposing document setting out the regulations of the Official Secrets Act. I read it carefully and noted that one of its solemn provisions

laid down that I would disclose to no one, but absolutely
no one, what I was being paid by the department or anything else about the financial affairs of the organization—
which of course was financed out of the secret vote. Then
I signed a declaration that I had duly taken it all in and
realized the appalling penalties I would incur if I committed a breech of security.

"Aha!" I said to myself. "Now I understand why they
would not tell me where we were going, even though they
knew I was bound to find out ninety minutes later." I was
deeply impressed. And that was the origin of my gaffe.
For hardly had I been taken across to Dick Crossman's
little office in a long, much-partitioned hall, which in time
of peace was the ducal riding school, when a breathless
messenger burst in on Dick and me.

"Mr. Delmer, you are wanted on the telephone, sir," he
panted.

"I'll take the call in here," I said.

"You can't, sir," said the messenger. "It is Lord Beaverbrook who wants you, and the call is on the green line.
You'll have to take it in the box."

I had no idea what the green line could be, other than
a bus service. "Some sort of a special ministerial telephone, I expect," I said to myself, as I ran through the
long corridors with my guide. When as last I got to the
telephone, there waiting for me was the deep rasping
voice that had ruled my destiny for the last fourteen years
of my life.

"Tom" said the Minister of Aircraft Production in Winston Churchill's government, "how are you getting on?
How are they treating you?"

"I am only just settling in, sir," I replied, "but I hope
to do all right."

"What are they paying you?"

Into my mind flashed the Official Secrets Act and its penalties, also the exceptional discretion of my companions in the car. Without a moment's further thought I replied as stiffly to Lord Beaverbrook as they had to me. "I am afraid, sir," I said, "that is something I am not allowed to disclose."

From the other end of the green line came an exclamation of gurgling anger and disgust. "Ugh," said Lord Beaverbrook to this young puppy whom he had trained and who was now biting the hand that had been about to feed him. "In my position I can know any man's salary. Good-bye to you, Tom!" and he hung up.

I never heard another word from him until the war was over.

Lord Beaverbrook, however, so much resented what he regarded as my "patronizing arrogance" that he told the story of my outrageous reply not just once but, as I learned many years later, at least a score of times. Beaverbrook had not only been on the point of making up my salary to its former total for the duration of the war, he had also been about to make me a present of some shares in the *Express*.

But much as I regretted missing this bonus, what I regretted even more, when I learned of this background to the boss's call, was that I should have seemed ungrateful and impertinent to a man for whom I have always had affection and respect.

As I rode around in the car with the "O.H.M.S." on its windscreen in those early days, I always hoped that one of my Fleet Street friends would see me and say, "That fellow Delmer must be doing something terribly important. Look at that enormous car!" Very soon, however, the glamour of the car wore off, and the cold truth was borne in on me that I had no real job and no real work.

I had a small office to myself in a hush-hush building in a cul-de-sac off Berkeley Square. It contained a couple of very hard chairs, an unvarnished deal table, an In-tray and an Out-tray, a filing cabinet, and a set of official stationery, all impressively marked "W. D. Box 100. London S.W.1." But except for the "Daily Digest" with exerpts from the press of the "Enemy, Satellite, and Occupied Countries" my trays were empty. And apart from writing and delivering two or three talks every week for the German service of the B.B.C.—unlike the other British speakers, I wrote mine in German, not in English—and attending a planning committee or two at Woburn Abbey, I seemed to have no work, and certainly no importance. In my disgruntlement, I even began to think of returning to Lisbon. I had an invitation to do so from my friends at the Admiralty. My Lisbon S.I.S. boss too had been clamouring for me to come back.

Admiral John Godfrey, the Director of Naval Intelligence, had got to the point of asking for my transfer to his staff, when at last I was offered a real job by my psychological-warfare bosses. Leonard Ingrams did the offering. This truly brilliant man combined a key job in the Ministry of Economic Warfare with another in the cloak-and dagger organization S.O.2, later renamed S.O.E. (Special Operations Executive), which was responsible for the organization of resistance, sabotage, assassination, and kindred enterprises. He had yet a third job in S.O.1, as my department was called. In truth, he was a star operative on the British side of the secret war of wits, and I had the greatest admiration for him.

"How would you like to run a new R.U., Tom?" said Leonard.

"What's an R.U.?" I asked.

"A Research Unit—didn't you know?"

"No, I didn't. What do they research?"

Leonard looked at me with mock astonishment. "I had no idea our security was as good as all that," he said. "Do you mean to say you have been with us now for the best part of eight weeks and you've still not found out what a Research Unit is? A fine reporter you are!"

Somewhat huffily I retorted that I did not now consider myself to be a reporter, ferreting out secrets, but was concerning myself strictly with my own business. "And if you want me to take charge of any research work, for heaven's sake cut the mystery and tell me what it's all about!"

Leonard laughed. R.U.'s, he explained, had nothing to do with research. "R.U." was simply the cover name our organization used for its Freedom Radios, the units broadcasting from England on the special transmitters of the department and pretending that they were doing so from somewhere inside Hitler-occupied Europe.

"We used to have two German R.U.'s," said Leonard, "one was a right-wing station operated by a former Reichstag deputy of Brüning's Centre Party, who is living over here now as an émigré. But that folded up when the old boy fell ill, and now we have only the left-wing station. It is operated by a group of German Marxists, and calls itself *Sender der Europäischen Revolution* [Radio of the European Revolution]. It appeals to workers to shake off the Fascist yoke, and all that stuff, and preaches a doctrine of European Community, good will, and Marxism. Your friend Dick Crossman takes a sort of benevolent interest in it. But in point of fact the Germans are left to operate it on their own. Not really a terribly good idea."

Dick Crossman and his wife, I learned, presided over the secret house in which the "European revolutionaries" lived and worked. Dick sat in on some of the team's conferences, gave them general advice, and passed them odd bits of intelligence. But the team—most of them members of a left-wing group called *Neubeginn*—resented any kind of British editorial interference.

"We now want to start up a new right-wing R.U.," Leonard said, "and I have suggested that you take charge of it with full editorial and political control. The Germans under you would say and do what you tell them to say and do. No more nonsense about freedom and independence. What do you think of that?"

"I think it sounds fine."

"Well, think it over. Then shove down on paper a plan for your R.U. One thing, by the way, you should state is that you will work in close conjunction with S.O.2 and fit in with their operational plans wherever required. That will enable me to give you a little protection from our woolly-minded Socialist colleagues, should they start shooting at you. And in any case, there are ways in which your R.U. can help S.O.2. You'll learn about that in due course."

Tory Leonard Ingrams was bitterly suspicious of Socialist Dick Crossman, who had recently become director of the German section of our department, and he feared—groundlessly, as it turned out—that Dick would try to squash any attempt by me to introduce a fresh approach and fresh ideas.

"Oh, and one other small point," Leonard added in the offhand throwaway manner he always adopted when he thought something particularly important or particularly funny. "You know the Germans have recently launched a British left-wing Freedom Radio. 'The Workers' Challenge' they call it. Old ladies in Eastbourne and Torquay are listening to it avidly, because it is using the foulest language ever. They enjoy counting the F's and the B's. Well, my Minister * thinks we should reply in kind, and, as he is a Socialist, he thinks a right-wing station would be the appropriate one to carry the filth."

"That's okay by me," I laughed. "If he wants crusty, trenchant language, he shall have it. I shall make a special study of barrack-room German."

"Go to it then, Tom. And let me have your paper as soon as you can. It is a great chance for you to show your ingenuity. There are no limits. No holds are barred."

---

* The late Lord Dalton, at that time Dr. Hugh Dalton.

That was the beginning of the trail which was to see the building up of a powerful new weapon of psychological warfare, the legend of which I would find reverberating in Germany long after the war was over.

But as I sat down in my austere little office to think out a scheme for the new R.U., I was without any sense of this. What I did feel was that the German service of the B.B.C., as it was being put over at this time, had got itself into a groove, and a bad and unprofitable groove at that. The German news bulletins, edited by my colleague Hugh Carleton Greene, the former Berlin correspondent of the *Daily Telegraph*, were right enough. They were straightforward and—with some lapses owing to carelessness or credulity—accurate. But the talks were terrible. They sounded like émigrés talking to émigrés or, as I used to say at the time, like Maida Vale calling Hampstead, not like London calling Berlin. They were addressed not to the mass of Germans who supported Hitler and his war of aggression but to the infinitesimal few who wanted to lose it. To the ordinary German they were bound to sound like arid enemy propaganda and would be dismissed as such.

I had therefore been urging that the B.B.C. at this stage of the war should go all out to build up its reputation in Germany as a reliable source of news; that it should concentrate on well and clearly written news bulletins, on talks containing information rather than views, and interpretation of information rather than comment. Argument, I suggested, should be kept to a minimum and appeals eliminated altogether. But it was useless. The B.B.C. went on just as before. An analysis of the B.B.C. talks in German between October 26, 1941, and December 6, 1941, shows that "ideological humanitarian appeal" constituted twenty-one per cent of the output, "argument" took up thirty-two per cent, twelve per cent of the talks assumed a friendly audience of anti-Nazi pacifists, and thirty-five per cent looked forward to "revolution or active opposition."

In my view, all this was a waste of breath and electric power. The Germans, I was convinced, would begin to listen and react to that sort of thing only when they had realized that the war was lost and that it was better for them to abandon Hitler than to fight on. To stimulate the Germans into thoughts and actions hostile to Hitler before this stage had been reached, they would have to be tricked. Trickery and deception, however, were tasks which lay outside what it was possible or desirable for the B.B.C. to undertake. A new weapon of psychological warfare was needed for this purpose. Perhaps the new R.U., I thought, could make a first experimental probing in this direction, in much the same way as the commando raids being carried out at that time against the coast of Norway and France seemed to be a probing experiment with a new technique of amphibious assault. In analogy to "black magic," "black mass," and "black market," my friends and I called this new psychological attack "black propaganda."

There had, of course, been "black propaganda" and "black radio" broadcasts against Hitler before this. In the early years of the Third Reich I had sometimes listened to the "secret transmitter" which the ex-Nazi Rudolf Formis operated from the garret of an inn at Zahori in Czechoslovakia—until on the night of January 23, 1935, a squad of S.S. men crossed the nearby frontier and shot Formis down.

Then, in the autumn of 1939, I had heard another "freedom radio." It was operated for the French government from a transmitter just outside Paris by Willy Münzenberg, the Communist propaganda genius who had so brilliantly faked the legend that the Nazis had lit the Reichstag fire. Münzenberg himself had let me into the secret of his "freedom station" one evening as we dined together in a private room at the La Perouse restaurant in Paris.

The Formis station, like Münzenberg's "freedom radio," Neubeginn's "European revolution," and the other British station which had closed down, had one thing in common. They were straightforward opposition radios, appealing to the German people to rise against Hitler, denouncing the war, vaunting the strength of the allies, and generally behaving like an enemy propaganda broadcast, except that where the B.B.C. said "you Germans" they said "we Germans." As I thought about the station I was to run, I decided that a new approach was needed.

"I think we should try out a new type of 'black radio' on the Germans," I suggested to Leonard, when I went to talk things over with him again, "one that undermines Hitler, not by opposing him, but by pretending to be all for him and his war."

The idea obviously appealed to Leonard. He asked me to elaborate. I told him that with a super-patriotic platform for the new station we ought to be able to get across all manner of subversive rumour stories under a cover of nationalist patriotic clichés. I told him that Hitler had once said to me, "There is an inner pigdog in every man." "We must appeal to the 'inner pigdog' inside every German in the name of his highest patriotic ideals," I said. "Give him a patriotic reason for doing what he would like to do from self-interest, talk to him about his Führer and his Fatherland and all that sort of thing, and at the same time inject some item of news into his mind which would make him think, and if possible act, in a way that is contrary to the efficient conduct of Hitler's war." We would have to be told, of course, I added, what our people at the top actually wanted the Germans to do.

"I think you are on the right lines, all right," said Leonard. "Get that paper written. And don't forget to include my little slogan among your campaigns."

"Which one?"

"You can't bomb a currency," Leonard intoned like a priest chanting the credo, "but you can destroy it with whispers."

A few days later I put up my paper. Rex Leeper * the top boss of my department, minuted it: "A novel and promising idea. Please go ahead with all speed."

Dick Crossman also approved.

Such was the basic formula for this first "black radio" I was now designing, and by and large this psychological judo which exploited the impetus of the enemy's own ideological preaching to turn it against him was to remain the prescription for almost all our German "black radio" campaigns that followed.

One other break with tradition I planned for this new unit: the broadcasts should not sound as though they were addressed to the public. I remembered the way I had sometimes found myself listening to the salty conversations of ships' captains talking over the radio telephone at sea. I would try to make the German listener believe that he was eavesdropping in much the same way on radio talk not intended for his ears. As he twiddled the knobs on his set, he would suddenly find himself tuned in to what sounded like the signals traffic of a clandestine military organization sending ciphered instructions to its secret cells all over occupied Europe. In between the cipher messages a die-hard of the old Prussian school would use the transmitter to give the members of the organization his caustic and salaciously outspoken views of what was going on—views which, while being spiced with plenty of inside information, would show him as loyal and devoted to the Führer, but scathingly contemptuous of the "rabble" that had seized

---

* Sir Reginald Leeper, G.B.E., later Ambassador to Greece, later still to the Argentine, today Director of De Beers Consolidated Mines, Ltd., and Chairman of its London committees.

control of the Fatherland in the Führer's name. The station in fact would seek to be a nightly demonstration of a growing split between the conservative elements of the Army and the radicals of the Nazi Party.

To add a special touch of irony, I decided that the nameless leader should be introduced as *Der Chef*—the chief. For this was the title by which I had heard the members of his immediate entourage refer to Hitler as I travelled around Germany with him during 1932 and 1933. The station itself we would call *Gustav Siegfried Eins*—signallers' German for our "George Sugar One"— and leave it to the listener to decide what these cabalistic initials signified. Did they mean *Geheimsender 1* (Secret Transmitter 1), or *Generalstab 1* (General Staff 1), or perhaps, as Leonard Ingrams suggested, *Gurkensalat 1* (Cucumber Salad 1)? I had no idea, nor did anyone else. But we were soon to hear the most intriguing theories being reported back to us from Germany and elsewhere abroad.

Gustav Siegfried Eins went on the air for the first time on the evening of May 23, 1941. It was a rough and by no means ready performance, this first one, for Der Chef had to appear without an adjutant to announce him—an appalling solecism under the social protocol of the Third Reich, where even the lesser dignitaries of the Party and the Armed Services never ventured forth without having at least one aide-de-camp in attendance. Nor had I been able yet to coach Der Chef out of a bad habit of dropping his voice monotonously at the end of each sentence.

But there was no avoiding it. The Pioneer Corps Corporal who was to play the part of Der Chef was the only member of my team to have arrived so far at the discreet red-bricked house in the little Bedfordshire village of Aspley Guise, which had been assigned to serve as the top-secret home for me and my team. Der Chef's adjutant was not yet through his security check, and we could not wait for him any longer. It was urgent we get on with the job, whether he was there or not.

It was urgent because only twelve days earlier the impossible had become accomplished fact: Hitler's deputy, the faithful Rudolf Hess, had parachuted into Scotland and presented Britain's political warriors with a priceless opportunity for causing confusion among our enemies. And in those twelve days it had become clear that Der Chef must get in on the act. For to the amazed chagrin of Dick Crossman and the rest of us, Winston Churchill was giving the B.B.C. no opportunity to exploit it. No information was being passed to the propagandists beyond the bald announcement that Hess had arrived and had been made prisoner. Worse than that, the B.B.C. and the *Luftpost*, a news sheet dropped on the Germans by the R.A.F., were asked to abstain from all speculation and comment. It was almost as though Churchill feared that, if the facts about Hess's "peace mission" leaked to the British public, there would be a rush by Britain's phantom "Peace Party" to unseat him, and avail themselves of Hess's services.

Der Chef, however, was not subject to the restrictions of truthfulness and obedience to policy imposed on the B.B.C. If he had no facts, he could invent them. So it was up to him to get going and do his little bit to exploit the situation. It could in any case only be a very little bit. For in its first broadcasts a "black radio" can only have the tiniest of audiences, operating as it does on a short-wave frequency, enjoying no preparatory publicity, and relying exclusively on the few chance knob-twiddlers who may happen to tune in on it at the right moment.

Punctually at half past two in the afternoon of May 23, 1941, a small black limousine drove up the larch-hedged gravel drive to our villa. A khaki-uniformed girl driver saluted smartly, and Der Chef, still in his Pioneer Corps battle dress, climbed in, followed by me. Twenty minutes later we stepped out again in what looked like a London stockbroker's more than comfortable country retreat. Rhododendron bushes, spreading chestnuts, and a few venerable monkey-puzzle trees hid a lawn from which came the click of croquet mallets.

"You're sure this is the right place?" I asked the driver. And I was even more puzzled when I went inside. For there, confronting my astonished eyes, were a shiny mahogany table with books and a vase of cut flowers, a large settee and easy chairs, an elegant staircase leading to what would be the bedroom stories, and a grand piano, with a fresh and pretty blonde tinkling something that sounded like Mozart's "*Eine kleine Nachtmusik.*" Nothing suggested that this was a recording studio of the Secret Service.

"I was just about to apologize and retreat when the blonde got up from the piano and came towards us.

"G.3?" she inquired brightly, announcing our unit's code number, as she gave us the medicated smile of a dentist's receptionist. "We have everything ready for you, if you will follow me." And forthwith she led the two of us into a billiard room. The billiard table, however, was shrouded in dust covers, and the windows were shuttered and curtained. Three chromium-plated R.C.A. microphones twinkled at us invitingly under a strip of ultra-modern fluorescent lights. One microphone was suspended from the ceiling, a second topped an adjustable stand, and the third stood on a very business-like desk with two chairs in front of it.

"Let me adjust this so that you are comfortable," said the blonde, more like a dentist's receptionist than ever. "Are you going to be sitting or standing?"

Later, when Gustav Siegfried Eins and Der Chef had won a large audience in Germany, all kinds of theories were spread by word of mouth as to his identity and the location of his transmitter. One, mentioned in his reminiscences by Paul Schmidt,* Hitler's Foreign Office interpreter, was that Der Chef operated from a barge on the river Spree. Another was that he kept on the move through Hitler's Europe, dodging from hideout to hideout. All theories coincided in assigning primitive and extremely uncomfortable quarters to Der Chef and his intrepid signals unit. Had his listeners been able to take a peep at the surroundings in which his messages were, in fact, recorded, our audience would, I am sure have shrunk to zero.

Der Chef, in that first broadcast, began very soberly by announcing his call sign and then dictating some code signals.

"Here is Gustav Siegfried Eins. Here is Gustav Siegfried Eins," he repeated monotonously for about forty-five seconds. And then, "Calling Gustav Siegfried Achtzehn, here is a message for Gustav Siegfried Achtzehn. . . . Calling Gustav Siegfried Achtzehn, a message for

* Dr. Paul Schmidt, *Der Statist auf der Gallerie*, Bonn, 1951. Schmidt says G.S.1 was the "cleverest propaganda from the British side." From his description of G.S.1, however, I think he has muddled it with Soldatensender Calais, which came later.

Gustav Siegfried Achtzehn. . . ." There followed a message in a number code. It was not a high-grade cipher,
and, when broken and decoded by the monitors of the
Reich Central Security Office, as it was bound to be, I
reckoned it would produce quite an acceptable flurry in
the Gestapo dovecotes all over Germany. For the message
said, "Willy meet Jochen Friday row five parquet stalls
second performance Union Theatre." There were hundreds of Union Theatre cinemas all over Germany, and I
fondly imagined leather-coated Gestapo thugs attending
everyone of them on the look-out for "Willy" and "Jochen."
For the Gestapo with their radio-detection instruments
would be quick to fix our signal as coming from Britain.
They could not ignore the possibility that Willy and
Jochen were British agents, and that the message to them
was genuine.

Then, at last, code dictation done, it was time for Der
Chef to launch into his special address. He was answering
queries, he said, which had followed his last message. (Of
course there had been no previous transmission, but I
thought it a good idea for him to talk as if there had been
several, in order to cause trouble for the German Security
monitors. They would be accused of having missed them.)
In that message, so Der Chef let it be understood, he had
warned that this obscenity of a dilettante deputy Führer
(Hess) was about to do something idiotic and he had ordered his comrades to lie low because of the witch-hunt
which was bound to result from the fellow's folly. He had
been off the air himself for a few days as a consequence.
But now the coast was reasonably clear again and he
could answer the queries.

"First, let's get this straight," rasped Der Chef. "This
fellow is by no means the worst of the lot. He was a

good comrade of ours in the days of the Free Corps. But like the rest of this clique of cranks, megalomaniacs, string-pullers and parlour Bolsheviks who call themselves our leaders, he simply has no nerves for a crisis. As soon as he learns a little of the darker side of the developments that lie ahead, what happens? He loses his head completely, packs himself a satchel full of hormone pills and a white flag, and flies off to throw himself and us on the mercy of that flat-footed bastard of a drunken old Jew Churchill. And he overlooks completely that he is the bearer of the Reich's most precious secrets, all of which the obscenity British will now suck out of him as easily as if he was a bottle of Berlin White-Beer."

Dramatic pause.

"I must, however, deny one thing that some of the lick-spittles in the Führer headquarters are putting around," Der Chef went on. "Namely, that the fellow flew to Britain under orders of the Führer. That I am convinced is quite out of the question. The Führer would never have authorized a man with such an intimate knowledge of our operational plans to go into enemy country. And that is proved, too, by the drastic way the Führer is dealing with those who have, by their negligence, permitted this grave blow against the future of our fatherland to be struck—namely the security snoops, who if they had been anywhere near as good as they say they are, would have stopped the poor idiot in time. Unfortunately, however, that supreme obscenity of a Reich Security Chief, to get himself out of the mess, has seen fit to arrest a number of men—leaders of industry, leaders of the *Abwehr*—true German patriots, all of them, men of the deepest national devotion and Fatherland-loyalty, men whose one fault was that they misjudged the nerve strength of this so-called deputy leader and placed before him, in the last days of April, the grave misgivings which, owing to the hedge of liars and sycophants that surrounds him, they had been unable to place before the Führer himself."

There followed a list of alleged arrestees. The amazing thing is, that though we invented them all, several of the men we said had been arrested actually had been detained on suspicion of having been initiates of Hess's schemes, as it turned out later.

A certain Dr. Jahncke, for instance. I remembered having heard of him as the top espionage expert in Hess's office. So we put him on the list. And to my great pleasure, when I visited Germany after the war I learned that Der Chef had not misled his listeners. Nor did I have the slightest idea that when I got Der Chef to talk of "a grave crisis" and "dangerous developments ahead" Germany was in fact on the verge of the most dangerous development since 1939—Hitler's invasion of Russia.

Der Chef finished his transmission with an undramatic "That is all for now. I shall be repeating this—all being well—every hour at seven minutes to the full hour. *Immer sieben Minuten vor voll!*"

As I listened to the playback—the whole performance had been recorded—the bit I liked best was the denunciation of Churchill as a "flat-footed bastard of a drunken old Jew." Here, with one phrase, which cost no one any broken bones, we had won credibility as a genuinely German station. No member of the great German public, I felt convinced, would suspect that British propagandists could be capable of using such outrageous language about their beloved Prime Minister. This was a phrase, I decided, which was well worth repeating in other broadcasts.

The corporal and I were just being ushered out of the house when one of the recording engineers, a long, lanky man in tweeds, with spectacled eyes and wavy locks, leaned over the banisters and hailed me.

"Don't you think, Mr. Delmer, that G.3 should have a signature tune?" he asked. "Makes it easier for the listeners to tune in, you know. I should be delighted to fix you up with one—anything you like."

I thought for a moment. "A signature tune is not really in character with an army signals station, is it?" I said. "But you are right, it will help our listeners. And that is what we are after—listeners."

So there and then I got my new musician friend—Jim Dougherty was his name—to sit down at his piano and record for us the answering phrase to the call-sign of Hitler's own Deutschlandsender. This German equivalent of the B.B.C. used the first few bars of a pleasant little eighteenth-century folk song by Ludwig Hölty, as it was played on the carillon of the Potsdam garrison chapel.

> "*Üb immer Treu und Redlichkeit* . . .
> Always practise troth and probity . . ."

tinkled the Deutschlandsender. And now Gustav Siegfried Eins replied with the second line played on what sounded wonderfully like a cracked piano stationed in some primitive front-line billet:

> "*Bis an dein kühles Grab.* . . .
> Until your cool, cool grave. . . ."

It remained Der Chef's signature tune until he broke off in mid-transmission one evening eighteen months later, caught by the Gestapo at last!

Who was Der Chef, and how did he come to join me?

Corporal Paul Sanders was a Berliner of about my own age who had earned his living as a writer of detective stories. In 1938, sickened by the outrages against the Jews, he had turned his back on Germany and come to Britain. On the outbreak of war he immediately enlisted in the Pioneer Corps and was sent to France. When I first met him in April 1941 he was in a London bomb-disposal squad, risking his life day after day to dig out the Luftwaffe's time-bombs and remove their fuses. Not content with this hazardous job, he had volunteered to be parachuted behind the German lines in one of the cloak-and-dagger commandos of S.O.2. That was how Leonard Ingrams had come across him, and Leonard passed him on to me. I liked him enormously, this man with the sallow face, watchful observant eyes, and aristocratic hawk nose. His voice seemed to me just right for Der Chef as I envisaged him, virile and resonant with that slight trace of a Berlin drawl which I had found so often in the speech of Junker officers of the Kaiser's guards regiments.

The second man, Johannes Reinholz, was a German journalist. He was a genuine German Conservative who had fled to Britain with his Jewish wife only at the last moment in 1939—just before the war broke out. Reinholz had worked with the right-wing opposition to Hitler first under the leadership of Walter Stennes, then, after Stennes had escaped to China, under such doughty old Pomeranian Junker antagonists of Hitler as von Oldenburg-Januschau and von Rohr-Demmin.

I was much relieved when the Security people at last allowed Reinholz to join me, for the Corporal had not been able to get the hang of what I wanted, and in those earliest days I was having to write most of Der Chef's talks myself. Now Johannes Reinholz took on that task, and very well he performed it. He also played the part of the aide-de-camp in the broadcasts, dictating the code messages and introducing Der Chef. His metallic baritone and his clipped accents, pregnant with generations of heel-clicking, goose-stepping, command-barking Pomeranian forebears, gave just the right military tone to the station. And when he announced, *"Es spricht der Chef . . . The Chief speaks . . ."* I could almost see Hitler himself walking gravely and stiffly up to the microphone in the small interval the Corporal allowed to elapse before, solemn and deep-voiced, he went into his act.

The advent of Reinholz worked wonders in the Corporal. Now at last he began to get the knack of how to handle his voice at the microphone. With every transmission he was growing more and more into the role of Der Chef. One day he asked me whether he could alter the script to suit his way of talking. I immediately agreed. His alterations were superb. Those salty, vividly impudent Berlinese phrases I had hoped for after my first conversations with him at last began to blossom forth in all sorts of unexpected places. Soon the Corporal asked me whether he might write a piece on his own. He did, and it was a masterpiece, caustic, witty, even moving. I now had two good writers.

But what G.3 did not have was intelligence material with which to give body to our campaign of subversion by rumour. In those earliest experimental months we had to live off our own knowledge and our own imagination. As Goebbels would have said, we were "sucking the news out of our fingers." Fortunately we had the stories and personalities I had brought back with me from my inter-

rogation of Jewish refugees in Lisbon with which to give
flesh, colour, and background to our inventions. Around
the foremen, engineers, and Nazi Party pepmen from my
Lisbon notebook we were able to build up some convincing inside stories. Reinholz was able to clothe any inci-
dents we liked to locate in Pomerania with details of old
von Rohr and his cronies at Demmin. And Max Braun, the
Socialist leader who had led the anti-Hitler front in the
Saar, was able to help us a great deal from his own Socialist intelligence contacts in Europe and his remarkably
acute reading and interpretation of German newspapers.
Max was the third man to join my team.

When I had first met Max Braun seven years earlier in
the Saar at the time of the plebiscite I had thought him a
pathetic and rather ridiculous figure, as he stood on the
platform at the "status quo" rallies, his dumpy potbellied
figure swathed in a grass-green Socialist version of the
Nazi brown-shirt uniform. But over the four years that we
worked together during the war, I got to know him not
only as a brilliant intelligence expert but as a most upright and sincere German patriot. It is one of Germany's
tragedies that Max Braun died in April 1945, just when
the war was won and his country needed his services
most. I believe that had Max Braun been able to influence
the decisions of the German Socialist Party after the war
we would not have seen that party become the ineffective
unrealistic bunch of sterile office-seekers whose weakness
has caused Germany to be left without a competent opposition to the illusionist eastern policies of Chancellor
Adenauer.

I have given Max Braun's real name because his true
identity was never secret. It was disclosed the morning
after his arrival. Foolishly I had given him the cover name

"Albert Simon" through ignorance of the old rule that cover names should, whenever possible, preserve the initials of the true name. Sure enough, the very first morning, before I could intercept him, Max came down to breakfast in a beautiful silk dressing-gown with the initials M.B. embroidered on the breast pocket. Reinholz, who already the previous evening thought he had recognized the newcomer from his newspaper pictures, now did a "Dr. Livingstone, I presume?" "Simon" confessed and the secret was out. I learned the lesson.

And when at my request my friends from Spain's International Brigade, Albrecht Ernst and Alexander Maass, were contacted by Leonard's cloak-and-dagger friends and brought over to Britain to join me from Lisbon and French North Africa respectively, I was most careful to see that their new initials were identical with their old ones.

7

What baffled me about the Hess episode was the astonishing reluctance of our authorities to handle his case with the realism and practicality the British normally show when faced with an opportunity of this kind. We behaved as though Hess were some dangerous Trojan Horse planted in our midst, a booby trap which might explode in our faces at any moment. Not only were the political-warfare agencies prevented from exploiting Hess as they could have and as Hitler feared we would, but even the Intelligence people failed to apply to the interrogation of "Captain Horn," as he first called himself, the ingenuity which they applied so successfully to their other prisoners.

Let no one say that there was nothing we could have got out of Hess. Even though his deputy Bormann had latterly been taking over much of his work, Hess was still a member of the special Defence Council, a trusted confident of the Führer, and the repository of much valuable political, economic, and strategic information. We could have made great use of what he knew for psychological-warfare operations, even if it had been of no immediate military usefulness.

The deception experts also could have used him in confusing the German High Command and Germany's allies. But from the very beginning the handling of Hess was amateurish—as was made clear to me very soon. For within less than three hours after Hess's landing became known in Whitehall I myself was involved in this deplorable masquerade.

On Sunday, May 12, 1940, the Corporal and I were in our red-brick villa rehearsing for Der Chef's debut when Valentine Williams telephoned me the astounding news and asked me to come over right away and see him in his office at the Abbey.

"Cadogan," * he said, "wants someone who knows Hess personally to go up to Scotland to identify and question him. We must be ready to start at once."

"Who's we?" I asked.

"Oh, I am going with you," said Valentine. "Hurry! Rush!"

But when I got to the Abbey, Valentine told me the mission was off. The Foreign Office had managed to get hold of Ivone Kirkpatrick,† and he was going instead. I

* Sir Alexander Cadogan, Permanent Undersecretary of State at the Foreign Office.

† Later Sir Ivone Kirkpatrick, G.C.B., Permanent Undersecretary of State at the Foreign Office.

was both disappointed and relieved—relieved because I had not thought it very bright of Whitehall to send me, whom Hess knew not as an official but as a journalist. What was more, he would remember me as the voice that had turned down Hitler's peace offer of the year before. I feared that even Kirkpatrick was not the ideal emissary. For, though as first secretary at the British Embassy from 1933 to 1938 he had occasionally met Hess at diplomatic functions and Hess would probably remember him, he was not nearly exalted enough in rank to satisfy Rudolf Hess's parvenu hunger for an interlocutor of high influence and social position. I was already convinced that it would be necessary to flatter Hess if we wanted to get anything out of him.

But this abortive mission to Scotland was not to be the end of my involvement with the handling of Hess. Two days after the trip to Scotland was cancelled, Valentine once more called me over to his office in the Abbey and put forward the suggestion that we should produce a bit of home news for Hess, which would make him feel so bitter against Adolf that he "would let his hair down at last."

I demurred a bit. "Odd sort of chap, Hess." I said. "It might take quite a bit to shock him. I cannot really see him talking to us just because his friend Adolf is being beastly to him. Flattery is the way to the heart of the Nazis, I've always found. Make him think we take him terrifically seriously. But best of all would be to give him a shot or two of a truth drug."

"Can't use drugs," said Valentine, who had been a Guards officer in the first war. "That's not done. Not in this country!" He glared at me, a friendly little glare, as much as to say, "None of your continental ruthlessness.

here, my lad!" "No," he continued, "I have an idea that might do the trick." And he proceeded to outline it to me.

Valentine's war-winner was that we should print a counterfeit page of Hitler's official newspaper, the *Völkischer Beobachter*. It would be an exact replica of a genuine page taken from the most recent *V.B.* to come into our possession since Hess's arrival. Except for one item. This item—to be written by me in the best *V.B.* style—was to contain news that would upset Hess and bring him over to us. The counterfeit page would then be inserted in the otherwise genuine *V.B.* and would be presented to Hess with his breakfast at the first opportunity.

"I suggest," said Valentine, "that you work out something on the lines that Frau Ilse Hess and her son have been shut up in a concentration camp."

I saw difficulties ahead of us. Did we have the right newsprint for the job, and the right type, and the right rotary press? However, who was I to worry about that? I had said my say. So I sat down and worked out two drafts for Valentine. Neither, I regret to say, was a masterpiece. But I like to think they were at least written in true German police-reporter journalese.

"The Chief State Attorney announces," said the first, "that Frau Ilse Hess, after prolonged and thorough interrogation by himself and Kommissar Dr. Braschwitz of the Political Police has made a complete confession. Frau Hess confirms that she smuggled nerve drugs, believed to be of British origin, into her husband's food. These drugs made Party Comrade Hess subjective to the hypnotic influence of British-inspired German traitors and produced the mental fog in which he flew to England.* Frau Hess

* For the *Völkischer Beobachter*, Scotland was part of England.

has been transferred to Munich for confrontation with the adjutants of Party Comrade Hess and other members of this sinister ring who are now in secure custody."

For good measure, I added a second item which I suggested might be inserted in the counterfeit of a local Munich newspaper, if we had one available for copying. The item, tucked away in an insignificant corner, would report the arrest of two women and a man who had caused a street disturbance on the evening of Sunday, May 12, by trying to interfere with the police as they were arresting a woman and her small boy at a villa in Harlaching. Harlaching was the suburb of Munich where Hess resided with his wife and son.

Valentine was delighted. Alas, as I had feared, when it came to printing the items, we suddenly discovered that the resources of the department were not equal to the job. Nor was the S.O.1 file of German personalities able to give me the name of a police official for the Munich district who would have been more suitable for the job of interviewing Frau Hess than my old Berlin antagonist Dr. Braschwitz. I made a mental note of these deficiencies and determined to remedy them for the future at least as far as our "black" work was concerned. A register of personalities high and low and founts of all the current German types, as well as a supply of German-made paper, were going to be essentials if we were to have any success in deceiving the Germans into accepting our products. And before many months had passed I had succeeded in laying the foundations for all these things.

But on this day of May 16, 1941, we had to confess defeat. Ultimately the item was printed in English in a London newspaper, Hess being quite up to reading English newspapers. Several hundred copies had to be rolled off the rotary press in a top-secret special edition in order to get the one copy wanted for Hess. The rest were destroyed instantly.

In due course the newspaper was served up to Hess with his breakfast. The effect? Not what we had hoped. All that happened was that Hess accepted the bit about the British having drugs which made their victims subject to suggestion. From now on he refused to eat or drink anything unless he had seen someone else taste it first.

My first "black" operation had viciously backfired.

In my view, to break Hess down an indispensable preliminary would have been to flatter him by going through the motions of negotiating with him, preferably through a top-level "plenipotentiary."

Churchill did indeed make one effort to play Hess along in this way. He sent a genuine cabinet minister to see him in the rambling Victorian country house near Aldershot called Mytchett Place, to which Hess had been moved in the meantime. Alas, the colleague whom he dispatched on this mission—on June 10, 1941, exactly a month after Hess had taken off from Augsburg—was that frigid, inhibited lawyer Lord Simon. I cannot conceive of a worse choice. For, brilliant as Lord Simon undoubtedly was in the cross-examination of witnesses, this was not the talent called for in dealing with Rudolf Hess at this stage. What was needed was a man of warmth, authority, and charm, who could prepare him for the Intelligence men.

The ludicrous fiasco that resulted from Simon's meeting with Hess could have been foreseen. Lord Simon (he spoke English, while Hess, interpreted by a Dr. Maass, spoke German) began promisingly enough by informing Hess that he was "able to receive his mission with government authority." Hess, pleased and flattered, launched eagerly into a long and well-argued account of the motives that had brought him to Britain. There was no trace in his intelligent and lucid exposé of the "amnesia" or "schizophrenia" and "paranoia" which later protected him from all further interrogation.

He had flown to Britain, Hess declared, in order to cut with one brave blow the tangle of inter-governmental red tape and prestige-consciousness which was keeping two Nordic brother peoples at war with each other. He wanted to make known to Britain the essential moderation of Hitler's peace terms for Britain, as he had learned them in the course of many conversations with the Führer.

Lord Simon listened with admirable courtesy and patience, called Hess *Herr Reichsminister*, was beautifully suave, but also—alas—ruthlessly and unnecessarily disillusioning. Item by item, he led Hess through the implications of his proposal that Europe should be a German sphere of interest in which Britain would have no say.

With every question from the Lord Chancellor, Hess became more and more tied up, more and more hostile and defiant. He was reduced to making threats. If we did not accept the terms he offered now, he said, the terms we would be compelled to accept, when we were defeated and brought to our knees, would be much worse.

As Hess blustered, Lord Simon completely forgot his Intelligence mission and fell more and more into the role of the heroic British statesman refusing to capitulate before a tyrannical enemy.

"I don't think your argument will be very good for the British cabinet," he said with smug understatement and an hauteur which would have been magnificent had he been faced with a victorious Hitler in Berlin instead of the defenceless prisoner Rudolf Hess in well-guarded Mytchett Place.

"You know," added Simon in his high, prissy voice, "there is a good deal of courage in this country, and we are not very fond of threats."

All this, of course, could have been grand stuff had the whole conversation been recorded on disks (tapes did not exist in Britain in those days) to be broadcast to Europe and to Hitler by the B.B.C. But no one had thought of this. And, even had it been suggested, I have no doubt the proposal would have been ruled out. As it was, the only effect of Simon's visit was that, when he and Kirkpatrick had left, Hess collapsed in despair. His plans, his hopes of glory, all had crashed about him. He determined to kill himself. And, indeed five days later, on June 15, 1941, dressed once more in his pale blue uniform of a Luftwaffe captain, he plunged dramatically over the banisters from the landing outside his rooms into the basement three floors below.

Poor Hess. He made a mess of this, too. Instead of leaping head first, he went feet first. So he did not kill himself, but merely smashed his pelvis and broke a leg.

But for the interrogators that was the finish.

There was one minister in Churchill's cabinet who could have cast a spell over Hess. Had Lord Beaverbrook been given the job of softening him up, he would in two or at most three interviews have laid all the psychological foundation the Intelligence men needed. Regrettably, Lord Beaverbrook, who at that time was Minister of Supply, did not see Hess until September 9, 1941, and then the two of them talked only for one hour. But even this short talk put Hess into a mood which clever interrogators could have exploited.

Beaverbrook had several advantages over Hess's other interlocutors, including Ivone Kirkpatrick. The greatest of them was that he was one of the men Hess had hoped to see and talk with when he flew off from Augsburg. For Hess had read many German diplomatic reports describing Beaverbrook as opposed to the war, as indeed he had been.

In neutral Switzerland, the Aga Khan had told Ribbentrop's amateur agent, Prince Max Hohenlohe, that Lord Beaverbrook was all for peace and compromise with Hitler. "Beaverbrook," so the Prince in a letter to the German Foreign Office on July 25, 1940 quoted the Aga Khan as saying, "is the only man who has the courage, the power, and the standing to bring about a change in England even against Churchill, since Churchill has for a long time been in Beaverbrook's pay." *

Another advantage Beaverbrook possessed was that Hess had met him a number of times before the war and had no difficulty in remembering his talks with him. Beaverbrook had paid several visits to Berlin between 1935 and 1939 and on each occasion he had talked at length with Hitler and Hess. They were talks in which Hitler, sometimes in the presence of Hess, had gone out of his way to impress his British visitor with his essential reasonableness and good sense—not without some success, as was shown by Beaverbrook's refusal to believe in 1939 that Hitler could be so foolish as to forgo the immense gains that avoidance of war would certainly have brought him.

Hess and Beaverbrook had already been exchanging

* *Documents on German Foreign Policy,* Series D, Vol. X, No. 228.

letters concerning the German invasion of Soviet Russia, when on September 5 Hess was informed that Lord Beaverbrook would be coming to call on him at Mytchett Place four days later.

I do not know whether what followed did so because Hess was still suffering from his sharp rebuff at the hands of Lord Simon. The fact, however, is that the prospect of meeting the man whom he had regarded as his most influential ally in Britain now filled Hess with nervousness and apprehension.

"He became moody and irritable and particularly sensitive to noises," reports Captain Johnston, the army doctor who had been put in charge of Hess at Mytchett Place. Hess began to complain of pains in his stomach, he gripped the beam supporting his broken leg, pulled himself up off the bed, and demanded morphine. Finally, he sent for the Foreign Office representative and said he was too ill to see Lord Beaverbrook.

Lord Beaverbrook did not let himself be put off by this. Dressed, as ever, in his sober blue serge suit, he walked into Hess's sick room, flung his soft black hat on a table, and advanced towards Hess with the outstretched hand and wide cheery smile of an old friend. It was the very opposite of the frozen formality of Lord Simon.

In no time, they were talking, not as wary negotiators, but as the cabinet ministers of two governments with conflicting views, each of whom was anxious to hear the other's opinions. Soviet Russia was the subject of their talk, as it had been of their letters.

Hess now stated that the object of his flight to Scotland had been to make peace with Britain "on any terms," providing that Britain would then join Germany in attacking Russia. It was an odd statement for him to make in view of the fact that he had not mentioned the coming attack on Russia with so much as a word when he had his talk with Lord Simon. And to Kirkpatrick he had denied point-blank that Hitler meant to attack Russia. Nor had the terms he put down in writing at the time of his talk with Simon suggested Germany's readiness for peace with Britain "at any price."

But Lord Beaverbrook, unlike Lord Simon, did not hold him up with argument or quibbling. He wanted to hear what Hess had to say. And he heard plenty. Hess's main theme was that the British were wrong if they hoped that the conflict with the Soviet Union would so weaken both Russia and Germany that at the end of it Britain's nineteenth-century hegemony over Europe would be restored.

He told Beaverbrook that a victory for England as the ally of the Russians, would be a victory for the Bolsheviks and sooner or later would mean Russian occupation of Germany and the rest of Europe. England, he said, would be just as incapable of preventing this as any other nation. Hess was apparently convinced that the Soviet Union of the future would dominate the world if its power was not quickly destroyed.

That prophecy, of course, was part of the propaganda theme which the Germans had begun to broadcast to the world as soon as Hitler's troops began their march into Russia—the theme of Germany's God-given mission to defend the civilized world against the Bolshevik East. I am sure that Beaverbrook was no more impressed by the argument when it came from Hess in 1941 than he has been more recently when it was used by Chancellor Adenauer to justify German re-armament. But he did not crush Hess with a haughty "It's no use talking that way to us." He listened to him with every show of sympathy and encouraged him to believe he had a potential convert before him. When the meeting was over, Hess was a changed man. Grinning cheerfully, he told Captain Johnston that he had enjoyed the conversation, and felt very much better now.

I say that if Beaverbrook had given Hess just one more dose of this treatment he would have had him in a state where this valuable prisoner would have been ready to talk—particularly so when the news of the German failure before Moscow began to penetrate his thinking. But there was no second dose. The Intelligence men made no special effort to exploit the euphoria induced in Hess by his hour with the Minister of Supply. He was allowed to shut himself off once more in the pose of apathy which was ultimately to degenerate into a permanent mental derangement. A great opportunity in the war of wits had been bungled.

Thursday, June 6, 1941, was a fresh, sunny day in the little village of Aspley Guise, and despite the bad news from Crete I was feeling good. For on my personal front of the war, things were beginning to look up.

Johannes Reinholz had joined the Gustav Siegfried team the previous day with his wife, and his very first script had shown that he was going to be able to write the kind of thing I wanted Der Chef to put over. A second point of satisfaction: Dick Crossman had asked me to take on a new assignment with the B.B.C. Together with him, I was to listen to Goebbels' star broadcaster Hans Fritzsche doing his weekly pep-talk for the German public over Radio Berlin. Then, an hour and a half later, I was to tear Fritzsche to pieces with a reply over the German service of the B.B.C.

"If we pull this off," Dick had said, "it will help enormously to build our audience. Millions of Germans listen to Fritzsche. If you do your stuff right, Tom, they'll all be wanting to hear you make him look silly."

As I have said, I had no great belief in the dry and dreary business of debating with the Nazis over the ether, an exercise of which the B.B.C. with its flock of would-be M.P.'s was over-fond. But this particular idea seemed different. It oozed human interest and listener appeal. The first clash with Fritzsche was booked for that evening, and I was looking forward to it. But just as I was about to get into the car which was to take me up to London the telephone rang. Leonard Ingrams was calling me.

"Why haven't you come over to the Abbey?" he asked. "Don't you know you are wanted at an important conference here?"

I told him no one had informed me, and that I was about to leave for London.

"You can get up to London later," said Leonard. "You simply have to be in on this thing. All the top brass will be there, and you may have to do some talking."

The stately ballroom of the Dukes of Bedford was already crowded when I got there. Sitting at long conference tables was the motley of university dons, advertising men, diplomats, motor salesmen, journalists, and officers from the Services that made up the top team of Britain's psychological warfare.

At a high table sat Lord Vansittart, Valentine Williams, Leonard Ingrams, Dr. Hugh Dalton, and some others whom I had not met before. Behind Dalton hovered a diffident, self-effacing young man carrying the Minister's brief case—his principal private secretary, Hugh Gaitskell.

Presiding in the Chair was the Department's own special boss, Rex Leeper, tall and spare, with the thoughtful, concentrated face of some old-time papal secretary. I had known Leeper before the war, for he had been the Foreign Office press chief. I admired Rex as one of the subtlest political brains I had met in the department, and my admiration was to increase as the war went on.

Rex had a flat, deliberately unemotional voice, guaranteed to make the most sensational announcement sound commonplace. But even he could not rob what he had to say now of its drama.

"Gentlemen," he said, when the last official had shuffled to his seat and lit his pipe, "I have obtained permission from the Prime Minister to reveal to you a piece of secret information which has been known to Mr. Churchill and the Chiefs of Staff for several weeks, but has until now been denied any wider circulation. He has authorized me to impart it to you—and to you only—in order that we may concert as early as possible our plans for the situation which we shall be facing shortly. Briefly, the information is that Hitler and his Wehrmacht are about to attack Soviet Russia. German armies have been secretly assembling on what I suppose will soon be called the Eastern Front. The actual invasion is expected to take place around the middle of June. The estimate of the Joint Intelligence Committee at their meeting yesterday was that June twenty-second is the most likely date.[*] You will all

[*] Churchill in the light of agents' reports had decided as early as the end of March that Hitler was going to attack Russia. The Joint Intelligence Committee, however, discounted these reports. While the Chiefs of Staff

agree, I am sure, that we should start planning now how best we should exploit this situation in both the overt field of political warfare and the covert. I will now call upon the heads of the regions for their suggestions."

This conference seemed to me a somewhat cumbrous method of planning, and indeed, not very long after, my journalist colleague Ritchie Calder was appointed head of a specially created Directorate of Plans which removed the necessity for over-large and over-long meetings of this kind. But here we were now, faced with several hours of verbiage. As the talk went on and on without anything but the obvious being said, my mind drifted off to other fields of speculation.

Into my daydreams broke the throaty, almost adenoidal voice of Rex Leeper. "And now, Mr. Delmer," he was saying, "will you please tell us what line that interesting character Der Chef is going to take?"

I felt nervous as I got up to speak. Oratory is one of the many accomplishments with which I am not endowed. "Der Chef, sir," I said, "is all for Hitler and this new war of his against the Bolsheviks. Der Chef will applaud and support the Führer's decision."

Lord Vansittart, sitting next to Leeper, roared with laughter, and barked, "Bravo, Delmer! Excellent!" But the rest of my colleagues knew nothing of Gustav Siegfried Eins. They stared at me in horrified incredulity.

"Der Chef, will insist that the Führer combine his anti-Bolshevik crusade against Soviet Russia with a cleaning-up campaign against the Bolsheviks at home—the Bolsheviks that is, of the National Socialist German Workers Party. He calls them *Die Parteikommune,* an interesting hybrid

decided on May 31 that an attack was imminent, the J.I.C. did not concede it until June 5.

made up of *Partei*, meaning the Nazi Party, and *Kommune*, the word by which the Nazis themselves used to refer to the Communists. Der Chef has collected a great deal of astonishing material about the Parteikommune which he will bring to the attention of the Führer."

Now they all laughed. Der Chef had at least provided the comic relief of the meeting. I travelled to London that afternoon for my first appointment with Fritzsche feeling a new elation and confidence.

The war against Russia was the making of Der Chef. He now became an entirely plausible figure. As he ranted against the Russian Bolsheviks in Moscow and the Party Bolsheviks at home, I felt that I might be listening to old Ludendorff. When things began to go wrong, Der Chef blamed all mishaps on the Party. He did not actually use the word *Dolchstoss* or refer openly to "the stab in the back," the favourite alibi of German generals, and, of course, he never used the word "Nazis," which would have smacked of propaganda talk. But with each new, carefully detailed story he told of the scandalous private and public life of the Parteikommune officials the moral was there: "While our brave soldiers are freezing to death in Russia because of the corruption of this Parteikommune crowd, who delayed getting the army's winter clothing ready in time because they were out for a bigger profit, these same traitorous swine are having a wonderful time feathering their nests in soft-job billets far from danger and privation." The Party was to blame, the Wehrmacht were the good men, the decent Germans, the true patriots.

I made the Nazi Party functionaries the number-one target of our attack because, in my opinion, the fanatical and dedicated officials of Hitler's organization were doing an amazingly effective job as the driving force behind the war effort of the German people. I was immensely impressed by the way Goebbels and his underlings, high and low, were succeeding in cheering and goading the Germans to ever greater efforts and ever greater sacrifices. If we could blacken these men in the eyes of the German public as a venal and slothful "privilegentsia" which demanded everything from the common man but made no sacrifices itself, we would have struck a mortal blow at a vital nerve of Germany's war morale. Not only that—we would be giving the ordinary German a splendid excuse for any falling short in his own devotion to duty: "Why should I put up with this," he would be able to say to himself, "when those party swine can get out of it all?"

Der Chef told how party highups used their inside knowledge to secure privileges for themselves at the expense of Germany's war economy. But when doing so, he was always at great pains to reveal exactly how the Nazi bigshot had done his foul deed, in the hope that listeners would follow his dastardly recipe themselves. This was what Leonard Ingrams called "operational propaganda" —propaganda which made people do things. And sometimes it worked.

In one of his transmissions, for instance, Der Chef denounced by name the wives of a number of high Party officials in the Schleswig-Holstein area who, he said, had rushed to the clothing stores (also named) and bought up all the woollen goods and textiles to which they were entitled by their clothing coupons. Why? Because these traitorous whores had learned from their obscenity husbands that the Fatherland's supplies of textiles were running out, owing to the needs of the army in Russia, and that any folk-comrade who did not cash his clothing coupons now would not be able to buy anything at all a little later.

Sure enough, about six weeks later, when I was looking through a Kiel newspaper which had been published shortly after Der Chef's philippic, there it was—the report of a run on the clothing stores. And to my great satisfaction, the editor made things worse by reiterating our most effective argument. "If everyone behaves like this," he wrote, "there will be nothing left for anyone, and the clothing coupons will be valueless."

We never attacked internationally known big shots such as Göring, Goebbels, and Himmler. They were the routine targets of all enemy propaganda. To give ourselves greater authenticity as a German station we went for the lesser-known local dictators.

Our stories were peopled with Burgomasters, District leaders, Local Group leaders, and even Cell leaders, with whose goings-on, both private and public, Der Chef showed an astonishingly intimate acquaintance. We spread over them a slime of obloquy as foul as that which they themselves had spread over the Jews. Not even the sexual extravagances of those who came under Der Chef's microscope were safe from his detailed and truly evangelistic denunciation.

In fact, to equip our heroes and heroines with the appropriate fetishisms and perversions—beloved of German audiences—I had to do a considerable amount of research in the works of that great authority on sexual aberrations, Dr. Magnus Hirschfeld. I believe Dr. Hirschfeld, had he been able to hear Der Chef, would have felt that the burning of his books by the Nazis had been avenged at least in part. And, of course, these outspoken and unabashed diatribes added enormously to the listener appeal of the station.

But Gustav Siegfried Eins was doing far more than that. With every broadcast a new legend was being drummed home: the Army is against the Party, the Army is against the S.S., the Army is against the Gestapo. . . . It was the legend that was to be our platform, the notional justification of most of our "black" operations. And, alas, in the years after the war it was to prove a most dangerous boomerang.

In the earliest weeks of Gustav Siegfried's activities the stories with which Der Chef spiced his homilies were entirely fictitious. For some of them the ideas and the material came to us from the special Rumour Committee. This was a small body of experts from the various services and the Ministry of Economic Warfare who met in conclave once a fortnight and compiled a short list of rumours which secret agents were to put around for German consumption in such centres as Lisbon, Zurich, Stockholm, and Istanbul. Around the nucleus of one of the committee's rumours which I had selected from the list—the rumours were called "sibs" from the Latin *sibillare*—to whisper—we built up a detailed and colourful story.

Most of our sibs, however, and the stories to go with them, we concocted ourselves. And, unlike other writers of fiction, we took great pains that the *dramatis personae* figuring in them should whenever possible be genuine living persons, employed or residing at the addresses Der Chef gave them. Also that they should be persons who, as far as rank and calling went, fitted the role ascribed to them.

How did we get these names and addresses? Out of the German newspapers and magazines. Even before Max Braun had joined us, while I was having to act as my own intelligence expert and archivist, I had begun a file of personalities, high and low. I collected them from the news columns of the German newspapers, from the announcements of births, deaths, and marriages, from the small advertisements. If I required an engine driver living in the district of Kassel, or a grocer's shop in Berlin's Hansa district, my files could provide them.

Often, too, newspaper articles provided the inspiration for a Gustav Siegfried story—as, for instance, when I read a feature article in one of Dr. Goebbels' periodicals which praised the blood-transfusion units of the Nazi medical service and obligingly singled out for special mention, by name, certain meritorious doctors and nurses.

"I think you might have a go at these folk-comrades," I said to the Corporal, handing him the magazine. "They have been guilty of criminal carelessness. As you no doubt know, they have been collecting most of their blood from Polish and Russian prisoners. And they have been treating these Polish and Russian blood donors just as though they were good, clean Germans. Believe it or not, they have been taking their blood without first giving the fellows a Wassermann test. One of our splendid old army doctors—Simon [i.e., Max Braun] will give you a name and a hospital—grew suspicious when some of our brave wounded, who had received transfusions, developed unpleasant symptoms. He made a random Wassermann test of the blood sent to his hospital and found that twelve per cent gave a positive reaction. Our army doctor immediately notified the Parteikommune scum—these fellows in the magazine—and suggested they destroy their stocks. And what do you think they had the gall to answer? 'Venereal diseases,' they said, 'are not transferable by blood transfusion, and there is no point in doing a Wassermann or destroying existing stocks.' And so these traitors, to cover up their negligence, are not only refusing to notify the units to whom they have sent the infected blood, but are continuing to send out more from the same sources, so that more and more infected Slav blood is being pumped into the men who have given their own clean German blood for the Fatherland. How do you like that, Corporal?"

The Corporal liked it very much, and the next evening Der Chef broadcast the harrowing tale.

It was not long, however, before I began to build up a supply of intelligence from sources other than newspapers which helped us to provide a more and more suitable background for our rumour stories.

One invaluable source of the kind of intelligence essential to our work were the monitoring reports made at the prisoner-of-war cages. These recorded verbatim the highly interesting conversations between newly captured German prisoners of war. The prisoners, unaware that the walls of their quarters, and even the trees in the garden, contained hidden microphones, freely revealed the favourite grouses of the German servicemen and many titbits of gossip that came in useful. They also gave us many new slang expressions that had come into use since the war, and enabled us to bring Der Chef's soldier language up to date. I found too, that abbreviations such as "Teno" for *Technische Nothiffe*—i.e., Technical Emergency Service, employed for repairing air raid damage and so forth

—gave a particularly authentic inside-Germany sound to Der Chef's oratory. And I therefore made a special collection of them.

At first I only saw these monitoring reports occasionally. Valentine Williams had them, and when he did let me see them I had to read them in his office at the Abbey. But soon I succeeded in laying hands on my own contraband supply, smuggled to me by Colonel A. R. Rawlinson, the Deputy Director of the interrogation cages, who realized their importance to our operations.

Another source was the letters intercepted by the postal censorship on their way from Germany to neutral America—North, Central, and South. They were an inexhaustible mine of material. There was Genevra Wolff-Limper, for instance, the young American-born wife of a Cologne industrialist, who wrote splendid gossip-rich letters to her girl friend Mrs. Ruth Stradling, somewhere in Nevada. Genevra Wolff-Limper and her husband moved in the exalted circles of Cologne's young Nazi burgomaster, Herr Winkelkämpner, and Gauleiter Grohé. As she was full of ingenuous wonder at all that was going on around her, and described everyone she met and the parties at which she met them in beautifully naïve "gentlemen prefer blondes" detail, Der Chef was able to fake up some most convincing stories about what we denounced as the sybaritic life of the Cologne Parteikommune and their goings-on.

I can well imagine the fury and anguish of party comrade Winkelkämpner as he listened to Der Chef describing the magnificent sugar cake baked in the shape of Cologne Cathedral with which Herr Winkelkämpner regaled his guests at a party just after the sugar ration had been drastically cut for ordinary folk-comrades. He must have wondered who the traitor was. But I am sure that neither he nor the Gestapo ever guessed her identity. For "black propaganda," whether it was Gustav Siegfried or one of our later ventures, never used a piece of intelligence straight. We always "improved" it so that its source became unidentifiable.

When, for instance, I learned that Dino Alfieri, Mussolini's Ambassador to Berlin, was shortly returning to Rome for consultations, Der Chef did not announce this as news, as the B.B.C. or Reuters would have done. He did not say, "It is learned that Signor Alfieri is shortly returning to Rome for consultations. In diplomatic circles it is believed that the probable purpose of his journey is to discuss, etc. . . ." Gustav Siegfried's task was to exploit this piece of intelligence, not merely to communicate it. And Der Chef's reaction was to demand Alfieri's recall. So that when this favourite of Ribbentrop's did, in fact, leave Berlin a few days after Der Chef's broadcast, his journey was seen as proof of Gustav Siegfried's allegations.

The Alfieri broadcast was one of Der Chef's best, and it is still reverberating today. For his story was accepted as the truth. It even crept into diplomatic dispatches, and thence into Ciano's Diary.

In justification of his demand that Alfieri must go, Der Chef recounted how a German officer (full name and rank stated), had come home unexpectedly on leave from the East Front. In his Berlin flat (street and house number stated) the officer discovered his wife *in flagrante delicto* with the Ambassador. The Kamerad, reported Der Chef, drew his service revolver and would have shot the Ambassador there and then, had not this cringing coward of a macaroni gone down on his knees and pleaded diplomatic immunity. So, instead of shooting him, the Kamerad had beaten up the spineless creature until he could neither see, hear, nor stand. Then he had bundled the fellow into a car and had delivered him to his embassy.

Ciano, in his diary for July 3, 1941, recorded that "Alfieri's star appeared to be on the wane in Berlin" and that the Duce had laughed heartily when he heard how Dino was beaten up by a German officer.

Our best source of information, help, and inspiration—apart from Leonard Ingrams and his Ministry of Economic Warfare—was the Admiralty. And it was to the Admiralty and the Naval Intelligence division, in particular, that I owed the intimate relationship which soon grew up between my "black" unit and the Fighting Services. In its turn, it was this collaboration with the Intelligence and Operational Planning sections of the services which caused what had begun as a pin-prick rumour operation to develop into the major weapon of psychological warfare it ultimately became.

When I ask myself today why the Navy should have been the first of the services to discover and support us, I find I can put down a number of factors. For one thing, the Navy was fighting an all-out war from the beginning without any respect for the phony war imposed on the Army and the R.A.F. by the French. They had contact with the enemy. They had prisoners and they had intelligence of the kind that could be useful to us. For another, I had personal friends in Naval Intelligence. Ian Fleming * had introduced me to his boss Admiral John Godfrey, as soon as I arrived back from the campaign in Poland in 1939. And when I had told Godfrey in April 1941 that I

---

* After the war Ian Fleming achieved considerable fame as the author of a best-selling series of adventure novels featuring that heroic British Secret Service agent, James Bond.

would not be able to go to Lisbon for him after all because of the new "black radio" job I had been given, he was immediately interested. He saw at once that propaganda of this kind could be of value in the attack on the morale of the U-boat crews. He also recognized that we could be of help in misleading his opposite numbers in the German Admiralty's Intelligence division—though this was a function we did not develop until we possessed a more elaborate means of communicating with the enemy than Gustav Siegfried Eins.

Above all, this shrewdest of our wartime directors of Naval Intelligence saw the great advantage that "black" had over "white"—as the overt broadcasts of the B.B.C. and the R.A.F. news-sheets came to be called—through its ability to use intelligence rather than to reproduce it, a faculty which safeguarded the security of N.I.D.'s sources.

Admiral Godfrey was so impressed with the possibilities of psychological attack on the enemy crews that he set up a special propaganda section and asked me to come to the Admiralty to coach the officers of the new section in the elements of the art during its first weeks.

The Admiral had installed his personal staff in a vast barn of a room immediately adjoining his own very comfortable inner sanctum. Somehow this outer workshop— N.I.D. 17 was its Admiralty title—reminded me of the Arab banks I had visited in Tangier and Beirut.

Ian Fleming, the "chief clerk"—his code number was 17F—sat at a desk guarding the glass door to the boss's room, which overlooked the Horse Guards Parade. At a dozen desks of varying shapes the other "clerks" beavered away at stacks of papers. The "clerks," however, were all naval officers, and their papers were not bills of exchange and freight letters but top-secret reports. Each desk represented a special field of Intelligence activity and each had its special code number: N.I.D. 17a, N.I.D. 17b, N.I.D. 17c, and so on. Now a new desk had been moved into N.I.D. 17 for the propaganda section. And this section too received its code letter—the last in the alphabet.

I felt considerable trepidation the first time I called on the officers of N.I.D. 17z—my "pupils," as Ian insisted on describing them. I feared they would resent the intrusion of a civilian. But the R.N.V.R. lieutenants sitting at the new desks could not have been more friendly and respectful.

There were three of them the first time I called. One was Robert Harling, a young man with the laughing, big-eared, long-nosed face of a medieval court jester and the shrewd appraising eyes of a physician. He was an artist typographer in civilian life, Ian told me, as he introduced us. (Robert Harling is today editor of London's *House and Garden* and author of several best-selling novels of suspense.) The second, whom Godfrey had picked to command the section, was a bony, sandy-haired Scotsman called Donald McLachlan. (Today he is the editor of *The Sunday Telegraph*.) He had been a don at Winchester, and had spent a short time in the Berlin office of *The Times*, had then worked for several years on *The Times'* foreign desk. The third was a young Marine officer called David Astor (today The Honourable David Astor is the editor of *The Observer*). But Astor had been posted to another unit by the time I next visited the department.

It only took a few visits to convince me that we could not have a better officer to service "black" with intelligence material and ideas than the methodical and imaginative ex-schoolmaster McLachlan. He had been brought out of the Army by Admiral Godfrey in 1940 and trained

in all branches of Naval Intelligence. His latest duty in
N.I. had been the ideal preparation for "black." For Godfrey, as though he had sensed the kind of thinking we
were going to demand of Donald McLachlan, had made
him secretary to the F.O.E. (Forward Operations Enemy)
sub-committee of the Chiefs of Staff which appraised
enemy intentions over the whole war front, and it had
been Donald's special duty to write a paper every week
on the war at sea as it would appear to a German Intelligence officer.

But I was delighted with the new section for yet another reason. Up to this time the Admiralty in common
with the other Fighting Services had left psychological
warfare to their public relations department, and I had
found that the public relations officers had neither the access to the kind of intelligence material we needed nor
the understanding for our indirect subversive approach
to the enemy. This was no fault of theirs, for their job was
the straightforward one of projecting the splendour and
invincibility of the British Navy to the world through
newspapers and radio. They were not conditioned for the
devious approach needed for deceiving and tricking the
Germans.

Admiral Godfrey's plan had been for N.I.D. 17z to conduct its attack on the German crews through the B.B.C.
as well as through "black." But, although Carleton Greene
made time available for McLachlan and Harling to produce a special naval programme on the B.B.C., he would
not let them write a special naval news bulletin. The news
had to be written by the B.B.C., and no outsiders were
allowed to interfere with it. The operatives of N.I.D. 17z
were therefore confined to commentaries, which was dis-
appointing. In my view, and that of Donald McLachlan,

carefully selected news items, skilfully presented, are the most subversive propaganda force of all.

The result of this B.B.C. obstinacy was that the Admiralty turned more and more to "black." And soon, as the reader will learn, "black," with the Admiralty to back it, intruded into the most sacred preserve of the B.B.C. with a live news broadcast of its own. What the Admiralty liked about "black" was its ability to make statements, about sinkings for instance, without the Admiralty being held responsible. Had they been broadcast by the B.B.C., on the other hand, they would have been quoted as official Admiralty statements. (The B.B.C., of course, cannot be blamed for this.)

Moreover, the Navy had been impressed by the evidence that now began to come in, that Gustav Siegfried had built up a substantial audience in Germany and that Der Chef's stories were getting around. The new formula appeared to be working.

Gustav Siegfried's left-wing stable companion, the *Sender der Europäischen Revolution,* had produced little or no reaction in Germany. Nor had its right-wing predecessor. German prisoners seemed never to have heard of either. Der Chef, however, after only a few weeks produced a crop of startling "comebacks," as we called the bits of direct and indirect evidence that a station was being listened to.

What pleased me most was finding that some story we had invented was being retailed as fact by the Germans without any mention of Gustav Siegfried as the source. Great was my delight, for instance, when in the P.O.W. monitoring reports I found a freshly captured German Luftwaffe officer telling the story about Nazi boss Robert

Ley and the diplomat rations which Der Chef had invented and broadcast only three weeks before.

It was a good little story.

The father of a kitchen maid who had recently left her employ in the Ley household had telephoned the Ley major-domo to ask for his daughter's ration cards to be sent on to her. "This is the Palais Ley," grandly answered the major-domo. "We have no ration cards here. We don't bother about them, you know. Here we have diplomat rations."

The so-called diplomat rations had been instituted by the German government for foreign embassies in Berlin and certain government departments that had to entertain for representational purposes. Gustav Siegfried Eins made out that the party bigshots had all got themselves fixed up with diplomat rations as a way of evading the rationing laws to which the common man was subject. The Ley story we had invented as an example. And here was the proof now out of the mouth of this Luftwaffe officer that Germans had accepted our story and were passing it on.

We plugged the diplomat-rations racket with such effect that Goebbels and Ley had to lay on a special campaign to counter it. Robert Ley himself went on record in Goebbels' newspaper *Der Angriff* ". . . we National Socialists know no such thing as diplomat rations. Every man, whether he is a Reich minister or a Reich leader, has to live on his rations just like any ordinary workman, mechanic, and official. The normal rations are enough. I myself am a normal consumer and live on them. . . ." *

But by the time they got around to this démenti we were able to quote the decree authorizing special rations

* *Der Angriff*, October 12, 1943.

for diplomats and party officials with representational duties (BEM.1,237/43 of 26.1.1943). We were even able to give them the colour of the certificates and the exact scale of the diplomat rations.

There were plenty of other "comebacks." The most entertaining of them all, however, was one that showed up the greatest danger inherent in "black" operations—the danger of misleading your own side.

In those days of the summer and autumn of 1941 the Americans still had an Embassy in Berlin. And just as Franco's Foreign Office used to show the Duke of Alba's dispatches from London to the Germans, so did the State Department allow the Foreign Office to see the reports they were getting from Berlin. In due course, Foreign Office dispatch boxes with copies of these reports made their way up to Woburn Abbey, where they were carefully scrutinized for anything that might help us with our picture of war-time Germany.

Valentine Williams was reading the report of one of the American service attachés when his eyes lit on a passage that filled him with mischievous triumph. The American reported that there had been a dramatic increase in the hostility of the Army to the Nazi Party since the invasion of Russia. The Army, he said, had gone so far as to set up a radio transmitter from which a nameless officer referred to as Der Chef was broadcasting violent attacks on certain sections of the party. An ever-increasing number of Germans, said the American diplomat, were listening to the broadcast of this officer. The German government's attempts to locate his transmitter and have it shut down had so far failed, probably because an important Army authority was shielding the group of which the officer was the spokesman.

Valentine Williams called me in and congratulated me. I felt a little less sanguine about this "comeback" than Valentine, because I suspected that the American officer might be writing with his tongue in his cheek, in order to tell us that we were being heard. But further dispatches came in, each quoting Der Chef at length. Each insisted that the emergence of this station was a most significant indication of the increased strength and confidence of the anti-Party underground in the Army. I was forced to agree with Valentine that we appeared to have deceived our American friends.

Valentine Williams now called a conference to decide what was to be done. It was by no means desirable that the Americans should be under the illusion that they had only to sit on the fence a little longer and Hitler would be overthrown by his Army. But could we warn them, without disclosing our operation to the whole world? At last it was decided that David Bowes-Lyon, the brother of the then Queen, who was our Washington representative, should call on President Roosevelt at the White House and reveal the truth to him on the strict understanding that it was for Roosevelt's ears alone.

David performed the task admirably. Roosevelt, instead of being chagrined at the thought that his diplomatic agents had fallen for such a simple deception, chuckled and chortled as though the whole affair had been specially set up for his amusement. Unfortunately, however, Roosevelt's ideas of security were not as strict as ours. The President could not refrain from telling his friends about the trick the British were playing on the Germans, and soon the story of Gustav Siegfried Eins was all over Washington.

When the United States came into the war, Rex Leeper

was besieged by Americans demanding to be initiated into the arts and techniques of "black propaganda." One good result of this was the close and profitable collaboration between the emissaries of the Office of Strategic Services and myself. It was a collaboration which, like that with our British Fighting Services, became the basis of the most important and successful work my unit performed.

Gustav Siegfried Eins continued to defy the Gestapo and burn up the ether with its sulphurous broadcasts until the end of October 1943. Then I decided that we could make even better use of the Corporal in a new capacity.

So Der Chef had to die—"caught at last." Alas, in dying he suffered the only bad slip-up of his long career. For he died twice.

A transmitter engineer, knowing no German and unaware of the final nature of the broadcast—complete with Tommy-gun salvo and gruff "Got you, you swine!"—went through his usual routine and repeated the record an hour after the broadcast that was supposed to be his last. Fortunately I heard it.

I have never met anyone else who did.

Frascati's was my favourite restaurant in war-time London. Its gilded Edwardian cherubs, its plush chairs and elderly waiters held a nostalgic echo of my Paris eating places. I could be sure of meeting no one there who knew me, and there was ample space between the tables so that my guests and I could talk without being overheard. But the most compelling attraction of all was that the bins in Frascati's cellars held a collection of clarets and champagnes which was unrivalled in the London of 1942. Many of my most successful "black" ventures were born there under the inspiration of a Moët Chandon 1919 (I have an almost necrolatrous passion for old champagne) and a superb Ausone 1923.

No suggestion, however, was more fruitful or more important than that which Donald McLachlan put to me at a Frascati lunch just before Christmas 1942. That meal with Donald saw the conception of the counterfeit radios *Deutscher Kurzwellensender Atlantik* and *Soldatensender Calais* ("German Shortwave Radio Atlantic" and "Soldiers' Radio Calais").

Camille, our Niçois waiter, had just made his customary promise of gastronomic prestidigitation: "I have somethings upper ma sleeve for you, gentlemen—moshroomps on toast."

Donald had politely savoured the aged Moët Chandon, as though he shared my admiration for it. And now we were ready for business. "I have a very important proposal for you from the Admiralty," he began in his methodical way. "You know we are now conducting a knockout offensive against the U-boats. We have a whole arsenal of new weapons for detecting and destroying them, which will make going to sea in a U-boat about as attractive as a cruise in a coffin. It may well be that we shall cause the first real crack in the morale of a German fighting service. And if the U-boatmen crack, it is bound to spread to other arms. Do you agree?"

Donald had a trick of asking people whether they agreed when he knew they most certainly did. I remembered only too well the Kiel mutiny of the German Navy in the previous war, and how it spread its infection all over the country.

"Well, in view of all this, the Admiralty planners are anxious to step up our psychological-warfare attack on the German Navy and the U-boat crews in particular. The main instrument of that attack should, in their view, be not the B.B.C. but 'black.' What do you think of reinforc-

ing Gustav Siegfried with a new station specially beamed
at the U-boats? How about a 'black' news bulletin?"

Donald, of course, knew that a "black" news bulletin,
mixing truth and calculated fiction, had for long been my
dream—if only to try out my ideas for a new and livelier
style of news writing and news selection. I longed to show
the B.B.C. the difference between the stodgy news presen-
tation of the old-fashioned journalism to which the B.B.C.
bowed down, and the sharp and vivid style of my side of
Fleet Street which I hoped to adapt to radio. I wanted to
demonstrate the mass appeal of the significant "human
story," until now absent from the air, the technique of
"personalizing" the news. But how could it be done?

I reminded Donald how I had tried to launch a "black"
news bulletin with a station called *Wehrmachtsender
Nord*. It was a short-lived venture. Very soon I had come
to the conclusion that it did not sound right, because, like
all "black" transmissions at that time, it had to be pre-
recorded. Radio news, to be news, and to sound like news,
I had discovered then, must be broadcast live. It must be
up to the minute, changing from bulletin to bulletin. But
unfortunately our "black" studios could not handle live
broadcasts. And after a few weeks of experimentation I
had abandoned the recorded *Wehrmachtsender Nord*.

"If we could get facilities for a live broadcast, then I
am all for it," I said. "We could have a counterfeit forces
programme ostensibly for the benefit of U-boat crews and
the troops in France. It could model itself on those forces
stations the Germans have set up in Belgrade and Lvov.
But how on earth are we to get the facilities for live transmissions? Besides, they'll turn live broadcasts down on
security grounds."

"Don't forget you have the Admiralty behind you," said

Donald. "A word from Charles Lambe to Dallas Brooks *
will work wonders. And as for security, surely all you need
is a switch censor?" (A switch censor sits by a switch while
a speaker is broadcasting, and can cut him off by pressing
a button if he deviates from the approved text.)

I was still unconvinced because of the lack of a studio.
And then I suddenly had an idea. My department had recently put up a huge 600-kilowatt medium-wave transmitter at Crowborough, and had built studios for it at
Milton Bryan near Woburn. The transmitter had been designed and built to drown the voice of the enemy station
and impose its own voice on it by superior strength. But
for the time being it had been lent to reinforce the B.B.C.
No one was using the studios at Milton Bryan, so why
should we not be allowed to use them? The other regions
would be sure to protest, but with the help of the Admiralty we might be awarded the necessary priority. Donald
and I left Frascati's in a state of high elation—not due
exclusively to the Moët Chandon—determined to fight for
the right to broadcast live, an unheard of innovation for
"black."

Robert Bruce Lockhart, who had become Director General when Rex Leeper departed to be Ambassador to the
King of Greece, was a cautious Scot, and circumspect almost to a fault. But when I put our revolutionary project
to him, he accepted it with an alacrity amounting to enthusiasm. I was impressed. Bruce was too old a hand in

* Major General Dallas Brooks of the Royal Marines was Deputy
Director General of my department and in charge of relations with the
Services. Captain Charles Lambe, R.N., at that time was Deputy Di-
rector of Plans at the Admiralty. Before he died, he rose to the Navy's
highest rank as First Sea Lord. Dallas Brooks became Commandant
General of the Marines, and at the time of writing is Governor of the
Australian State of Victoria.

Whitehall politics not to be aware that a live news bulletin, complete with music, greetings from home, and all the other attractions of a German forces radio, was going to bring us slap up against the powerful interests of the B.B.C. Just as the Church of England regards the British heaven as its established monopoly, so did the B.B.C., in those days before commercial television, regard the British ether as theirs.

That we would start with only six half-hour short-wave broadcasts an evening in no way lessened the daring of Bruce's decision in my eyes. For I had told him that we meant to extend this as soon as we had gained confidence and proficiency. We meant to have continuous all-night broadcasts. And he cannot have failed to realize that before long we would go even further and ask for the department's 600-kilowatt transmitter to be taken from the B.B.C. and handed over to us so that we could broadcast on medium wave as well as short wave. But Bruce showed no qualms.

He agreed to let me have the exclusive use of the studio for my team and immediately ordered additional prefab huts to be erected in the studio compound, to house the Intelligence unit with its files. Clearly the voice of the Admiralty conveyed through Dallas Brooks had been most eloquent and suasive. For the first time in the department's history Bruce Lockhart was able to tell his ministers that a Fighting Service had proposed an operational task.

Early in the new year my team and I took possession of "M.B.," as the Milton Bryan studio and its compound were known. It consisted of about five acres of grass and tarmac in the centre of which stood a neat and functional two-story, red-brick building which from the outside looked

like any of the new factories and workshops then being
built. Around it stretched a twelve-foot-high mesh-wire
fence topped by vicious-looking barbs. A squad of special
constables guarded the place, and at night they patrolled
the fence with those German sheep dogs which in Britain
we rather stupidly prefer to call "Alsatians." They also
had an armoury of rifles and Tommy-guns, with which
they practised on a special shooting range—just in case.

Everything at M.B. was the last word in up-to-dateness
and efficiency. As operators for our telephone switch-
board we had no amateurish war-time recruits but three
girls of established trustworthiness, who had been trained
by G.P.O. London and had served there for years before
the war. To be trained by G.P.O. London is for telephon-
ists like a fellowship at All Souls. My girls looked down
on the Abbey operators who were *mere* graduates of
Cable and Wireless.

Two telephones stood on my desk. One bore the coveted colour green, which meant that it was a "scrambler"
and that over it I could talk to other executives on the
"scrambler level" in complete confidence of secrecy, knowing that anyone trying to listen in would hear nothing but
a meaningless jumble. "Black," thanks to the Admiralty,
had arrived. Now it was up to us to justify expectations.

On February 5, 1943, after three weeks of rehearsals
and dry runs, the *Atlantiksender,* as the Germans soon
called it, opened its maiden broadcast with a shrieking
pipe melody as its signature tune. It had been recorded on
a Hammond organ by my versatile musician friend among
the radio engineers. In accordance with what, by now,
was a tradition—for we had given birth to several other
"black" stations since Gustav Siegfried first ventured on
the air—the script for the speakers was written in such a

way as to suggest from internal evidence that this was not the first broadcast of a new station, but the umpteenth of a series which the clumsy monitors of Reichsmarshal Göring's radio security service had somehow contrived to miss.

But the enemy monitors did not, in fact, miss it. By the time our third transmission of the evening was going out their jammers were after us in full hue and shriek.

The launching of the Atlantiksender had meant, of course, that I had to take on fresh staff and re-organize my unit. True, I had considerably enlarged my original Gustav Siegfried team in the twenty months that had gone by since Der Chef's first broadcast. We had moved from our discreet red-brick villa into a much larger house. It had once belonged to the owner editor of a news-sheet known in sporting circles as "The Pink Un." (In uncanny premonition of our activities there he had named his house "The Rookery.") But I still had nothing like enough personnel to staff this ambitious new enterprise. I had to look around for fresh talent.

Amazing good fortune blessed my search. From a then moribund department of the Foreign Office I managed to extract as my chief intelligence expert Clifton Child, a young education officer from Manchester. Child had an almost supernatural genius for ferreting German news from the most unpromising sources. I am sure he could have been one of the greatest news editors Fleet Street ever possessed, if only he could have been persuaded to join a newspaper after the war instead of rejoining the Foreign Office, as he has done.

Leonard Ingrams and the Ministry of Economic Warfare generously seconded to me C. E. ("Tom Brown")

Stevens, the Oxford ancient history don, who today tells his Oxford undergraduate pupils that only a course of black propaganda will give them a full understanding of Caesar and Cicero! Stevens' truly historic contribution to psychological warfare was made, however, before he joined my team.

One morning Leonard Ingrams walked into his office at M.E.W. "Got any ideas today for the V-Committee?" asked Leonard. The V-Committee was the small body of propagandists planning the "V for Victory" campaign which was being sent over on the European service of the B.B.C.

"Well," said Tom Brown, sucking on his dreadful old pipe, "have you ever thought of the letter V in Morse code —dot-dot-dot-dash? It fits the opening bars of Beethoven's Fifth. Just an idea."

With Max Braun and a team of university-graduate girl researchers to help them, Child and Stevens now headed a first-class intelligence team. It was as gifted in its own specialized work as the equally mixed intelligence groups of professional officers, lawyers, biologists, and the like, in the service ministries, who in those last years of the war showed themselves far and away superior not only to the Germans but to our Russian and American allies as well.

Tom Brown—he was given that nickname when, as a twelve-year-old, he arrived at Winchester for his first term wearing a top hat, a dickie, and a made-up tie—was our walking encyclopædia.

Day after day, week in week out, Child—that extraordinarily painstaking and gifted man—provided us not only with items beautifully apposite to the campaigns we were running but with "scoops" which built up the belief in Germany that Atlantic had its agents everywhere.

As deputy to myself in running the Atlantiksender, I secured Karl Robson from the War Office. Karl, a tall, haggard, dark-eyed Hamlet figure, was the ideal counterpart to my own bulky, over-ebullient self. His job was difficult, for I was determined to introduce a new kind of radio language into our broadcasts. I meant to make listening easier for German listeners just as British popular newspapers had made reading easier for their readers.

"We are having none of those long classical sentences with the all-important verb left to the very end," I said at the first rehearsal. "We are going to use easily understood colloquial German in short sentences. None of our stuff is going to sound as though it is being read aloud from some learned periodical." That was not too easy to put across with Germans who had been brought up to regard anything simple and colloquial as ungrammatical and as "bad German."

My second demand was that our news items must have what I called *Hörfang* in their opening phrase. *Hörfang* was a German word meaning "listen-catch," which I had invented.

"The difference between the way we are going to write our news items and the way the Deutschlandsender and the B.B.C. write theirs," I said to the team, "is the difference between the English way of reading figures and the German. We say "eighty-three"—eighty being the operative word—while Germans say "three and eighty." In our items the operative phrase will come first to catch the listener's attention and give him an idea of what the item is about from the start. *Verstanden?*"

Karl and I had to see that these little rules were applied, and he did it very well.

As my chief news writers in addition to Albrecht Ernst —my friend from Spanish war days and Lisbon—I had a one-time Berlin art dealer, Hans Gutmann, and Dr. Albert, a former press attaché of the Austrian Legation who had remained in Britain when Hitler took over his country. To Alex Maass, another veteran of the Spanish war, I gave the important job of chief disk jockey. Alex put together the dance music that was both an important listener attraction of the station and, by its distinctive style, a kind of continuous call sign.

We took a great deal of trouble over getting the right music for the station. Some of our records were the latest German hits specially flown over to us by Mosquito from Stockholm, where "Joe" Parrott (today British Ambassador in Prague) with his press-reading team did a wonderful job collecting information for us and other little items such as these disks. Other records were specially made for us at M.B. by a German band under that accomplished musician Henry Zeisel. Zeisel and his band had been touring North Africa when they were captured by the Eighth Army and sent back to Britain. Now with my American radio colleague, John Kebbe, to direct them, they were carrying on their good work of entertaining Hitler's Wehrmacht on the Atlantiksender.

The American O.S.S. men with whom we were now starting to co-operate supplied us with the latest and best American dance music. They even arranged for German-speaking artists, such as Marlene Dietrich, to make special recordings for us in German.

Marlene, of course, like the other artists had no idea she was recording her songs for a counterfeit. She was led to believe that her songs would be sent over on a German broadcast of the Voice of America. This was why, when

she visited Europe, I was reluctantly compelled to keep
her voice off the air so that she should not hear herself
singing on what was ostensibly a Nazi radio. Poor Marlene! She never learned the truth until she revisited her
native Germany after the war and the new chauvinists
pelted the "traitress Marlene" with rotten tomatoes.

But we had yet another supplier of music—the band of
the Royal Marines. General Brooks arranged for it to come
up to London from Portsmouth for a top-secret recording
session in—of all places—the Albert Hall. One of the tunes
the Marines recorded for us was a catchy Berlin music-
hall song called *"Es war in Schöneberg im Monat Mai."*
(Louis Armstrong, visiting Berlin many years after the
war, found the melody so attractive that he produced his
own swing version of it.)

I had chosen it as the theme song of the Atlantiksender's
special navy programme, because, as we had learned from
prisoners, it was a favourite with the U-boat men and they
had made up some bawdy new verses for it. René Halkett,
a nephew of the Wehrmacht's former Chief of Staff General von Fritzsch, sang the new vocal bits. He was the
most versatile member of the team, and seemed to be able
to do anything, whether it was writing, speaking in dialect,
or singing and accompanying himself on an accordion or
a guitar.

The first line of the new U-boat version went: *"Ich war
in St. Nazaire in einem Puff. . . ."* which means, "I was
in a brothel in St. Nazaire. . . ." Fortunately the band-
master colonel conducting the Marines did not ask me to
translate the rest of the words.

My most important source of staff for our operations
was the German Wehrmacht itself. From U-boats sunk in

the Atlantic, from Rommel's harried armies in North Africa, from the German aircraft shot down over Britain and over Libya an ever-increasing stream of prisoners was now pouring into the interrogation cages run by my Intelligence friends in London and nearby.

These prisoners provided a prolific flow of information useful to our campaigns. They also provided me with a new reservoir of talent, for among the new prisoners were a number of Germans so antagonized by Hitler and the moral and physical destruction he was imposing on their country that they wanted to seize the first opportunity to hasten his end. From the ranks of these men I selected some of my ablest fellow workers. Several have remained trusted friends of mine to this day.

One of them, a young artillery major, scion of an old Prussian family steeped in army traditions, had been the 1-A Intelligence officer of his regiment in North Africa. Wolfgang von Virchow, as I called him, had an accurate and retentive mind. He became number one of the little team which under the direction of Molly Fitzpatrick, a witty young German-speaking Irishwoman, wrote the special "Army Programme." Like its naval counterpart this consisted of bits of service gossip, news of the movements of units, criticism of weapons and other titbits likely to entertain, mislead and subvert the German soldier. Virchow also advised the news writers on their interpretation of the military news, and he was invaluable in helping us to avoid solecisms of language, procedure, and the other pitfalls of the counterfeiter.

The German Air Force provided me with an entire three-man crew who were testing a new German night-fighter—two officers and a sergeant. The three of them were determined anti-Nazis. They did not belong to any resistance group, but, talking together, they had discovered that each of them had the same idea—to get to Britain and there join up with other Germans fighting Hitler on the British side.

They were carrying out their test flights from a German airfield in Denmark when their great opportunity presented itself. To their base was sent the very latest and most up-to-date Messerschmitt night-fighter to leave the works. It carried the new electronic equipment which the German Air Force Command felt confident was at last going to put a stop to the British night-time bombing raids on Germany.

Though they realized that they might be shot down and killed by the Germans or the British before they could land in Britain, they decided to fly the plane over and present it to the R.A.F. as an earnest of their desire to fight Hitler. They were not shot down. They managed to land their plane intact on an Essex airstrip. Of course, they should never have been made prisoners of war at all. But unfortunately their names were sent through to the International Red Cross before the British authorities realized the mistake they had made.

When the three—Steiner, Wegely, and Obermeyer—had given all their information to the R.A.F. interrogators, they were offered to me.

Any Germans who listened to the Atlantiksender, or the medium-wave Soldatensender which was soon coupled to it, will remember the diatribes of the angry Bavarian voice in the Luftwaffe programme, denouncing the impossible conditions under which he and his comrades were expected to fight the enemy. That was Sergeant Sepp Obermeyer, a red-haired, typically stocky Upper Bavarian with a face that was just like his voice. At first his talks had to be written for him. He also required endless coaching before he could speak naturally before the microphone. Then one day, just like Corporal Paul Sanders when we were starting the Gustav Siegfried broadcasts, Obermeyer asked me whether he might alter the script to suit his own style of speaking. I was delighted, for I guessed what was coming. And, sure enough, soon this rustic Bavarian mechanic began writing his own talks. First-class talks they were too, simple, salty, and sincere. Steiner and Wegely, with Squadron Leader Norman Roffy from Air Intelligence 3 to supply them with technical intelligence, and one of my own old hands to coach them in the art of writing, between them put out a first-rate programme of gossip, technical news, and grumbles for the Luftwaffe similar to that which Major von Virchow handled for the Army.

The German Navy and the U-boats, which were the first and original target of the Atlantiksender, were particularly well represented by recruits from the cages. Our ablest and most resourceful U-boat man was Eddy Mander, a bright little Hamburg guttersnipe who before the war had been a wireless operator with the Debeg, the German equivalent of Marconi. Mander held the rank of a *Flotillen Oberfunkmeister* (flotilla chief radio petty officer), which was about as high as an N.C.O. could rise. But he was full of bitterness against his own officers and against the Nazi leaders. His personal experiences had gradually changed him from a devout Nazi at the beginning of the war into a gifted and resolute adversary of the Third Reich.

In 1939 Mander had been serving with the German Merchant Marine. He was the chief wireless officer on the *Altmark* when, her holds crammed with captured British merchant seamen, she was herself boarded off the Norwegian coast by the British destroyer *Cossack*. Mander escaped, becoming a British prisoner at that time by jumping overboard and running for the coast across the ice-floes. Even though he was hit in the right lung by a British machine-gun bullet, he managed to keep going until he reached land.

As soon as he was well enough to go to sea again he was called up by the German Navy. Much to Mander's resentment, the Navy insisted on ignoring his expert proficiency as a wireless operator. The naval radio men made him go through their radio training course from its most elementary beginnings. That soured him.

Then he was caught out in a black-market deal with coffee and court-martialled. He was given a choice of death sentences: transfer to a penal battalion in the foremost line of the Russian front, or three more Atlantic cruises in a U-boat. Mander chose the U-boat death. But he was lucky. Though his submarine was sunk on the second night out of his first cruise, he himself was fished out and taken prisoner.

With him into captivity he brought his U-boat codebook containing all the latest ciphers, and a great hate of Hitler's Navy.

Over a British naval transmitter Mander then got his first revenge. With the British to help him he sent out a series of cipher signals which directed two German U-boats to a rendezvous. There they were pounced on by the waiting British. The boats were sunk, and their crews joined Mander in captivity.

What made Mander invaluable to my team at M.B. were his technical knowledge, particularly in matters of signals and radar, his wide range of acquaintances among

U-boat crews, and his wonderful gift of racy German lower-deck slang. He was adept at thinking up new grouses. And when it came to suggesting how U-boat men might delay the departure of their ship—and prolong their lives—by petty and unattributable acts of sabotage, not even our own naval experts were more fertile.

Mander was the mainstay of the team writing the naval programme. At the end of the war Mander was repatriated. But he died soon after his return—of tuberculosis, it is stated. Needless to say, there is another story that he met his death at the hands of former U-boat men.

Frank Lynder, the son of a Bremen bookseller and publisher, was the captain of the naval team, its number-one writer, intelligence researcher, and speaker. His Bremen accent had just the right nautical ring to it. Not that Frank was a German naval man; he was a coffee broker, and came to me from the same Pioneer Corps bomb-disposal squad as Paul Sanders. Lynder had been its sergeant while Sanders was the corporal.

Frank, who today is the London correspondent of Hamburg's Springer group of newspapers, joined my team, never having read or written anything more literary than an invoice. But he soon showed a flair for searching out the unexpected, all-revealing detail and writing little items which had what my classics master at St. Paul's would have called a "charming Platonic simplicity." On a blackboard in his office he chalked up the various campaigns which Donald McLachlan had laid down for him to follow. Every time an item went out in support of one of these campaigns, Lynder marked it on his board as assiduously as a German student of philology counting up the accusatives-cum-infinitive in Otfried for his doctor's thesis. And if Frank Lynder found that any campaign was being neglected, he was like a terrier after a rat in seeing to it that this neglect was remedied at once.

It was Frank Lynder too, who, with his girl research assistant, read the letters which the U-boat men in the P.O.W. camps in Britain and Canada were sending and receiving from home. He and his secretary noted down every bit of gossip and family news in a huge card file in which they also included the marriages, births, and deaths announced by U-boat families in German newspapers. On the basis of this file the Atlantiksender's "Sailor's Sweet-heart"—Agnes Bernelle, a daughter of the Berlin play-wright and theatre-owner Rudolf Bernauer, whom we called "Vicky"—was able to startle the German Navy men by sending out birthday greetings not merely to the U-boat men themselves but also to their families, congratu-lating them on the birth of a son or daughter and generally showing an intimate acquaintance with the private affairs of her "dear boys in blue."

Vicky was incredibly good at it. The treacle in her voice would never let you suspect that this Circe had lost half her family in the gas chambers of Auschwitz.

No less a Nazi potentate than the dynamic little Dr. Goebbels himself provided the cover for the Atlantik-sender's subversive broadcasts—he and his official news agency, the *Deutsche Nachrichtenbüro*. Goebbels, in order to assure to the D.N.B. news a fast distribution over the whole of Hitler's far-flung territories, had set up a wireless teleprinter service by means of a so-called *Hell-schreiber*. I managed to get hold of a Hell-schreiber receiving set, which the D.N.B. London correspondent had inadvert-ently left in his office when he fled to Germany at the out-break of war. Reuters now had it—the D.N.B. office had been in the Reuters building—and Christopher Chancellor, the head of Reuters, nobly yielded it up to me when I asked him for it.

On this Hell-schreiber we now received Dr. Goebbels' news service in M.B. at the same time as the German newspapers and radio stations were receiving it. And, being faster workers and less inhibited than the teams working for Goebbels, we were able to put his news on the air before our Nazi competitors.

We used some items as cover to give ourselves authenticity as a German station purveying official news. To others we gave a subversive twist so that when listeners heard them on the German radio later they read our tendentious distortion as the truth hidden "between the lines." The Hell-schreiber told us of decorations and promotions in the Wehrmacht, it gave us the official communiqués and the speeches of the Nazi Party orators proclaiming their unshakeable faith in the Führer and final victory. From these we would give brief and damningly deadpan excerpts. From the D.N.B. Hell-schreiber we also got our invaluable sports news, which was magnificently edited for us by the veteran Ullstein sports reporter Dr. Willy Meisl. In short, without the Hell-schreiber we would never have been able to follow the formula which enabled us to put over the poison in our news bulletins without making it sound like enemy propaganda. "Cover, dirt, cover, cover, dirt, cover, dirt" was the approximate rhythm we followed—"dirt" being what we called the items which we hoped would make our listeners think and act on lines displeasing to their Führer.

The D.N.B., however, was not the only debt we owed the "propaganda dwarf." He himself occasionally made a personal appearance on the Atlantiksender to give it ad-

ditional authenticity as a German station. And so did the
Führer. For, when Goebbels or Hitler delivered one of
their speeches over the German radio, we picked it up
from the German network and relayed it over the Atlantiksender.

"The Deutsche Kurzwellensender Atlantik, in common
with all other stations in the Reich network," said our
announcer on these occasions, "now takes you over to the
Sports Palace in Berlin, where you will hear the address
of the Führer, *Wir schalten um* . . ." As Harold Robin,
the brilliant and ingenious chief technician of the radio
unit switched over and Hitler took over from Sepp Obermeyer or Vicky, a roar of Homeric laughter echoed through
M.B. It was a trick that never lost its appeal. Many were
those in the team who begged me to let them interrupt
Goebbels or the Führer with a rough comment or two.
We could have done so very easily by switching in and
out again. But I was firm. "One operation at a time, my
children!" I said. "We are doing this for cover, cover,
cover and nothing else. No dirt this time!"

Even in our subversive items we took care to keep to
the Goebbels idiom. We talked of the Allies as "the enemy"
and adopted whatever pejorative epithets were current at
the time. Raids by the bombers of the R.A.F. and the
United States Air Force we referred to as "terror raids"
and the raiding crews we called "terror flyers." But despite
all the cover and the blandly matter-of-fact authority of
even our most outrageous news items, I could not help
feeling that our cannier listeners would soon come to suspect the unorthodox deviation of the Atlantiksender from
the routine output of the other stations as being due to
something more than the remoteness of the radio's putative home in France from the dynamic Doctor's central

control. Even if they did, however, I calculated the station would still remain effective, partly because it always spoke from a patriotic and "national" German viewpoint— and this was bound to be more insidious and psychologically effective than a straight enemy broadcast—and partly because listeners caught tuning us in would welcome the excuse that they had only listened in the belief that Atlantik was German.

It was amazing, however, how many Germans were genuinely taken in, and did in fact believe the station to be a German forces radio. Quite early we received indisputable evidence from a prisoner that for several days the sergeant at the Wehrmacht equivalent of an N.A.A.F.I. station in Tunis had piped the Atlantiksender into the recreation huts "because the music was so marvellous— *so fabelhaft.*" Only when an officer reprimanded him did he realize he had been entertaining his comrades with a forbidden enemy station.

In the nine months that the Atlantiksender remained on its own, broadcasting exclusively on short waves, the team developed into a hard-working crew of perfectionists. Talks and news items would be rewritten again and again, until we got them as I wanted them. Immense trouble was taken over small detail. "Accuracy first," I used to tell the writers. "We must never lie by accident, or through slovenliness—only deliberately."

As we put out news bulletin after news bulletin, and service programme after service programme, an entire system of subversive campaigns developed, based on those campaigns we had originally created in the Gustav Siegfried days. But now they had been elaborated and perfected as a result of Clifton Child's research and ingenuity.

In item after item we gave examples of the "inequality of sacrifice" between the common man and the "privileged" party functionaries. There was enough truth to them to give our allegations complete plausibility and make them stick in the minds of our listeners. Germans wanted to believe ill of their Nazi Party overseers, and we gave them the "facts" with which to back up their suspicions.

Party functionaries, we showed, were exempt from front-line service. (We could quote a genuine decree exempting officials of the Goebbels propaganda ministry from military service.) If they were sent to join the forces, they did so only for a short token period and then returned to their posts on the "home front." Regularly once a week we put out a list, entirely genuine, of Party officials who had left for their period of token service and others who had returned.

The wives and daughters of Party highups, we said, were exempt from the call-up of women. Their families were exempt from providing billets in their homes for evacuees or bombed out families, as ordinary Germans were compelled to do. (Quite true. Reasons of security and secrecy no doubt dictated this exemption. But why should we point that out?) Party highups were permitted to move their offices and homes away from the much bombed-urban districts, while the ordinary worker had to stay put in the town to fight fires. We gave innumerable examples of the defeatism of the Party highups. They were selling the businesses they had acquired in occupied countries, knowing that they would soon be leaving. They were smuggling their money to safe accounts in Switzerland and South America.

We encouraged our listeners to defiance and disobedience not by appeals but by news items showing that control had slipped from the hands of the German authorities. It was safe to defy them and their police. For such police as had not been called up for military service were old and decrepit. In our sports news Willy Meisl stressed the defeat of police teams. "They're such a lot of elderly crocks, they can hardly run, let alone kick a ball." In bulletin after bulletin we plugged the crime wave, the spate of unsolved murders. Air raids, we showed by innumerable examples, made police control impossible. "The authorities do not know who is missing because he has been killed, and who is missing because he has deserted."

The files and registers on which the police relied were being destroyed in the raids. Under cover of the bombing more and more prisoners were escaping from custody. The same enemy explosives which were sending the house walls crashing down, were destroying the whole edifice of Himmler's security system. In almost every bulletin we illustrated these themes with news items, some true, some invented, but all of them plausible.

The news of the day, however, was our main concern. When Goebbels announced that he was distributing a special "air-raid bonus" of chocolate in the workshop canteens, in addition to other food—he did so in order to attract absentee workers back to their factories—we added in the blandest and most matter-of-fact style that this "bomb chocolate" had been spiked with drugs like Pervitin to stimulate the bomb-fatigued workers to extra energy and extra productivity.

When we learned that families bombed out during the "terror raids" on Hamburg were being evacuated to eastern areas such as Poland, Slovakia, and Ruthenia, we reported the epidemics of typhoid and cholera allegedly raging in those areas. We did the same for the *Kinderland-*

verschickungslager, the short and snappy name for the special camps to which evacuee children were being sent. We did not, of course, put out the news of these epidemics in the KLV camps as a straightforward announcement. We dressed it up—often something like this: "Dr. Conti, the Reichsführer for physicians, has congratulated the medical officers at the KLV camps in the Gau Wartheland for the selfless devotion with which they are fighting the diphtheria epidemic among the children in their care. He has expressed his great satisfaction at their success in overcoming the tragic lack of medicaments, and reducing deaths to an average of sixty a week."

We never gave up trying to make our Wehrmacht listeners worry about what was happening to their families at home. We even made them worry about what those evil men, the Party bosses, would do to their wives should they have the misfortune to lose their lives while fighting for Führer and Fatherland.

Hitler himself was of the greatest help to us in this campaign, for he had an impulsive way of rushing out decrees which were intended to sustain and comfort his men but which when twisted a little by us had just the opposite effect. One example was his decree about posthumous divorce. Hitler must have heard or read somewhere that it was a great scandal that women against whom their soldier husbands had started divorce proceedings would be saved from the consequences of their adultery if the husband was killed before the hearing of the case was concluded. Forthwith he issued an order, on April 1, 1943, that not only should all such divorces be carried through to the bitter end just as though the soldier were still alive but that divorce proceedings must also be instituted in those cases where a dead soldier would *prob-*

ably have started proceedings against his wife had he lived. The fact that he might not have known of his wife's infidelity before he was killed was immaterial. Henceforth it would be up to the state prosecutor and the Party authorities to sue in the dead man's name in order that no faithless wives of soldiers should bear their dead husband's name, inherit his worldly goods, and collect his pension.

It was a gift, and we went to town on it in a big way, not only on the Atlantiksender but with printed leaflets as well.* The Führer's decree was of course an invitation to us to report, as we did in convincing detail, that Party bosses were using it to frame and blackmail the widows of our comrades. To forestall such blackmail, said the Atlantiksender, many comrades were sending their wives legally certified letters of renunciation, duly witnessed by their commanding officers, in which the man stated expressly that he would not consent to a posthumous divorce, no matter what his wife might have done or be accused of having done.

To help our Services listeners to visit their families and see for themselves what was going on at home, we reminded them that if their home had been bombed they were entitled to compassionate leave under an order—OKW order 967/42g of August 28, 1942—which Clifton Child had discovered among the captured documents. To help them still more—service, after all, is one of the best ways of making friends and influencing people—we put out lists of the streets which had been bombed in German towns during the raids of the previous evening. These lists became a regular feature of our programmes and impressed the German listeners enormously, for our reports

* See Appendix, page 292.

were fast and accurate. So fast and so accurate were they that German intelligence men checking them decided we must have agents in the bombed cities reporting to us on secret transmitters.

The belief has survived to this day. In that ridiculous German thriller film about the Soldatensender Calais— the medium-wave extension of the Atlantiksender which followed later—agents of the big fat boss of M.B. pop up in the middle of an air raid on Essen to tap out their messages to him. "Bombs have fallen on the Kettwiger Strasse in Essen and destroyed houses numbers seven to twenty-five," they flash, or "Incendiaries have struck the administration buildings of the Krupp works in the Altendorfer Strasse. The entire complex is on fire."

Most certainly we put out reports like this, and often embroidered them with graphic detail as well. But we did not receive our intelligence from agents. Our reports were based on information given us by the raiders themselves. Within minutes of the bombers' return from Germany a squadron intelligence officer who had examined the pilots would be on the "scrambler" to me to tell me where the raiders had been, what they believed they had hit, whether they had dropped mainly incendiaries and caused big fires or had been dropping block-buster high explosives as well, and so on.

This information, however, useful as it was, would not by itself have enabled us to compile those detailed street-by-street reports which so impressed the Germans. The main source for these were the photographs brought back by the R.A.F. Mosquitoes which flew to the bombed areas immediately after every attack to check the damage. My friends in Air Intelligence rushed the pictures to M.B. by motorcycle dispatch riders as soon as they had been printed. A special section in Clifton Child's intelligence team then interpreted them with the aid of stereoscopic viewers. To help them, they had a whole library of German town plans and Baedekers.

In charge of this work was a young German Rhodes scholar whom the R.A.F. Intelligence men had specially trained for me in the art of reading their reconnaissance photographs. Peter von Schlabrenhorst took a justified pride in his work, and he not only compiled the lists of the streets bombed in the latest raids but insisted on going to the microphone and giving them out himself. They were remarkably accurate.

Those reports, on the other hand, in which the Atlantiksender described a raid that was still in progress and gave precise details of what buildings and streets were on fire, or the harrowing eye-witness accounts of men and women and children being caught up in the melting asphalt of the Cuxhavener Strasse, or of Local Groupleader Schickedanz ordering the Teno to blow up the crowded shelter in the Buxtehuder Platz while the folk-comrades were still inside it—these were all fiction and guess-work. From the bomber pilots we knew approximately when and where the bombs had fallen, where fires were raging. We filled in the rest with the picture we wanted to present. Our listeners accepted these reports as true because the rest of our damage and air-raid reports had been so accurate.

Needless to say, the Atlantiksender paid great attention in its output to news campaigns intended to stimulate surrender and desertion. Prisoners of war, we showed, were going to have an unfair advantage over the fighting men when "peace broke out," for the enemy had set up excellent training courses for them to learn trades and professions in the prison camps. Many of them, too, were working outside the camps and being paid well in pounds and dollars—money which would have a high value at the end of the war, compared with the useless German mark.

Tucked away somewhere in most bulletins was an item about deserters. The International Red Cross, our favourite source for these, would report the increase in the number of German soldiers crossing into Sweden, Switzerland, or Spain, and the fact that, while many had been interned, the majority were earning good money in good jobs. The German authorities, it would be repeated again and again, were not able to take the threatened reprisals against the families of deserters because—and here came our old tag line—"they do not know who is missing because he has been killed, and who is missing because he has deserted."

Not all the news broadcasts, however, of the Atlantik-sender, and the medium-wave station with which it was soon to be coupled, were directed at the enemy. One of the most interesting and successful of our operations had neutral listeners as its target—the neutral firms and businessmen who were breaking the allied blockade by trading with Hitler. Most of these firms were being punished effectively enough by the Ministry of Economic Warfare, which put their names on a so-called "statutory list." This meant that they were under boycott and blockade. Any firm dealing with them would also find itself proscribed and commercially excommunicated. But there was a second list of firms who were only suspects. Their names were not published. British officials, however, had orders to put the evil eye on them whenever they could.

"Tom Brown" Stevens got hold of this "black list" of

suspects from M.E.W. as well as the secret file which revealed both the reasons for suspicion and the personal
background of the suspect firms' directors. The next thing
was that these neutral businessmen heard the secrets of
their private and commercial lives being publicly exposed
on our radio. Usually, their reaction was to protest to the
nearest British authorities, who, of course, denied any
connection with us. We then waited to see whether they
would mend their ways. If they did not, we followed up
with further broadcasts about them. As a rule, however,
one broadcast was enough.

One typical case was that of a firm of Swedish ex-
porters who were buying ball-bearings in Sweden and
smuggling them to Germany, thereby undoing the effects
of our bombing. Our story about the firm was so accurate
and so ribald that the Swedish authorities felt deeply hurt
in their national pride. They made unofficial representa-
tions about it to the British Ambassador, Sir Victor Mallet.

"We had our eye on this firm," said the Swedes with
injured dignity. "We were waiting to prosecute them,
when we had enough evidence. Now your broadcast has
warned them."

Sir Victor replied that he had no knowledge of the
Atlantiksender, and nothing to do with it. Then he sent me
a rocket through the Foreign Office.

M.E.W. however, were pleased with us. For the Swedish newspapers had taken up the story we had put out,
and the directors of the Swedish firm, fearing more Atlantiksender publicity, had cancelled all further deliveries
to Germany.

"It's blackmail by 'black,'" I said, congratulating "Tom
Brown."

The Navy programme was the first special programme for a Fighting Service which we launched, and in an astonishingly short time we had evidence that it was proving effective. My friends at the cages where German prisoners were interrogated told me that the Atlantiksender was helping them considerably. "You are doing all our preliminary softening up for us," said the R.N.V.R. Commander in charge of U-boat interrogation. "The men arriving now have all been told by their officers that the Atlantiksender is British. But they are so impressed by the universality of the Atlantiksender's intelligence service and the completeness of its information on everything to do with U-boats or themselves and their families, that they say, 'The British know it all anyhow. So I may as well make things more comfortable for myself by answering their questions.' Before you started the Atlantiksender it took us weeks to get them to that stage. Now they're in the ready-to-talk condition before they even get here."

Having seen what we could do, the Admiralty Intelligence people helped us more and more. Donald McLachlan was even able to arrange that N.I.D. agents in France should signal back such apparent trivia as the results of the football matches between U-boat crews. We were thus able to announce them within a few hours after the game.

"The Seventh U-Flotilla St. Nazaire," announced the Atlantiksender, "this afternoon beat the Second Flotilla by three goals to two in their football match at Lorient. The two teams are now celebrating at the Café Réunion. Congratulations on an excellent game. Goal scorers were . . ."

As we gave their names, Frankie Lynder attached to each one of them some little bit of gossip and badinage culled from his files.

Sometimes we would call up a U-boat which the Admiralty experts told us was likely to have left on a cruise, and play it some "special-request" music. The radio petty officer of *U-Luther* told me, after he had been captured, how much this trick had scared him when we played it on his boat. "We had sailed under all the usual secrecy— strict radio silence and all that—" he said, "but we had not been at sea for more than two days when Atlantik calls us up and plays us some special music. It's a mighty unpleasant sensation, I can tell you, to feel that you're being watched like that, and that the enemy knows exactly where you are." Which, of course, the enemy did not.

Another little trick which impressed our German listeners was that we announced decorations and honours for U-boat men before the German authorities themselves had done so. How did we manage this? By careful study we had worked out the number of tons which a commander had to sink before Admiral Doenitz conferred on him the appropriate decoration. We knew what the various commanders were managing to sink. Our files told us the rest. (Stevens successfully applied the same technique to German food rations. Again and again with the help of the experts at the Ministry of Economic Warfare he enabled us to announce a reduction or an increase in German rations before the news had been announced by the German Ministry of Food.)

The result of all this was to raise the prestige of the Atlantiksender as a rapid all-seeing purveyor of news to such heights that we were given credit for scoops which we had never in fact brought off. An illustration of this was the Luftwaffe officer commanding the German Air Force squadrons in the Bay of Biscay area. When he was shot down into the sea and made prisoner, he said to his first interrogater, "No good my attempting to keep anything secret from you fellows. You know it all anyhow. The Atlantiksender the other day even broadcast a verbatim report of my top-secret conference with the Navy on board a blockade breaker in the Gironde estuary. They told all about it within a few hours after the conference. Incredible!"

It was incredible, too, for it just was not true. What had really happened was that we had learned from the Admiralty that five armed merchant vessels were lying in the Gironde estuary with steam up. There was a possibility, the Admiralty thought, that the ships would try to break through the British naval cordon and make for Japan. So, just to play on the crews' nerves and show them that their secret was a secret no longer, we decided to pay them the honour of a special musical serenade.

"And now," said Vicky at her most dulcet, "by special request of the comrade blockade-runners who are getting awfully bored down there in the Gironde estuary while they await orders to sail, I am going to play a little selection of music from our brave allies in the East, a little foretaste for our comrades of many an *Ohrenschmaus* [ear feast] to come!" There followed the most cacophonous jumble of Japanese and Chinese records to be found in the archives of His Master's Voice. A day later we followed this up with more Japanese music and a talk on the difficulties the Luftwaffe were raising about the Navy's demands for air cover during the break-out. This was a very reasonable guess in view of what we knew from Air Commodore "Tubby" Grant and his colleagues in Air Intelli-

gence 3 of the number of fighters and reconnaissance aircraft available in the Biscay area.

By a helpful coincidence the Luftwaffe commander had
gone aboard one of the blockade-runners for a conference
with the naval commander of the expedition a little earlier
that very afternoon. He had been much irritated by the
officious security precautions of the naval men. Sentries
with fixed bayonets had been placed outside the ward-
room, and before the men would talk at all they made him
read the German equivalent of our Official Secrets Act,
sign it, and swear a solemn oath that he would talk with
no one about what he learned from them.

As soon as he got back to his quarters at the air base,
the Luftwaffe commandant switched on the Atlantiksender. The first thing he heard was Vicky's Japanese
concert, which was followed by the talk on the inability
of the Luftwaffe to provide adequate air cover.

"I laughed and I laughed till the tears ran down my
cheeks," he told the British interrogating officer. "There
was the Atlantiksender not only revealing Japan as the
destination of the trip, but giving a sentence-by-sentence
report of what had been said at this top-secret conference
behind the closed doors guarded by the sentries with fixed
bayonets. It was *kolossal*. And what a showup for those
stuck-up Navy fellows. But how on earth do you do it?
I suppose you had the place miked by your agents."

Admiral Godfrey tried to use the Atlantiksender for
deception purposes as well, and many were the ingenious
double bluffs that were carried out at his suggestion. For
it was a reasonable surmise that the German Naval Intelligence men devoted much close study to our broadcasts. For instance, when the Germans came up with a

new anti-radar device called Aphrodite—a ludicrous-looking rubber balloon released from the U-boat and floated on the waves with the intention of deflecting the R.A.F.'s electronic rays from the submarine—John Godfrey asked us to run a special "anti-Aphrodite" campaign. The Germans, he calculated, deducing from this that the Admiralty was worried about Aphrodite, would hold on to the balloon device, although it was, in fact, worse than useless.

His bluff worked. The Germans, despite the evidence they must have had of Aphrodite's failure, remained faithful to their toy balloon for an unbelievably long time.

This technique of publicly discussing German technical devices which the German security officers had said were super-secret was so successful with our U-boat listeners that we started using it in our transmissions to the German Air Force and Army as well. But it was the Admiralty who set the example to the Air Ministry and War Office by releasing the secret technical material to us to make these talks possible. We indulged in learned discussions of *Mücke* and *Wanze,* the latest secret weapons against our radar, and of *Zaunkönig,* the new German torpedo with an automatic homing device.

But, of course, our main concern was with the crews—our constant object being to set them against their officers. We had plenty of opportunities for doing so. For, as the war went on, considerable feeling developed between the old petty officers, veterans of many dangerous cruises, and the young commanders who would be put in charge of a U-boat after taking part in not more than two or three voyages as first or second officers. It was easy for us to suggest that these young officers, with their hunger for Knight's Crosses, were the natural enemies of their crews. And Eddy Mander saw to it that our grousing went straight to the petty officer's heart.

What with the appalling death rate among the U-boat crews and its exploitation by the subversive broadcasts of the Atlantiksender, that crack in German naval morale which Donald had talked of during our lunch at Frascati's had, by the end of October 1943, become a wide and gaping fact. It was time for us to go a step further. It was time for us to start softening up the German forces in France in preparation for the invasion of Europe.

Before we ever reached this stage, however, an entirely new set of problems was dumped on my plate. For both Dick Crossman and I had been promoted. Dick was made Director of Political Warfare against the Enemy and Satellites ("White"), and I was appointed Director of Special Operations against the Enemy and Satellites ("Black"). That meant that I now had over-all charge of the "black" assault on Hitler's satellites in addition to that on Germany itself.

Into new barracks hastily erected in the compound of M.B. marched Intelligence teams, editorial writers, speakers, and secretaries from Italy, Hungary, Bulgaria, and even Romania. Our canteen became a tower of Babel, as dark-eyed gypsy beauties from the Balkans flirted with my fair-haired German prisoners over toad-in-the-hole, powdered-egg omelettes, Spam fritters, soybean sausages, and the other irresistible delicacies from the repertory of wartime cooks.

The arrival of the Italian and Balkan teams in our midst certainly sharpened up the attack against the German forces. I was now able to see that our campaigns against the morale of the German occupiers received support from these regions. We, in our turn, were able to pick up some of their campaigns. Fortunately for me, the Englishmen directing the "black" stations of Italy, Hungary, and the Balkan countries were all skilled at their job. I knew only very little Italian, and no Hungarian, Bulgarian, or Romanian. So I would not have been able to give them the kind of editorial help I did with our German output, had it been needed.

The Italians were my first concern. As Mussolini's regime staggered and reeled under demoralizing defeats, first in Africa then in Italy itself, we launched fresh stations and fresh campaigns to hasten its end. The two most important of these were (1) Radio Livorno, an operation designed to help bring about the surrender of the Italian Navy, and (2) a counterfeit of the German-sponsored Radio of the Italian Fascist Republic.

Radio Livorno was the name we gave to a station which pretended to be operating on behalf of the Italian "resistance" from the radio cabin of an Italian warship, lying in the Livorno base. Night after night "Livorno" called the Italian ships at Spezia, Genoa, and other North Italian naval stations. In eloquent anti-German invective our speaker—a Maltese officer of the British Army—warned his comrades of the Italian Navy to be on guard against the Germans, particularly against German attempts to board and seize their ships. Night after night too, "Livorno" ordered the Italian patriots of the Navy to make no move without orders from itself. I waited anxiously for the Germans to launch a counterfeit of our tricky operation. To my relief, they failed to do so. The minds of the *Abwehr* apparently did not work along those lines.

Then, as the time for action approached, we began to

let it become clearer and clearer that "Livorno" was negotiating with the allies for the "liberation" of the Italian
Navy from the Germans. When, at last, the great day
came and "Livorno" on September 10, 1943, gave the order to sail, the Italian ships obediently upped anchor and
sailed for Malta, the rendezvous "Livorno" had given
them. There they surrendered to Admiral Cunningham
and General Eisenhower.

The whole "Livorno" operation had been run in the
closest contact with the Admiralty, who told us day by
day the rough gist of the messages they would like
"Livorno" to put out. It all went off so smoothly and successfully, that I was convinced that the Italian Navy chiefs
knew "Livorno" was the voice of Cunningham, and
obeyed it as such. But there was one man who did not
suspect it. This was our Maltese speaker, Randolph
Imozzi; he was convinced that by his vocal efforts in front
of the microphone he and he alone had brought about
the surrender of the Italian Navy. When the surrender
was announced, he put on his best uniform and paraded
before me in my office, fully expecting me to pin a decoration on his chest. Alas, I had no medals to bestow, only
compliments. Of these I gave him a feast. And he de-
served it, for never did a man work harder and more
enthusiastically.

Our counterfeit of the Radio of the Italian Fascist Republic required much technical skill. And though its results were not as dramatic as those of Radio Livorno, I
reckon we received fair dividends for the effort invested.
But, even if this counterfeit had been completely without
effect, it would still have been worth the work we put
into it, for it gave us experience with a new technique

which was to prove invaluable when later we came to mount a similar operation against the Germans.

It was Goebbels himself who presented us with the opportunity for a try-out against the Italians. Otto Skorzeny and his S.S. commandos had recently rescued Mussolini from his Italian anti-Fascist captors and enabled him to set up a Fascist Republican government under Hitler's protection in Northern Italy. Goebbels immediately provided him with a radio station so that he could continue to inspire the Italian public with his "dynamism."

This Fascist Republican Radio was a short-wave affair, transmitted from Munich on two frequencies simultaneously, and broadcasting not continuously, but for half-hour periods. I decided that the Doctor was not being sufficiently generous to the Duce and that we should remedy his niggardliness by giving Mussolini a third station with a short-wave frequency right alongside the other two.

I suggested to John Skeaping, my British colleague in charge of the Italians, that all we had to do was pick up the beginning of the Munich Italians' broadcast and relay it over our transmitter; then, at the right moment, we would break off the relay and come up with our own announcers and our own stuff; finally, when we had said our say, we would pick up our Munich friends again and allow them to finish their broadcast over our transmitter.

"How do you think you're going to be able to find the opening for the change-over, and how are you going to be able to blend the two programmes without the fake being obvious to all?" John asked.

But as it turned out the operation did not prove as dif-

ficult as all that. The Munich Italians played right into
our hands. They had divided their speaking programme
into three sections, each carefully separated from the
other by intermissions of military and patriotic music. All
we had to do was relay the first leg of their programme,
then come in with our own music and news when they
began the second. The trick was to make sure that the last
items of our news and announcements were so worded
that we could cut off in mid-paragraph and switch back
to the relay when Munich's music introduced the third
leg of their programme. Does it sound complicated? It
was. But after a fortnight's assiduous rehearsing our Italians were ready to go. And we could not have had better
speakers. They were two prisoners of war who, before
being called up for the Italian Army, had been professional announcers for Radio Italia.

What I hoped to achieve with this operation was that
Italian listeners searching for the Duce's station on their
dials would tune in to us by mistake as often as they
tuned in to the genuine Fascist Republican station. And,
much to the satisfaction of John and myself, and the Italian announcers and script writer, that was how it did indeed work out.

After only a few days of the operation the Duce's Munich men were indignantly and vehemently denying that
they had said the appalling things which monitors all
over the world reported them as saying. We got them so
tangled up in denials and counter-denials that in the end
Dr. Goebbels decided he must shut down his short-wave
broadcasts altogether. He gave them time instead on
Munich's medium-wave radio, to the great indignation of
the Bavarians, who were furious at losing their own radio

entertainment—a fury which we were to exploit to our profit only too soon.*

I am ashamed to say that one of the "mistakes" which the Fascist Republican Radio (our edition) perpetrated was to be inexcusably rude and hostile to His Holiness the Pope. The Vatican's protests were carried by Italian newspapers everywhere. Another silly thing the Fascist Republican Radio (our edition) did was to give advance news of the government's intention to devalue the lira. This produced a most satisfactory run on that currency. We also publicized an alleged arrangement by which the Allies were supposed to have declared a "mercy zone" which they had promised not to bomb in order that the inhabitants of the industrial cities of the Italian north could take refuge there and stay alive. We did so by broadcasting Mussolini's indignant denunciation of unpatriotic Italians who were leaving their work in the cities to take refuge in the "mercy zone."

Of the Balkan operations, there were two that stand out in my memory. One was designed to sabotage the supply of Romanian oil to Germany. Under the motto "Keep the oil underground; don't let the Germans play havoc with Romania's one great capital asset," we transmitted week in and week out a course of fourteen simple lessons in oil-well sabotage prepared for me by one of the British oil engineers I had met out in Romania at the beginning of the war. When the fourteen records had been transmitted, we started them all over again from the beginning.

The simplest of the lessons was, "If you see a valve or a stopcock in the oil fields just give it a turn as you pass."

* See report to Munich's Gestapo Chief Freiherr von Eberstein, quoted on pages 128–130.

I thought this such an attractive device that, without consulting my engineer friend again, I ran a similar campaign for the Austrian oil fields under the slogan *"Gehn ma drahn"*—roughly, "Let's take a turn—let's have a dance!"

But when, on a visit to Vienna after the war, I asked Mr. Van Sickel, the Canadian pioneer of the Austrian oil industry, whether our campaign had achieved any results in Austria, he hooted with derisive laughter. "Give the valves a twist, my boy, is splendid advice for mucking up the Romanian oil wells. But it won't work here. We have a different system for our oil wells, and there are no stopcocks and valves for you to turn!"

The other Balkan operation was Bulgarian. Believe it or not, our Bulgarian team set up a freedom station that was meant to sound like a Bulgarian freedom station run by the Germans. Roughly, its line was the same as if a Goebbels freedom station claiming to be British had broadcast in English—"Ve Prittischers must help ze Führer lipperate our gountry. . . ."

In order to put this one over convincingly, we had to find among the German refugees in Britain two who could speak Bulgarian with a strong German accent. We found them. They were excellent, and, for those who understood Bulgarian, wonderfully funny. I am told that this counterfeit of a counterfeit did a lot to make the Germans in Sofia look ridiculous. Everyone thought them responsible for a clumsy and insulting fake. And well may it have been so. For, as I used to tell my team, the simplest and most effective of all "black" operations is to spit in a man's soup and cry "Heil Hitler!"

10

At three minutes to six on the evening of October 24, 1943, Johnnie Kisch * was sitting, as usual, in front of the battery of grey painted receiving sets in his low ceilinged cabin at the B.B.C. monitoring station in Caversham. Johnnie had a boring job. His sets were tuned to the stations in the German radio network, and it was his task to watch for variations in their programmes—variations which suggested that the Germans were trying to put some secret code message across to an agent, or that Goebbels was up to some new trick in his propaganda

* At the time of writing, J. H. Kisch is the London editor of the German magazine *Quick*.

warfare. But there never were any variations. Night after night, day after day, Johnnie had to listen to the same dreary speakers churning out the same dreary propaganda. "The impregnable fortress of Europe, Hitler the champion of Western civilization against the Bolshevik hordes, the Jewish conspiracy . . ." Deadly stuff. Johnnie felt very sorry for himself.

Absent-mindedly he twiddled the knob on the set which was tuned in to Munich. It was now six o'clock on the dot. And then it happened. With a crash of drums and a blare of trumpets a jubilantly boisterous German march burst from the set. It was so loud that Johnnie immediately leaned forward to turn down the volume. As he did so, a voice which Johnnie had never heard before announced in crisp soldier German, "Here is the Soldiers' Radio Calais, broadcasting on wave bands 360 metres 410 and 492 metres. Coupled with it the German shortwave Radio Atlantic, on wavebands 30.7 and 48.3. We bring music and news for comrades in the command areas West and Norway. We shall now play dance music."

Johnnie had never heard of the Atlantiksender; he had specialized in the medium-wave band. And so he was amazed by the exhilarating dance music which was snappier and dancier than anything he had heard over the radio before. Johnnie reached for the telephone to call his superior.

"Hey Bob," he said, "there is a new German forces station broadcasting from Calais. Very powerful signal and really excellent music. It's on almost the same wave band as Munich."

"Right," said Bob. "Let me have a report."

At half-past six Johnnie called his superior again. "You really must listen to this station yourself, Bob," he said,

"I cannot make it out. It seems to be much more out-spoken than most of the German stations. They are putting out the usual German crap, but in between there are items which are quite different from the normal run. And I don't know whether they deliberately intended it as irony, but immediately after a quotation from that very optimistic speech of Gauleiter Sauckel, they had some very depressing news from the front in Russia. I wonder what's up?"

A few minutes later Johnnie Kisch, who is an intelligent young man, was able to make a pretty shrewd guess at what was up. A messenger arrived, and in an envelope marked "Secret" he handed Johnnie Kisch a D-notice—so-called because it was issued under the war-time emergency law known as the Defence Regulations. It was the same notice that had already gone out from the Ministry of Information to the editors of newspapers and news agencies.

"No reference will be made," it said, "to the radio transmissions of Soldatensender Calais or the Kurzwellensender Atlantik or to the contents of their broadcasts."

But in Germany, in German-occupied France, and the Low Countries there were many listeners who heard this first broadcast. And they had no D-notice to help them. They accepted the new station at its face value as a German station, and listened to it with wonder and pleasure. A less enthusiastic but equally attentive listener was Dr. Joseph Goebbels. Four weeks after the Soldatensender had first gone on the air he recorded in his diary for November 28, 1943, "In the evening the so-called Soldatensender Calais, which evidently originates in England and uses the same wave lengths as Radio Deutschland—when the latter is out during their air raids—gave us something to worry about. The station does a very clever job of propaganda, and from what is put on the air one can gather that the English know exactly what they have destroyed in Berlin and what they have not." *

Yes, we had made the medium wave at last. And not only did we have the powerful 600-kw transmitter nicknamed "Aspidistra" broadcasting us at full blast, but Harold Robin had also linked with it a small half-kilowatt mobile transmitter which he and his men had trundled to a spot on the coast near Dover where it was directly opposite Calais. Just a little touch for the benefit of those trying to get a fix.

But what a fight it had been to get authority for the new station and to pry "Aspidistra," the most powerful transmitter in Europe, from the grasp of the B.B.C.! Although "Aspidistra" had only been lent to them by our department, long possession had made the B.B.C. regard it as theirs by right. That it should be transferred to those rough, vulgar fellows of the "black" was unthinkable. But after almost four weeks of papers, meetings, and arguments the B.B.C. had been made to give way.

Ivone Kirkpatrick had been my chief antagonist. "'Black' is all right on short wave," he said with the clipped dogmatic self-assurance of the military man turned diplomat, "but if you get on the medium wave with all your lies and distortion, you will undermine the whole currency value of British propaganda as a purveyor of truth." Kirkpatrick represented the European Service of the B.B.C. in the counsels of the Political Warfare Executive, and as a high-ranking diplomat he carried great weight, particularly with Bruce Lockhart, who was

---

* Joseph Goebbels, *Diaries, 1942–1943,* edited and translated by Louis P. Lochner (New York, Doubleday).

a former Foreign Office man himself, and naturally coveted the good opinion of his senior colleagues.

But Bruce Lockhart was away ill at the time this decision had to be taken, and General Dallas Brooks was presiding over the Department in his place. General Brooks was a Marine, and what counted with him were the views of the Service ministries, particularly those of the Admiralty. The Service ministries, led by the Admiralty, were all for letting "black" have "Aspidistra" and some medium-wave frequencies. For the time had arrived to soften up the Germans in preparation for the invasion of German-held France. In the opinion of the chiefs of staff, the B.B.C. with its inhibitions and its passion for ideological debate was not quite sharp enough an instrument for this purpose. Something new and more ruthless was needed in addition to the B.B.C.: Soldatensender Calais.

Even the name "Calais" required approval before we could use it. The allied cover plan was designed to have Hitler and his Intelligence men believe that Calais and the area around it would be the main target of the invasion, and that Normandy was merely a diversion for deception purposes. If we named our transmitter Soldatensender Calais, would that make the Germans think the threat to Calais was bluff? In the end it was decided that it would not affect their decisions one way or the other, and I was allowed the name with its euphonic elegiac rhythm.

"Mind you don't let me down, Tom," were Dallas Brooks' last words to me before we let loose. "I'm taking a big gamble on this. If you make a mess of things it will be my head that rolls in the sand!"

I too feared that there was a danger here. Our staff was

only about one-third of that for the B.B.C.'s German service, and here we were putting out constantly changing
news bulletins with three service programmes every evening instead of just one, as we had been doing up to now
on "Atlantik."

"Calais has got to be absolutely first class for the first
six weeks," I told the team in our conference the next
morning. "We are going to have a lot of critics listening
in, and some of them will be trying to catch us out. So
there will be no leave for anyone for four weeks. *Einverstanden?*"

The team—émigrés, P.O.W.'s, and all—agreed with enthusiasm. They were grand fellows with tremendous *esprit
de corps* and a truly German pride in their work. And
when we did take our leaves again the standard set in
those early programmes never sagged. Instead, we improved all the time. But there were anxious moments. The
first was caused by Lindley Frazer, who was seconded
from my department to act as its chief liaison with Carleton Greene and the B.B.C. Lindley rang me on the department's internal telephone one evening soon after "Calais"
had started.

"Tom," he said, "unless I was badly mistaught at Balliol,
the philosopher Spinoza was of the Jewish race and religion."

"Lindley," I said with the cheerfulness of a television
quiz-master awarding a prize, "you are right! How can I
help you?"

"Well"—Lindley now crashed heavily down upon me
—"it seems a little improbable to me, in view of the
philosopher's race, that there should be a Spinoza Street
in Nazi Frankfort on the Main today. However, I just
heard G.7 [our code name for the Soldatensender] an-

nounce that R.A.F. bombs had dropped last night in Frankfort's Spinoza Street."

"Oh dear, oh dear!" I said, now very small indeed. "Thank you very much, Lindley. I'll look into it right away."

My heart was in my mouth. I feared we had fallen victims to a pre-Hitler Baedeker. But as good luck had it, we had not. The town plan Schlabrenhorst had worked on was up to date. For some reason, the Frankfort municipal fathers had gone on calling Spinoza Street Spinoza Street even after Hitler had taken over, and I was able to reassure Lindley that Calais had not slipped. But it was just the kind of mistake that could have tripped us up.

The reception of the Soldatensender by the German public did not justify the gloomy foreboding of Ivone Kirkpatrick. Very soon after we started, reports began to come in from prisoners and other sources showing that the German public, far from dismissing it as a clumsy hoax, were eagerly lapping up the Soldatensender and accepting its "candid and outspoken news reports" as evidence that the Reich propaganda men had to tell many truths to the Wehrmacht which they kept from the German civilian public. Poor little Dr. Goebbels was inundated with reports from Himmler's police officials and from the Gauleiters telling him of the havoc the Soldatensender was causing.

One report in particular caused me great joy when a copy of it turned up among a bunch of captured documents. It was from the Bavarian Ministry of the Interior and was addressed to Freiherr von Eberstein, the Munich Chief of Himmler's S.D. Security Service. I passed it with my compliments to Kirkpatrick.

Security Service of the Reichsführer SS   Munich 13
SD—Directing Sector Munich   Franz Joseph Street 38
III C 4—AZ 17/43—Dr.Kn/Hi   16.3.1944.
[Stamped: Bavarian State Ministry of the Interior: 20 March
    1944]
Transmitted   Marked for
on 18.3.44.   SS Obergruppenführer and General of Police
               Freiherr von Eberstein
SS Obergruppenführer   Ref: Reception and effect of the trans-
               missions of the Soldatensender
               Calais among the population.

Since October 1943 increasingly frequent references are
being made by the population to the transmissions of the radio
station which calls itself Soldatensender Calais and concerning whose nationality people are not clear.

The chief effect of the station's news transmissions, which
have been described as psychologically excellent, emerges
from its practice of giving absolutely unexceptionable information, which has also been carried verbatim in the German
News Service, and mixing in with it a number of isolated, more
or less tendentious items. This has caused large portions of the
population to believe that Soldatensender Calais was a German station, perhaps one of the many Soldatensender started
up in the occupied territories also without anything about them
being officially communicated to the population. That the reports of the Soldatensender Calais often had a sharpness otherwise nowhere to be found in the German News Service was in
some cases explained by the population on the following lines:
"After all, they cannot present the soldier at the front with the
same propaganda as they sell us at home. They have to be
more honest with the soldiers at the front."

As was shown in the course of the last two months of the
year 1943, Soldatensender Calais, which originally transmitted
on a wave length around 360m. and only later started to
broadcast on the frequency of Munich, owes a large part of

its audience to one quite special circumstance. Since September 1943, it will be remembered, the Reichssender Munich carried in the evening hours transmissions for Fascist Republican Italy which, as they continued, caused the greatest indignation among listeners here and forced them to dial other stations in order not to lose their evening's entertainment. They twiddled and found the Soldatensender Calais, which was coming through with extraordinary power and held the population with its news service.

Since the New Year, observers in Munich and the provinces point out with all urgency that the transmitter has caused the greatest unrest and confusion among the population by news concerning the situation at the fronts and at home and that the population is showing ever-increasing trust in the station's news service, as its reports have shown themselves more or less correct. There is general agreement that the majority of the opinions expressed among the population concerning the situation at the front are derived from the news of the Sender Calais which, in the words of a Munich radio expert of note, with Belgrade and the Luftnot-Sender Laibach belongs to the three most listened-to radio stations.

Politically responsible observers demand with increasing urgency that action should be taken against this station with all means at our disposal, and above all that the population must be enlightened as to its character as an enemy station. As this had not been done so far, the population feels it has the right to listen to the station, on the one hand because they cannot help listening to it on the Munich frequency, and on the other hand because its effectiveness is not being interfered with sufficiently.

As it has not been possible to reduce listening to Soldatensender Calais by confidential hints as to its origin, it was considered justified that the station should be powerfully jammed.

But this jamming had unpleasant consequences, particularly of late. The noise of the jammer mobilized against Calais made reception of the Reichsstation Munich quite impossible in many parts of the Gau Oberbayern and particularly in the Munich town area. Calais itself, on the other hand, could be received clearly. The Reichssender Munich is completely drowned (and it is noteworthy that many people have identified the jammer put on against Calais as an enemy jammer attacking the "German station" Calais).

In view of the very grave effects of this enemy station from a morale and propaganda point of view it seems very necessary to limit as far as possible the effectiveness of the Soldatensender Calais, for the attempts to jam it that have been made hitherto must be considered insufficient in the light of the listener reports received here.

per pro [signature illegible]
S.S. Sturmbannführer

On the strength of this note, Giesler, the Gauleiter, sent another shorter note to Dr. Goebbels repeating most of these points and asking the minister to take steps against Calais.

In France too, the Soldatensender was causing the German authorities considerable misgivings about the effects of its "poison" on the "simple" minds of their soldiers. The High Command issued orders to unit commanders to lecture their men about the "poison transmitter Calais" and laid down the lines for the lectures in a special directive.

But I am happy to say we had plenty of evidence that despite the directive and the talks our audience was still growing.

11

For several weeks now, I had been carrying in my wallet a precious card marked with the cryptic word "Overlord" and under it my name and the security officer's signature. "Overlord," as all the world knows today, was the code name for the invasion of Normandy, and the card meant that I was one of the few taking part at this early stage in the planning of these decisive operations.

In fact, as far as I was concerned, my operations had already begun. To my unit had been assigned the task of "softening up" the German forces in the west. We were to try and produce in them a frame of mind in which they would show the least amount of resistance to the Allied armies, when at last the attack was launched. It was for this that Dallas Brooks had pried the giant transmitter from the B.B.C. and handed it to me. And we were already going ahead full blast. Now the general had gone one step further. He had ordered me to make a softening-up plan for the B.B.C.'s operations as well, and to see that they fitted in with ours.

I knew what I wanted to do with "Calais." I was already doing it. I knew too, what I considered the role of the B.B.C. should be at this stage. But were my friends at the B.B.C. going to like it, when I told them? Were they going to accept it? Or was I going to have another fight on my hands, like that with Kirkpatrick over "Aspidistra"?

My over-all objective was to try to lull the German troops in the west into the same false sense of security and sybaritic preoccupation with their creature comforts that I had seen the German propagandists induce in the French during the long phony war that preceded the German invasion of 1940.

On "Calais" we were already doing all we could to suggest to the Germans that the war in the west was no war at all, just a "Sitzkrieg" in which all military effort was futile and ludicrous. Worse than that, military efficiency was positively dangerous.

"Units which show themselves smart and efficient," said Calais, "are drafted to the Eastern Front. Promotion in France is a sure way to death in Russia."

The defeatist pun of Herr Schlicke, my Friedrichs Werdersches Gymnasium schoolmaster of the first war, *"Lieber ein heiles Kreuz als ein eisernes"* ("Rather an unbroken backbone than an Iron Cross") was embroidered by us in scores of variations. News item after news item illustrated the general theme that France was regarded by the O.K.W. (High Command of the Wehrmacht) as a theatre of inferior importance; and that in quality of manpower and armament the troops in France were far inferior to those on the Eastern Front, which was the operations area where Germany's fate was being decided. The idea behind this stress of the Eastern Front's priority was, that when the Allies attacked, we would be able to tell the German units in France that they had been written off by the High Command, that no reinforcements would be sent to them, no supplies. Their front did not matter.

I could not allow the B.B.C. men to come in on this campaign. If I did, they would be certain to show our hand in no time at all. They would want to put the campaign over in big lumbering talks and commentaries, not in subtly dispersed news items as we did. Much better, therefore, for the B.B.C. to stay right out of it for the time being. Their best contribution to the softening-up campaign, I argued, would be a stoic unawareness of any change in the west. All I would ask them to do was emphasize still further the rigours of the war in Russia and the immense resources of the Red Armies with their supplies of American materiel. Under no circumstances should either the B.B.C. or their allies of the Voice of America be allowed to indulge in any threats of the "We are going to crush you with the power of our invincible armada" variety. There would be plenty of time for that *after* D-day.

I put all this to Dallas Brooks, and he agreed and approved. But he too thought we might have a tough job in persuading my British and American colleagues in charge of the "white" to practise abstinence and self-restraint—particularly when they heard "black" campaigning away at the top of "Aspidistra's" overloud voice. I decided I had best find myself some influential allies in addition to Dallas Brooks.

So, together with Donald McLachlan, who had now been attached to the staff of Britain's Admiral Ramsay, the naval commander for "Overlord," in order that he might give us still better inside news, I set out to call on the Services planners concerned with the forthcoming operation, and explain our ideas to them. At the Combined Operations headquarters, in Norfolk House, we talked with Brigadier Arthur Head and Johnnie Vass. They were enthusiastic. I visited the newly arrived American General Robert McClure, who was to have charge of Psychological Warfare at SHAEF—the Supreme Headquarters of the Allied Expeditionary Forces. He promised his support. I dined with General Spaatz, the American Air Force Commander. And in his hospital room I consulted the British psychological warrior who carried the most weight with the Americans—Dick Crossman.

Dick had left London soon after he had been appointed Director of Political Warfare to the Enemy and Satellites ("White") to go out to North Africa. There he had been master-minding the highly successful Anglo-American psychological-warfare effort under McClure during the campaigns in Algeria, Tunis, and Sicily. But now he was back in London, and in hospital with a dangerous embolism which threatened his life—the result, not of enemy action, but of a ferocious wasp sting.

Dick, lying there in his hospital ward, with phlebitis

still creeping up his leg and threatening his heart, was all charm and enthusiasm. He had been listening to "Calais" as he lay in bed, he said, and it was the slickest thing ever.

"Of course," he insisted, "it is not 'black.'"

"No," I said, "it is something new. Donald and I call it 'grey.' It is between black and white. No doubt many of our German listeners realize we can't really be German. Nevertheless, they accept us gratefully, because we don't make that 'Boom, boom, boom' V-noise of the B.B.C. which betrays them to the Gestapo, and because we sound like ordinary Germans, not a lot of émigrés."

"Charming, charming," said Dick Crossman, "really charming! Wait till I tell the B.B.C.!"

But he did not, of course, betray my treasonable views about their announcers' voices to the B.B.C. and the Voice of America. Instead, when they too called on him in the hospital, he persuaded them that my plan was right, and quite properly had the support of the Services planners. The result was that when, a few days later, Donald, Dallas Brooks, and I faced my "white" colleagues and Carleton Greene, everything went off smoothly and the B.B.C. accepted the role I had assigned to it without objection. So, too, under instructions from McClure, did the Voice of America. And I am happy to report that by February 1944 Dick was sufficiently restored to hobble out on a stick and bring his influence to bear on the "white" planning at Supreme Headquarters.

The Soldatensender Calais did not use the Russian front only as a bogey to frighten Hitler's soldiers in France out of showing too much keenness and efficiency, and as a pretext for feeling "written off" "deserted" and "second class." We also used it as a stage on which to present mysterious new American "miracle weapons" against which resistance was useless.

The Americans, reported the Soldatensender, had been supplying the Russians with these ultra-modern "super-weapons." One of them was a phosphorous shell of unprecedented penetrative power which burst through the thickest armour and concrete and burned up everything inside it. It was this new weapon and others like it, we said, that were responsible for the latest German defeats in Russia. To my gratification, in one instance at least this propaganda had its effect, as we learned soon after D-day.

Through amplifiers an appeal had been made to Lieutenant General von Schlieben, who commanded the Fort du Roule blocking the American advance in the Cherbourg perimeter.

"You and your men have put up a gallant fight," said the voice through the amplifier, "but your position is hopeless. The only thing for you is to surrender while there is still time. Otherwise you and your men will be destroyed."

For a few minutes all was silence, and the team of psychological warriors feared they would be forced to admit failure. But suddenly a voice could be heard calling from the German position. It was General von Schlieben himself.

"I cannot surrender," said the general. "My orders are to fight to the last man and the last cartridge. It would be different if you could prove to me that our position is hopeless. If you could, for instance, fire one of those phosphorous shells . . ."

The Americans complied with alacrity. The nearest battery fired an ordinary common or garden shell at the fort. Up went the white flag, the great steel and concrete gate of the turret swung open, and out trooped the general with his men. In his huge great coat and steel helmet, the knight's cross gleaming under his heavy jowl, the general was the picture of gloom. But his honour had been salved, Fort du Roule was ours, and the way into Cherbourg was clear. The procedure was repeated with success on several further occasions by the Americans and ourselves at Concarneau and elsewhere.

But we had yet another motive for stressing the theme that "the true defence of the German fatherland is on the Eastern Front." I hoped that this "Calais" campaign might have a political impact on leaders of the German officers' corps.

We knew that the generals were becoming increasingly restive about the consequences of Hitler's interference with them and their strategy. "Peace feelers" were being noted with increasing frequency, and they were coming from men who claimed they had the support of the generals.

For some time already we had been attempting not only to speak in the name of this "army opposition," but to give its leaders the kind of encouragement that "white," as the official voice of the Allies, was unable to give them. We had been seeking to suggest to them that all they had to do was overthrow Hitler for us to be ready to start peace negotiations. For instance, when the *Frankfurter Zeitung* was closed down by Hitler and I produced a counterfeit of a "free" *Frankfurter Zeitung,* edited ostensibly by the German Resistance, I included in it a leading article on the need for the overthrow of Hitler and the establishment of a German peace government.

"Are the Western powers ready for peace talks?" asked the article. "We believe that in the light of first cautious contacts of German military circles in the West with the enemy we can answer this question in the affirmative. Only, we must act at last!" And there had been other similar gestures.

It seemed to me just possible that the generals might regard this "Calais" campaign as encouragement for their dream of revolt against the Führer followed by a separate peace with the West. Such a separate peace was, of course, out of the question. But if "Calais" by its repetition of the priority for the Eastern Front theme could trick the generals into action against the supreme war-lord, I was going to have no regrets. A coup by the generals, whether successful or not—even so much as the suspicion of an anti-Hitler conspiracy among them—would help to hasten Hitler's defeat. And as it turned out, we were to be rewarded here too.

When, in September 1944, I interviewed Otto John, the only survivor of the generals' conspiracy to get away abroad, I learned that our broadcasts had indeed been heard by the conspirators, and interpreted in precisely the sense I had hoped. I am sorry the generals ended their lives on Hitler's meat-hooks. But I cannot say that I have any compunction about having raised false hopes in them. For these men and their caste were the original patrons and sponsors of Hitler's movement. They were the profiteers of his Reich. And they only rose against him when it was clear that he and his war of conquest were doomed.

Critical readers may well object that I paid too little attention to the German conscience as an ally in the struggle against Hitler.

"What about the Church opposition to Hitler?" they might say. "What about Pastor Niemöller and Archbishop von Galen? What about the Scholls? What did you do to support and encourage them?"

I agree that on the Soldatensender I made little attempt to appeal to anything but instincts of self-interest and self-preservaion in our German listeners, both personal and national. When we suggested methods of sabotage to U-boat men, we did not approach them as pacifists or even as anti-Nazis. We told them in news items how other crews had successfully delayed the departure of their ship by unattributable acts of sabotage which we carefully described. To launch into a denunciation of the war as such at this pre-invasion stage would have been out of character for a "soldiers' radio" of the type we purported to be. Demands for an end to the war we did not begin to make until after the "peace generals," as we were to call them, had given us the green light with their rebellion of July 20, 1944.

None the less, we did make our "black" appeal to the humanitarian conscience of the Germans. We made it through a Roman Catholic priest. Father Andreas was a young Austrian of Styrian peasant stock who had received special permission from his order to speak on a clandestine radio under my direction. "Christ the King" was the name of this "black" station—"G.8" to the engineers.

What I had been looking for when I first decided to add a religious broadcast to my battery of "black" radios was someone like Father Muckermann, the intellectual German cleric who used to write brilliantly argued religious articles on social and political subjects for the Ullstein newspapers before Hitler came to power. Instead, I found this simple peasant priest, whose broadcasts, because of the earthy directness of their language and the beaming sincerity and goodness of the speaker, were

among the most moving radio talks I have ever listened
to.

Father Andreas usually opened by playing a few minutes of recorded music—Beethoven, Haydn, Bach, or
some of Nadia Boulanger's Monteverdi disks. That put his
listeners into the right contemplative mood. Then, having announced the name of the station, he would conduct
a very brief service with some more music, sacred this
time, before launching into his talk. In these talks Father
Andreas revealed to the Germans the infamous things that
were being done in their name to the Jews, and to the
Slav peoples of the East. He described the horrors of
Auschwitz, Natzweiler, and Mauthausen, concerning all
of which Clifton Child was able to brief him from our ex-
tensive intelligence reports.

He told of the monstrous "T.4" action—so-called because for a time the headquarters of the Nazi Euthanasia
Organization was housed at Tiergarten Strasse 4 in Berlin
—by which tens of thousands of sick persons were being
removed from hospitals and concentration camps under
the orders of a committee of Nazi doctors and sent to a
"mercy death" in the gas chambers.

He denounced the sadistic medical experiments of the
S.S. doctors with live prisoners, the no less cynical experiments in eugenics of the S.S. Lebensborn group which
mated S.S. men with unmarried girls in order to produce
a Germanic master race. He denounced the Nazi attack
on the German sense of family, the party's contempt for
all human and moral law. His material for these talks was
factual and accurate. It contained no inventions, no rumours. And his indictment of the "godless rulers" was delivered with a simple Styrian eloquence which made it a
hundred times more telling than had it been a religious

rodomontade of the Abraham à Santa Clara style which I originally had in mind for him.

So effective were his broadcasts that I seriously considered putting some of them out on the Soldatensender. We could have done so by pretending that we had recorded them from one of his transmissions. But in the end I decided against it. I did not wish to ruin another operation in which I had involved Father Andreas—without, I confess, taking him into the secret. For soon after he had begun his broadcasts, I asked my friends in S.O.E. and O.S.S. to have their rumour agents in the neutral capitals spread it around that this "Christ the King" radio was a "black" station secretly operated by the Vatican radio! That rumour caught on remarkably well, and in no time at all it spread not only to Switzerland, where the Father had a great following, but to Germany and Austria as well. It was superb "evidence" of the Pope's condemnation of the Nazi regime, and far too valuable to hazard by identifying Father Andreas even remotely with the "grey" broadcasts of "Calais-Atlantik."

Yet another "black" radio which played its part during this "softening-up" period was a workers' station. The underlying idea was that the speakers were anti-Nazi electronic engineers working in some large concern like Siemens which was building radio transmitters. They used the transmitters for their broadcasts on pretence of testing them. The call sign of the station was the Lili Marlene song. A Lili Marlene record would be played through once, then put on again, and at a point about a quarter or halfway through it would be roughly cut off and the voice of a proletarian anti-Hitler fighter would come on the air. Like some shop steward reporting to his committee, he gave news concerning conditions and grievances in various factories. He transmitted detailed instructions on factory sabotage, slow-down techniques, and methods of malingering. He also dictated short leaflets and stickers with slogans.

Just to make sure that the stickers did, in fact, make their appearance in Germany, we manufactured some of them ourselves. Agents of S.O.E. and O.S.S. took them to Germany and surreptitiously pasted them on lavatory walls and hoardings. I found one of them myself on the wall of a factory ruin in Essen, when I got there soon after its capture in 1945.

"Macht den Führer kalt," it said, *"dann wird die Stube wieder warm!"* "Make the Führer cold [i.e. kill him], then the room will soon be warm again."

12

As though to symbolize the *top* top secrecy of my work for "Overlord," I had been assigned an office on the topmost floor of my department's new headquarters in Bush House. It was a pleasant little white-walled room right under the roof of what then was still one of the tallest buildings in London. From its windows Betty Colbourne, my blonde, curly-headed young personal assistant could gaze across the grey tesselated desert of London rooftops beneath us all the way to the dome of St. Paul's.

And here, in this eyrie, high up over London, Betty and I now received our hush-hush callers—Poles, Danes, Norwegians, Frenchmen, Hollanders, Americans, and

British. They were officers of the underground Resistance groups in the German-occupied territories. Aircraft sent out by S.O.E. and O.S.S. had picked them up from secret airstrips right under the noses of Hitler's allegedly all-seeing S.S. guards. Then they had been flown to London for briefing in the roles that they and their groups were to play in the coming liberation of Europe. As part of that briefing they were now calling on me, so that I could learn from them what my unit could do to help theirs, and explain in what way they could help us.

As I listened to the lively, slim-waisted young Polish aristocrats, who seemed to know the latest and most fashionable London night-spots so much better than I did, it seemed incredible to me that only a few days earlier they had been in Cracow helping to publish a German-language newspaper with news items monitored from the Atlantiksender. Or that the tall young English colonel earnestly urging me to set up a new clandestine radio for the Slovenes had blown up the key signal-box of the railway junction of Laibach only the day before yesterday. I felt quite embarrassed by the deference with which these experts in physical disintegration listened to my exposition of the "black" possibilities of their work.

I had one major request for them: whenever they killed a German I wanted them to do their best to make it look as if he had been killed by Germans. "We want Hitler and the Gestapo to believe that they are faced not only with a Polish or a French underground but with a German anti-Nazi resistance as well."

To my great relief they all saw the point, and soon I had them as enthusiastic about planting evidence designed to trick the Germans into thoughts and actions inimical to Hitler's war effort as we were in manufacturing them.

I had plenty of samples to show them. One, designed to stimulate desertion to Sweden and Switzerland, was a leaflet got up to look exactly like a propaganda handout issued to officers by the O.K.W. under the title of *"Mitteilungen für die Truppe"*—"Information for the Troops." I produced a genuine German original so that my visitors could assure themselves that our forgery had the same format, the same kind of paper, the same print, and the same style of language. Our leaflet discussed the problem of the increasing number of desertions to neutral countries and called on officers to instruct their men not to leave the hunt for deserters to the overburdened and by no means numerous Field Police, but to watch out themselves for these treacherous cowards and prevent them from giving neutral countries a poor impression of Wehrmacht fighting spirit. The idea, I explained, was for members of the underground to leave this leaflet where a German officer might have dropped it and where it could be picked up by a German soldier. "A leaflet like this," I said, "will be a hundred times more effective in stimulating desertion than any propaganda of manifestly allied origin."

Another sample was a poster purporting to have been issued by the German Field Police.* It showed a poorly printed picture of a German soldier who was "wanted" by the German authorities for murder. The description of the man in the *Steckbrief*, like the portrait it went with, could fit almost any German soldier or officer in uniform. "Erwin Bauer," said the police notice, "was last seen in Oslo in the uniform of an S.S. captain, but is known also to have

* See Appendix, page 284.

used the uniforms of a Luftwaffe captain, an Army captain, and even of a party Sonderführer." The message of the notice was that the man was such a dangerous criminal that the Field Police asked for him to be delivered to them *alive or dead*. It was an open invitation to shoot German soldiers. And the invitation by implication included the Norwegians as well, for the notice was printed in both German and Norwegian.

"We have had some highly satisfactory results with this piece of 'evidence' in Norway," I told my guests. "The Haugesund underground managed to provide it with the correct rubber stamps of their local *Kommandantur* and post it up in quite a number of places, including the notice board of the German officers' mess in one of the hotels. They had a lot of fun before the Germans discovered what was up. Now, of course, if you would like to use it, we could probably fix you up with the correct rubber stamps, if you don't have them yourselves."

But nearly always my visitors already had all the German rubber stamps they required. I was amazed how well equipped these guerrillas were with the tools for forging German passes.

So, too, were we. For we had come a long way since that time in May 1941 when we could not forge a page of the *Völkischer Beobachter* for lack of suitable German type faces and newsprint. We now had our own special printing unit capable of producing counterfeits of any German document, from army orders to postage stamps and ration cards.

The genius responsible for the change was Armin Hull, who had come to us from a balloon barrage unit. He was a printer who had made a special study of German typography and printing techniques. Even before the war he regularly visited Germany and made a point of collecting specimens of German printing. He carried them all back with him in his baggage—newspapers, tram tickets, commercial and private stationery, business forms, police "wanted" posters, and anything else he could lay his hands on.

His greatest asset, however, from my point of view, was that he had an unrivalled knowledge of where to look in Britain for the printing types we needed in our operations. Before the war, the British printing trade had imported a good deal of type from Germany, but it was scattered all over the country. Bit by bit Hull managed to hunt it down until he had assembled a fantastic mass of founts in our secret composing room. I recall that on one occasion before this type collection was formed he visited six printing firms during two days or so to collect the lines of type we required for counterfeiting the letterhead of the Reichsbank. The final result was absolutely identical with the original, and probably only Hull could have achieved it.

He also had a first-class knowledge of the paper-making industry and arranged for British mills to counterfeit German papers and watermarks.

Nor was he at a loss if it became necessary for us to forge signatures and handwriting. Once we needed to forge a letter written by K. E. Krafft, one of Goebbels' tame astrologers. Hull produced the perfect forgery within three days.

"How on earth did you do this one?" I asked him, fascinated as I always was by his technique.

"Oh," said Armin at his most off-hand, "I looked up a friend of mine at Scotland Yard and asked him whether he knew a good forger who would like to serve his King and

Country in this way. He put me on to an artist doing time for forgery in Wormwood Scrubs, and there you are!"

Armin Hull was a great hand, too, at producing printing that looked exactly as if it had been produced by underground amateurs in a cellar. He had installed a tiny printing press in his office and often spent his evenings printing short runs of "sabotage" leaflets. He said that he could never find a professional printer capable of doing such work badly enough.

The fact of the matter was that Hull was a perfectionist. Not for him the *near*-perfect work which our opposite numbers working for Goebbels and S.D. chief Walter Schellenberg occasionally smuggled into Britain. I once showed him a little octavo-sized anti-Jewish leaflet which had been picked up in a Soho pub. To me it looked genuine. It had a London imprint; the type in which it was set was type we use in Britain; the format was British. But Hull took only one look at it and immediately pulled a small folding type scale out of his pocket.

"Made in Germany," he said when he had finished measuring. "This is set in Linotype Bodoni such as we also use in this country. But this lot has been cast on a German type body with a so-called Didot mould, which is fractionally larger than that for the English body and leaves a little more space between the lines. That, my dear Watson, gives it away."

"Humph." I pondered, and then a bright idea occurred to me. "And do you use the Didot body for our fakes?"

"Of course I do," Hull snorted indignantly. "The first thing I did when we started this work was to get all the necessary typecasting moulds converted from English to Didot standard."

One could not catch him out. He really was a champion counterfeiter.

Although our radio output had enjoyed top priority, my team and I had worked hard during 1941, 1942, and most of 1943 on producing what I may call "black literature." And there were quite a few bits of "evidence" which Betty and I were able to spread on the plain deal table of my office before our clients from the underground. We called them "evidence" because they often backed up in documentary or other form the stories and campaigns we were putting over on the radio.

There was a round saucer-size sticker, for instance, headed "Six weeks in dock," with instructions for German U-boat men on how to sabotage a submarine Diesel engine. We had "sold" this originally to the Norwegian underground, who had put it up all around the U-boat pens at Bergen and Trondhjem. Now I hoped to persuade the Poles to do the same for me at Gdynia and the French at Lorient and St. Nazaire.

The purpose of these stickers, as I explained to my clients, was not so much to get the crews to sabotage their boats, though it would be pleasant if they did, but to worry the German Security Service. If we could get the Gestapo flat-foots snooping around the boats, showing the U-boat men that they were suspect, that would help to undermine their pride and self-confidence, and weaken their fighting morale.

Similar thinking underlay another exhibit—our handbook teaching Germans how to malinger and trick their doctors into granting them a spell of sick leave. We had got this up in a number of different disguises—as a German Navy handbook on Physical Training, as a hymn-book, as a railway time-table, as an almanac, and even as a straightforward paperback of the Reclam Series with the title "*'Krankheit rettet' von Dr. med. Wilhelm Wohl-tat*" ("'Sickness saves you' by William Benefactor, M.D.").

One disguise which appealed to me, as a non-smoker, was a wafer-paper version which was packed inside a well-known German make of cigarette papers for smokers who "rolled their own." In the P.T. handbook, as in the hymnbook and the time-tables, the first few pages were identical copies of the German original. In the cigarette packets, too, the first papers were genuine cigarette papers. It was only when you got further inside all these "covers" that our "health instructions" made their appearance.

The techniques for malingering which we recommended had been specially devised by M.B.'s own "witch doctor," the late Dr. J. T. McCurdy of Corpus Christi College, Cambridge, a wise old one-eyed Canadian. McCurdy's peace-time job was to practise and teach the healing of mental illness. Now he revelled in applying his expertise against Hitler's Germans in the reverse.

Dr. McCurdy laid down two fundamental rules for ma-lingerers. Firstly, "the malingerer must give the physician the impression that here is a patriotic citizen, dedicated to his duty, who has the misfortune to be ill, despite him-self." Secondly the would-be malingerer must never tell the doctor that he is ill, that he is suffering from some specific disease, or volunteer symptoms. "One single symp-tom," said the handbook, "which the doctor has discovered by his own questions, is worth ten which the patient has volunteered."

Then the booklet proceeded to enumerate the symp-toms the patient should allow the doctor to discover in examination. It classified these symptoms not by illness, but by what kind of a leave was desired by the patient, whether he wanted a short respite from duty, a longer one, or whether he wanted to be exempt for the duration of the war.

"Our purpose in preparing this material," I explained to the officers, "is twofold, as in the case of the sabotage stickers. On the one hand I hope it will stimulate malingering among the Germans; on the other hand I hope it will cause German doctors who are warned about the handbook—as they are bound to be—to suspect malingering where there is in fact no malingering. I have high hopes that right now they are sending genuinely sick men and women back to duty, possibly even to spread infection, because they believe their symptoms have been faked up with the aid of this unspeakable fellow Dr. med. Wohltat."

My underground clients loved it.

Alas, things did not turn out altogether as I had intended. The German authorities were so impressed with the potentialities of Dr. McCurdy's handbook that they had it translated into English and shot it into the British and American lines. This version of our opus even outlasted hostilities. Copies of it were fetching a good price in London's Soho right up to 1952. For Britain's new Welfare State had put a premium on the wisdom it purveyed.

Among other samples of "black" printing I tried to sell to my foreign visitors, was an astrological magazine called *Zenith*. Armin Hull had got it up most beautifully with advertisements photocopied from genuine German astrological magazines. The text came from a famous Berlinborn astrologer, Louis de Wohl, whom I used to visit in his Piccadilly basement flat in Athenæum Court almost every time I was in London. He was a most sinister-looking creature, and it was with trepidation that, drawing partly on my knowledge of coming operations, partly on my store of propaganda campaigns, I sought to guide this new Nostradamus into lines which would fit our purposes of subversion.

There he sat, as I entered his den, a vast, spectacled jellyfish of a man dressed in the uniform of a British Army captain, puffing over-dimensional rings of smoke from an over-dimensional cigar—a khaki jellyfish in a spider's web of smoke.

As I nervously put forward my views on what I rather hoped the stars might be foretelling, he frowned at me with terrifying ferocity, as though to reprove me for my infidel cynicism. Then he would grab up a handful of astrological charts from his Chippendale escritoire and make some rapid astral calculations. This done, he would turn once more to me, his frown now relaxed into a patronizing smile. With the air of the master addressing a promising neophyte he would say in his guttural Berlin English: "How do you do it, my friend? It is most extraordinary. There is something very much like you say. In the . . ."

Then there would follow some to me completely unintelligible jargon about constellations, aspects, signs, and so forth. But I had to keep the straightest of straight faces when making my suggestions. For my astrologer always insisted that he would under no circumstances be prepared to prostitute his sacred knowledge to purposes of subversion, much as he abhorred Hitler and what he stood for. It was simply a most fortunate coincidence that what I suggested so often fitted in with what the stars did indeed foretell.

Undoubtedly he was a great artist in his field. And *Zenith* became a nice little sideline of psychological warfare. It contained horoscopes for Germany's leaders, prognostications for U-boats and aircraft according to the date and hour of their launching and sortie, and, of course, those general forecasts of woe or weal for persons born between certain dates without which no astrological magazine would be complete.

My respect for the sage's mystic integrity, however, did not preclude me from antedating some numbers of *Zenith* in order to include astoundingly accurate forecasts of events which had in fact already taken place. Thus Hitler's defeats at El Alamein and Stalingrad were astrologically foreseen in a *Zenith* number which bore the date June 1942, but had in fact been printed in March 1943. I felt that this little subterfuge would add weight to other predictions in the magazine which were concerned with developments far ahead of the date when our German customers would first find it lying around.

How did we deliver our "evidence" to our underground distributors? By the same canisters in which S.O.E. parachuted their supplies of arms to them. Our paper was stuffed into any gaps left between the automatic guns and plastic bombs. That was one reason why it was so specially necessary to brief these officers on the meaning and purpose of our bits of paper. Otherwise they might well have thrown them away as so much waste.

The Poles, in my experience, were the cleverest operators of all. From their bases in Poland they travelled over the whole territory of the Reich. And it was to the Poles that S.O.E. entrusted, on our behalf, the tricky job of posting letters inside Germany itself. The Poles, for instance, posted for us to German provincial newspapers the papier-mâché matrices with which we counterfeited the feature service of one of Goebbels' Nazi agencies. The Poles sent them to any number of newspapers for us. But the *Danziger Vorposten* was the only newspaper in which I was able to read one of our articles. It celebrated the fiftieth birthday of Admiral Doenitz. The article contained all the appropriate Nazi sentiments and was completely orthodox except for one sentence: "As a consequence of the loss of an average of thirty U-boats a month over the last half year," it said, "the Admiral has recently lost some of his pristine youthful freshness [*Jugendfrische*] and élan [*Schneid*]."

The other posting jobs the Poles did for us in Germany were more worthwhile than this elaborate pinprick operation against Doenitz. One consisted of posting letters to the relatives of German soldiers who had recently died in German military hospitals in Italy. Fortunately for us the German hospital directors made a practice of sending radio telegrams *en clair* to the local party authorities in Germany, asking them to break the news to the relatives. These telegrams were intercepted and passed on to me, and they gave us all the information we needed—the soldier's name, the address of his relatives, and the name of the hospital.

We now concocted a moving letter, written out in German longhand script on notepaper bearing the letter heading of the German hospital. Ostensibly the letter came either from a nurse or from a comrade of the dead man, who had entrusted it for posting to someone going to Germany on leave. Whoever the writer was, he or she had been with the dead man during his last hours, and was now writing to comfort his relatives. In moving terms the "friend" described the dying soldier's devotion to the

Führer, his unshakeable faith in ultimate victory, his last greetings to his relatives. Then, almost as an afterthought, he (or she) mentioned the diamond-studded watch, or the gold crucifix, or some other piece of valuable jewellery which the dead soldier had hoped to bring home as a present for his dear ones. "It has been specially forwarded to Herr Ortsgruppenleiter . . ."—and there followed the appropriate name—"to be handed to you by him personally or by one of his representatives."

When sufficient time had elapsed for the letter to be sent to the relatives and take effect, the Soldatensender took up the operation. In an indigant talk by Sepp Obermeyer or one of the other champions of the German servicemen we heaped vituperation on the miserable *Leichenfledderer* (corpse robbers) who did not hesitate to steal the effects of men who had died for their country. And, of course, we had many more cases and names to cite as instances of this kind of "crime" than just those in which we had—through our Polish allies—sent letters to the relatives.

On other occasions we used the same technique to tell the relatives that their soldier had not died of wounds but had been given a lethal injection. The Nazi doctor at the hospital, we explained through our nurse, had considered the man had no chance of becoming fighting fit again before the war was finished. The doctor had required the man's bed for soldiers with a better chance of rapid recovery.

In the ordinary way we did not distribute our counterfeit literature in Germany by R.A.F. bombers. That was a method I was glad to leave reserved for the official "white" leaflets. Not only would it have revealed the enemy origin of material we wanted to be mistaken for German, had we used the R.A.F., but our "evidence" could not have been placed in spots where Germans would discover it quickly and find it convincing. The perfect "plant" could only be accomplished by the human hand. We therefore depended on agents of the underground for our normal distribution.

But there were three counterfeits which we did drop from R.A.F. aircraft. The first of these were our forgeries of the German ration cards. The second was a rough leaflet multigraphed on sheets of Luftwaffe signals paper which we hoped would be accepted as having been dropped by Luftwaffe comrades of the ace fighter pilot Werner Mölders.

Armin Hull had been counterfeiting German ration cards for some time before I became aware of it. He was doing so for our friends in S.O.E. who required them for "travellers" operating in Germany. When I found some specimens of German ration cards lying on Armin's work-table I thought they were the genuine article.

"Could you counterfeit these?" I asked him, and I explained that if we could persuade the R.A.F. to drop them on Germany, we would be striking a powerful blow at Hitler's rationing system.

"Afraid you can't have them, though," said Armin.

"Why ever not? I know we are not allowed to forge bank notes. But these? Surely—"

"It isn't that. These belong to S.O.E. They *are* forgeries and they want them for their agents."

I could hardly believe it. "Show me the originals." I demanded.

Armin produced them. They were indistinguishable. The colours, the perforation, texture of the paper, the watermark—everything appeared to me to be identical.

It was a miracle. I decided to submit my plan to S.O.E., for I felt sure they would help when they heard it. And so indeed it turned out.

The S.O.E. chiefs' only stipulation was that we should not drop the latest issues on Germany. "We need these for our chaps working there," explained the colonel who was my liaison with the cloak-and-dagger men. "Besides, we don't want the Germans to know that we receive their ration cards here almost as soon as they are issued."

Instead of the latest issue he offered me some travellers' coupons which were valid throughout Germany. They had only one defect—they were due to expire fairly soon. I accepted them with enthusiasm. Armin printed vast quantities of these cards, and very soon the R.A.F. were dropping them on Germany.

"A little balm," I called it, "to take the hurt out of the bombs."

Goebbels' howl of protest at this British iniquity was so encouraging that we printed millions more ration cards and kept dropping them. Soon S.O.E. relented, and let us use the latest coupons and not only those about to expire.

Armin developed a splendid technique of mass forgery. As soon as he had heard from S.O.E. that a fresh consignment of German ration cards was on its way to him, he would call up his printers and the paper-maker and have them ready waiting in his office. While the printers made their offset plates, the paper-maker would be preparing the special watermarked paper, in the event that the Germans should have changed the pattern and a new batch was needed. The whole operation was completed at top speed. So expert did Hull's team become at the job that the R.A.F. would be distributing our forgeries within days after the new issue came from the German Food Offices.

The German C.I.D. circularized their offices to be on the lookout for our forgeries. In a special warning of January 14, 1944—we picked it up later among the captured documents—they issued a most painstaking analysis of the few points of difference they could establish between our forgeries and the genuine German coupons. But while these differences might be detectable by police equipped with special instruments I cannot imagine a grocer, or a baker, or an innkeeper being able to detect them in the rush of business. Considering the speed at which these counterfeits had been prepared, the police circular was a remarkable tribute to Hull and his team.

But Goebbels had a more imaginative countermeasure up his sleeve. When he found that the German printers and paper-makers could not beat Hull by altering the pattern of the coupons, Goebbels, brilliant artist that he was, counter-attacked with a stratagem which I rank among the most ingenious of the war. To back up his propaganda blast that the "R.A.F. forgeries" were "clumsy and easily detected" and "certain to land those who use them in the death cell," he got his own printers to fabricate some monumentally clumsy forgeries of ration cards. These he then displayed at Party meetings all over Germany as samples of "stupid British work by which no intelligent German could possibly be deceived." He followed this up with nation-wide publicity for the trials of *Volksschädlinge* (enemies of the people) who had been caught by shopkeepers trying to pass off the R.A.F. forgeries.

I was full of admiration for the little doctor's ingenuity at the time, and I still am. This was "black" against "black" at its most brilliant. But it did not deter the many thousands of Germans who used the ration cards we had dropped to provide themselves with a valuable addition to their calories.

When Armin Hull went to Germany in the summer of 1945, his German driver told him how he had lived for six weeks on our cheese coupons while he was on the run from the Gestapo. He had no idea that he was talking to the forger in person.

But the legend of the "clumsy" British forgeries spread by Goebbels has persisted in Germany to this day.

"Tell me, Herr Delmer," a young German recently asked me in Hamburg, "when the British dropped those counterfeit ration tickets, why did they not make a better job of it? Why did they drop cards that were so poorly faked that no one could use them?"

I told him.

I must confess that the success of the other R.A.F. job, the Werner Mölders letter, undertaken early in 1942, came as a surprise to me. For before launching it I had the greatest misgivings about entrusting any "black" job to the R.A.F.

Colonel Mölders, one of the most publicized fighter aces of the Luftwaffe, had been shot down by German flak near Breslau in the last days of 1941. It was almost certainly an accident, but of course we did not leave it that way when we learned of the peculiar circumstances of his end from a captured Luftwaffe officer.

Werner Mölders, said the officer, was a devout Catholic. He had become outspokenly critical of the anti-Christian Nazi regime after a British air raid on Münster, when the Nazis had insisted on taking over a convent there and expelling the nuns from it, among them his sister. Himm-

ler's S.D. had just begun to investigate Mölders' "treasonable outbursts" when the flyer was shot down and killed
as he was coming in to land on the airfield at Breslau.

Clearly this ambiguous death of one of the most popular
heroes of the Third Reich was bound to be much discussed
in Germany, and I determined to exploit it with every
means at our disposal. On Gustav Siegfried Eins Der Chef
delivered himself of a thundering denunciation of Himmler's Bolshevik canaille who had so treacherously murdered
this shining light of German manhood.

Next, I decided to fake a letter, allegedly written by
Mölders, expatiating on the doubts he and his comrades
felt about fighting for the atheist Hitler. I conceived it as
a piece of "evidence" with which to back up the Gustav
Siegfried campaign. But in this instance the typed word
was to have a greater resonance than the broadcast of Der
Chef.

As the addressee for the letter we selected the Roman
Catholic provost of Stettin, with whom, so the opening
sentence of the letter was made to suggest, Mölders had
been corresponding for some time. The "Mölders letter,"
as it came to be known throughout Germany, was defeatist. Sadly Mölders told the provost how more and more
of his comrades were being killed. The letter was rebellious. Rebellious against the Party, whom Mölders referred
to not as "the Party" or "the Nazis" but as "the godless
ones." And it informed the provost that more and more of
Mölders' Luftwaffe comrades were turning away from
"the godless ones" and seeking religion.

"There is nothing more beautiful for a man than to have
struggled successfully through all this slime of lies, injus-
tice, and perversion in order to find his way to knowledge,
to light, to the true faith." The letter suggested that

Mölders knew he was being hunted by "the godless ones" and that his days might be numbered. "If on my last journey no priest can be present," he concluded, "then I leave this earth in the knowledge that in God I shall find a merciful judge. Write again soon, my dear fatherly friend, and pray for your Werner Mölders."

It was urgent to have this moving document distributed in Germany before the Mölders story had lost its actuality. If we waited for a normal S.O.E. delivery, it might be months before it got through. So with considerable qualms I decided that, for this once, we would risk dropping a "black" job by the R.A.F. To make an air dropping plausible, I added a short introduction from an anonymous Luftwaffe man and had the whole thing reproduced on a copy that Hull had made of some Luftwaffe signal sheets we had found among a haul of captured documents. To any German picking up the sheets it would look, I hoped, as though they had been dropped by one of the night fighters sent up to chase off the R.A.F. bombers.

The R.A.F. airmen must have made a wonderfully lucky shot with their drop. In no time at all the "Mölders letter" was all over Germany. Courageous priests read it from their pulpits. The aged Field Marshal von Mackensen, shocked by the anti-Christian contempt for religion shown by the Nazi regime, had it copied out and sent to his friends. The B.B.C. and the Soviet radio picked it up.

Goebbels denounced the letter as a forgery. He made Mölders' mother denounce it too. But no one would believe them. For it was in keeping with the character of young Mölders to have written such a letter; he alone could have denounced it convincingly, and he was dead— murdered, so everyone believed, by the Nazis themselves.

The "Mölders letter" was such a success that about a

year later I asked the R.A.F. to drop another leaflet for me which purported to come from German fighter pilots. But this time, although the R.A.F. dropped several thousand copies of it—"white" leaflets, of course, were dropped by the millions—I got no reaction at all. The Goebbels propaganda took no notice of it, and I could find no prisoner who had ever come across it or heard of it. And yet it seemed to me an excellent job. The only difference from the "Mölders letter" was that this time we had not multigraphed our text on Luftwaffe signals paper, but had printed it on ordinary newsprint.

I did not mind our failure too much, for I transferred the operation to our radio and there it soon harvested its full measure of "comebacks." The leaflet—I give its full text in the appendix °—was an appeal by German fighter pilots to the public and their comrades of the Army against their commander-in-chief Major General Adolf Galland, who had complained of their lack of fighting spirit.

I did not commit another "black" job to the Air Force for dropping until very much later in the war, when the Germans themselves were having to supply their troops from the air and were dropping leaflets to them. I shall tell about that when I come to it.

Not all our "black" operations were counterfeit radio broadcasts or fake documents. What I called "Operation Tuckbox," for instance, was simply a financial transaction involving no danger to anyone and very little labour. I set it up early in 1944 as part of our softening-up campaign, and it had excellent results.

Certain firms in neutral countries such as Switzerland and Portugal, among them the German Hamburg Amerika

° See page 287.

Line, were advertising at this time that they could deliver food parcels to recipients in blockaded Germany. Germans with friends abroad who could pay in Swiss francs, Portuguese escudos, or American dollars could arrange to have hampers containing coffee, sugar, butter, tinned milk, and other scarce delicacies released to them from special depots in Germany.

We had been exploiting these shipments on the Soldatensender as a new angle for our "inequality of sacrifice" campaign against the "Party privilegentsia" who, we said, were the chief beneficiaries of this system. And then an idea occurred to me. For some time the Soldatensender had been putting out news items about the high wages in dollars that German prisoners in Canada and the United States were earning for the work they were doing over there as lumbermen, farmhands, truck drivers, and the like. Would it not be the most natural thing in the world for these German prisoners to want their folks in Germany to share in their good fortune? Why should they not send some of their dollars to Switzerland or Portugal in order to buy food parcels for the families in the fatherland? Well, if they would not, or could not do it themselves, we would do it for them through our S.O.E. agents in Switzerland and Portugal.

Frank Lynder compiled a list of relatives of U-boat P.O.W.'s and their addresses. My friends in S.O.E. and the British taxpayer did the rest. As the food parcels began to arrive (we read the thank-you letters the families sent to the putative donors in Canada), the news soon got around among the German fighting men of the splendid opportunities that awaited them in Canadian captivity. Enemy propaganda? Nonsense—look at the splendid parcel young Schöller had just sent his parents!

Some of the grateful parents became our best propagandists. One old baronial Lord of the manor in Pomerania was so moved by our little gift to him that he placed
it on a table in front of his house and made the whole of
his village march past the parcel to inspect what his dear
son Siegismund-Sizzo had sent his old father from "over
there."

A rather less charitable operation was one called "Braddock," which we set up a little later in the year.

We were indebted for this one to Winston Churchill
himself and the American novelist John Steinbeck. In his
novel about occupied Norway, *The Moon Is Down*, Steinbeck had told how Norwegian Resistance men set fire to
German stores. Churchill read the book late one night at
Chequers and decided that here was an excellent idea. He
gave orders for an incendiary device to be perfected for
the use of Resistance fighters throughout Hitler Europe.

A neat little thing it was, too, a tube about three inches
long of which you could safely carry several around in
your pocket. Winston gave it the cover name "Braddock."
All you had to do to get the Braddock working was to
pinch in the pointed end, push it into the Peasantführer's
haystack, the Gauleiter's sofa, or whatever else you
thought would make a good starting point for a fire, and
get out of sight. Fifteen minutes after you had squeezed
the end, the tube would burst noiselessly into flame.

Winston Churchill wanted the R.A.F. to drop this little
infernal machine during its raids on Germany, I was told
by my friends in Air Intelligence. But Sir Arthur "Bomber"
Harris, a tough and hard-headed man, refused to let the
R.A.F. carry any Braddocks. He indignantly maintained
—and, with all my admiration for Churchill, I think he

was right—that a load of bombs did more damage than an equivalent load of the Braddocks would. "I am not going to have my air crews risking their lives," said Harris, "for some damn novelist's fancy toys." Churchill gave way, and so Braddock had been abandoned and forgotten.

"But who has the Braddocks now?" I asked, when I heard the story. "They sound to me like an ideal weapon of psychological warfare."

It turned out that they were with S.O.E., and my opposite numbers there were only too happy to let me have them. I explained the plan I had for Braddock. We would have twenty or thirty thousand of them dropped every night by the American squadron of Flying Fortresses which were carrying leaflets to Germany. They would do this for me, I was sure. We would also print an appeal to the foreign workers in Germany in their various languages, instructing them to use this incendiary weapon against their Nazi oppressors, the aim of the operation being to make the Gestapo and the German public believe that many of the fires they saw raging around them were caused not by Allied incendiaries but by foreign workers using the Braddocks.

Not that I had any illusions that the foreign workers would in fact use them or that the Braddocks would cause vast fires. I had no hopes of the foreign workers because— contrary to the propaganda put out by my own department—I did not believe that the majority of foreign workers were "press-ganged into slave labour." I looked on them rather as willing collaborators attracted to Germany by the good pay and good rations the astute Munitions Minister Speer was giving them—a view in which I was confirmed after the war by Speer's right-hand man Willy Schlieker, the ship-building tycoon of today. As for the

Braddocks themselves, S.O.E. had warned me they might be "a little stale," and when I tried one out on my lawn it stubbornly refused to burst into flame. It did not even burn when I put it on the fire!

But that did not worry me. All I hoped for was that the Braddocks would turn the police and the public against the foreign workers and thereby reduce very considerably the value and efficiency of this hitherto loyal and devoted labour force. And, to judge by the reactions of the Goebbels ministry and the German police when the operation was carried out, it achieved all that and more.

The Germans were mobilized against the foreign workers, who, after being friends and helpers, were suddenly treated as the "Trojan Horse" within the citadel, an enemy to be feared. German newspapers published warnings to folk-comrades to be on the lookout for foreigners using the "cowardly incendiary packets" (*Brandpäckchen*). School children were sent out to try to collect them.

The official police gazette, the *Deutsche Kriminalpolizeiblatt* on November 3, 1944, put out a special edition warning police authorities. It was headlined "Enemy sabotage in the Reich by use of foreign workers and incendiary packs thrown from aircraft. Particularly important for posts of the *Geheime Staatspolizei!*"

And, of course, we did our best to help the Braddock campaign along with the other devices available to us. Our friends of the Polish underground and the other S.O.E. agents in Germany plastered the passenger compartments and lavatories of the German railways with notices issued in the name of the Reich Railways Administration, but prepared and printed by us, which called on folk-comrades to search under the seats for *Brandpäckchen* and if necessary to rip out any part of the fittings which they suspected might be harbouring one. The Soldatensender put out news items attributing fires we knew about from R.A.F. reconnaissance pictures to the foreign workers and their incendiaries. "Tom Brown" Stevens, too, by typically ingenious research contributed examples of alleged foreign-worker sabotage. For instance, when he noticed a number of identically worded death notices in a Leipzig newspaper which appeared to have been inserted by families all living in the same district, he guessed there must have been some kind of factory explosion there. From M.E.W. he discovered there were two factories in the area: one making munitions, the other a chemical works. As most of the dead were young women, he plumped for the chemical works. It belonged to a firm called Rudel and Fiedler. And, as we discovered later, he was quite right. There had been a great blow-up at Rudel and Fiedler's, only it had nothing to do with foreign workers and *Brandpäckchen* as we alleged. But who was to know that?

There was nothing occult or mystical about my confidence that I could persuade the United States Fortress squadron to do the job for me which "Bomber" Harris had refused to do for Churchill. The American pilots of the Special Leaflet Squadron had been working with me since the last week of April 1944. This squadron had come to Europe in 1942 as a regular bomber squadron—422(H) of the 305th Group. In October 1943, much to the disappointment of the crews, it was assigned exclusively to leaflet carrying. The leaflets were dropped in a special "leaflet bomb" designed by the squadron's inventive young armaments officer, Captain James Monroe. This was a cylinder of laminated wax paper 60 inches long and 18 in diameter. At an altitude of one thousand feet a fuse destroyed the container and released the leaflets. Instead of drifting for hundreds of miles, as in the early days of R.A.F. leaflet raids, when the leaflets were dropped any old how from doors and bomb bays, the leaflets—eighty thousand to each bomb—scattered over an area of about one square mile.

Night after night, these courageous young men flew in aircraft armed only with machine-guns on what they called their "milk run" over the German lines in France and Belgium, and far into the German hinterland, distributing our latest instrument of subversion, a daily newspaper, which I had named *Nachrichten für die Truppe* giving it a deliberately flat and neutral title, inspired by the O.K.W.'s *Mitteilunger für die Truppe* which we had so frequently counterfeited in the past.

Of all the enterprises I launched during the war, this "News for the Troops" is the one of which I am proudest. This was a joint British-American venture, and the readiness with which my American friends at O.S.S. and SHAEF's American psychological-warfare boss General Bob McClure placed a team of first-class editors and news writers under my orders, I still consider to have been the greatest compliment paid me at any time in my war-time career.

The newspaper team worked in yet another prefabricated barrack which had to be erected in haste in the M.B. compound. Every night, for 345 consecutive nights, they put the paper together from the news and talks of the Soldatensender, which they sub-edited and rewrote for print. For, of course, many changes were necessary to adapt our material written for radio to the style of a newspaper. John Elliot, whom I knew from my Berlin days as a painstaking and well-informed correspondent of the New York *Herald-Tribune,* headed the American team.

Dennis Clarke, who had been the *Express* correspondent in Vienna, took charge of its British counterpart. Dennis, as a gunner officer, had lost an arm and won an M.C. in the same North African battle in which young Virchow had been taken prisoner. But that did not stop the two of them from being the best of friends.

Dennis Clarke and John Elliot took turns editing the paper and submitting the page proofs to me or Karl Robson for final approval. Harold Keeble, today feature editor of the *Daily Mirror* group, supervised the layout in his printing shop at what had once been the Duchess of Bedford's model clinic and nursing home.

To print such vast quantities of a daily news sheet we needed a rotary press. John Mills, general manager of the Home Counties Newspapers at Luton, provided it. In printing shops and on presses that were already fully occupied putting out the seven provincial weeklies belonging to the group, he and his men turned out an average of two million copies of *Nachrichten* a night. Those Luton printers, as proud of *Nachrichten* as we were, looked on it as their special contribution to the annihilation of Hitler and worked smoothly and punctually without a hitch.

If the Soldatensender was what Donald and I called "grey" *Nachrichten* was a dirty off-white. Unlike other Allied leaflets it did not proclaim that it was issued by command of General Eisenhower or SHAEF. Nor did it, like "black" leaflets, claim to have some German or non-allied source. *Nachrichten* just dropped from the heavens, as an offering of the sublime objective truth. Unlike the Soldatensender, it did not refer to the Allies as the enemy. They were the Anglo-American forces or the Russians. The Germans were *Die Deutschen Truppen*. But whenever possible *Nachrichten* identified the German unit concerned—Infantry Regiment 919, the 21st Panzer Division, or the 356th Infantry Division, and so on. The talks which on the Soldatensender were delivered by a variety of voices always had the same signatory when used as articles in *Nachrichten*.

"Oblt. J.von Ö." stood for the mysterious figure who was our great authority on everything from the struggles between Doenitz and Schniewind in the naval hierarchy to the impossibility of fighting an air war without fuel or the "impossible" political interference with the army leaders' tactical decisions. Not that the mysterious Captain J.von Ö. (I always imagined our readers puzzling: "Can that be young Joachim von Örtzen? Or is it perhaps that fellow Johann von Öfterding?") was at all bashful about writing with expertise on some subject of home politics—such as, for example, the continued exemption from military service of members of Goebbels' Propaganda Ministry under the terms of an order—reproduced in facsimile—dating back to July 4, 1940.

Needless to say, we had no illusions that *Nachrichten* would be accepted as a German production—even though the *Oberleutnant* always wrote from the standpoint of a patriotic German officer. *Nachrichten* made no attempt to fool anyone. We merely refrained from underlining its Allied origin, for two excellent reasons: firstly, it would not have helped its effectiveness with our German readers for us to have added a byline, "Published by General Eisenhower"; secondly, to have done so would have meant that the Soldatensender, source of all the news and articles in the sheet, would no longer have been disavowable. To turn *Nachrichten* into a "white" news sheets—as some of the post-war critics of "black" suggested we should have done—would only have been possible if the B.B.C.

German service could have been used as its basis. This, for a variety of reasons, was impossible. Bruce Lockhart, Dallas Brooks, and I had considered all these points most carefully before launching *Nachrichten*.

Now, with the Flying Fortresses dropping our news sheet on the Germans night after night, I felt we were at last ready to play our part in support of the invasion. All that remained was to plan what our role should be on D-day.

13

As our fame spread in the world of the Secret Service, more and more visitors, both British and American, asked to be shown over M.B. with its studios, record library, intelligence files, and newspaper and radio news-rooms. Some of them, like General "Wild Bill" Donovan of O.S.S., even sat in on our morning conference and listened as Clifton Child and his intelligence officers produced their suggestions for news items and I directed how each item should be written and angled. But mostly my guests were satisfied with a brisk look around, a brief audition of the various stations, and the inevitable conference in my office, where we discussed at length how their organizations could help mine and what we, in return, could do for them.

When they had gone, I often found myself smiling wryly at the thought of what an odd impression we must have made on them. A more weirdly assorted group it would have been hard to find anywhere in Britain at that time; German refugees, German prisoners, Balkan beauties, Italians, Hungarians, Romanians, Bulgarians, British girl secretaries, British and American editors and executives—all jostled each other in the passages of M.B., talking their different languages and their assorted varieties of English. Each of them dressed as the fancy took him or her.

On one occasion a functionary of the Court of Admiralty met me and my team at a local cinema, bringing us a canister containing German films found on a captured German boat. I wanted to show the film to my team to give them an idea of German war-time life as seen through the eyes of Dr. Goebbels' cinema studios. As the men and girls tumbled out of the buses and into the cinema, the Law Courts official contemplated us with the severe and disapproving stare of a church-warden regarding a bunch of tipsy Teddy boys.

"You're something to do with the Ministry of Information, I suppose," he said when the last of my gang of wild Bohemians had disappeared inside the vestibule.

"Oh, no, not M. of I.," I said quite truthfully. Then I added wickedly, "As a matter of fact we are Foreign Office—diplomats, you know!"

He looked me over in dumbfounded amazement. And indeed I must have appeared an odd species of diplomat in shapeless grey flannels, khaki shirt open at the neck, my old suede jacket from the Spanish war, and a beard. The beard I had grown, not as a disguise, as has been said by some of the post-war German magazine writers elaborating their bits of tittle-tattle about the mysterious boss of the Soldatensender, nor even, as still others have said, to impress and terrify the members of my team. The simple truth is that I had found it hard to get razor blades. Once a week, therefore, on my regular trip up to London, I called at the barber's shop in the basement of Bush House. A cheerful little Whitechapel barber named Iky tended my beard. He called it "our beard" and treated it as though it were a piece of ornamental box hedge at Hampton Court. Each week he tried to cut it into a fresh shape.

"A spade beard today, sir?" he would ask, while the other barbers crowded in close to listen to him. "Or shall we continue with the Trotsky you're wearing now, sir, with perhaps just a shade more deviation to the left? No? Then how would it be to try something like this one I found on this tin?" And he produced an empty tin of Skipper's Sardines with a picture on it of a beard fringed skipper.

My team had expanded so rapidly that we had been forced to requisition extra houses in the village of Aspley Guise. The Germans alone now occupied seven houses, and as soon as new prisoners came in from Normandy we would have to take over yet another "desirable residence."

The villagers were much intrigued by the mysterious foreigners that strolled around their narrow lanes and village streets. No one knew who or what they were. Our men were forbidden to enter the local pubs, and the housekeepers and servants of our houses were all sworn to silence under the Official Secrets Act.

In my house, R.A.G., we lived well enough—much better, in fact, than most people in Britain. And we did so although we adhered strictly to the war-time rationing regulations. From Woburn Park we used to get venison, which was unrationed and unwanted, thanks to the obtuse refusal of the average Briton to eat this delicacy with which he is unacquainted. Our own chickens laid eggs for us, fed on meal and pellets for which we had given up our egg coupons. Vegetables were grown in our grounds by the gardener father of my highly efficient housekeeper and cook, Freda Maddy. The team collected mushrooms when out on their walks in the fields, and Isabel, to whom I had given "an expensive Paris education" in the culinary arts, as artist Peter Rose Pulham used to say, taught Mrs. Maddy the finer points of French cuisine. Moreover, my wine cellar was still well stocked, thanks to my wine-merchant friend John Hill of Hedges and Butler.

Somehow the story of R.A.G. dinners of mushrooms cooked in wine got around, and soon there was ugly talk of "foreigners living in luxury while Britons starved." It even got to the ears of my old colleague John Gordon of the *Sunday Express*. He sent a reporter to investigate "the scandal." The report was not published until after the war,* when the security ban forbidding any mention of our existence had been lifted.

"FAT-OF-THE-LAND" LIFE OF GERMAN P-O-W'S
MUSHROOMS COOKED IN WINE

said the headline, nicely calculated to excite the indignation of John Gordon's Scottish-Canadian master on grounds of both patriotism and thrift. The dispatch fully lived up to the headlines.

"The German prisoners who did broadcasting and propaganda work for Britain in civilian clothes had a good war here. . . . This alien propaganda corps, which included

* *Sunday Express*, February 17, 1946.

women, were lodged in big 10- to 14-roomed houses standing in their own grounds. . . . The men were all dressed in lounge suits or sports clothes. . . . Villagers told how the foreign contingent lived on the fat of the land. In one week last year, 434 pints of milk were delivered to the houses where the Germans and others were lodged.

"I was told how Continental delicacies were bought from Bedford for their table, how the best produce of a local fruit farm was allocated to them, how sometimes they dined off mushrooms cooked in wine. . . ."

How this piece would have rejoiced the victims of our "diplomat rations" campaign! Der Chef could not have done better.

Undeterred by this gossip, however, I continued to do my best to keep up the morale of the team, and gave "birthday parties" on each anniversary of Gustav Siegfried Eins and the Atlantiksender. The P.O.W.'s joined in all this with as much zest as our old-timers. So too did Father Andreas. "I was prepared for anything at M.B.," commented one of my delighted American visitors watching the Father at one such party. "But never, never, never did I expect to see a priest in a conga line!"

Soon I found romance blossoming between the British and Balkan girl secretaries and my new friends from the U-boats, the Luftwaffe, and the Afrika Corps. Young Virchow fell in love with Marianne, a very pretty girl of the Elizabeth Taylor type, and she with him. They announced their engagement. It created a big stir among the prisoners. Another officer reproached Virchow. He was a Bavarian monarchist with a family name known throughout Europe as long ago as the fifteenth century.

"How can you possibly do this? Your family will never forgive you!"

"I am sure they will approve," replied Virchow. "Marianne belongs to a very old and aristocratic Jewish family. Much older than mine or yours!"

Oh, that Hitler could have heard them!

14

Right up to the departure of the first waves of the invasion force the propaganda batteries under my command kept up their softening-up barrage. And by and large they did so along the lines we had agreed on at the start.

True, with the R.A.F. and the United States Air Force bombing the roads, railways, and bridges of occupied France, and Rommel racing from the Channel to the Mediterranean and back again to inspect his coastal defences, it would have been unrealistic for us to keep up our original *dolce far niente* insouciance and ignore the possibility of invasion. We just had to refer to it occasionally in our output. The main accent, however, remained

as before on the priority of the Russian front and the
O.K.W.'s alleged view that France was a minor theatre,
a mere training and recreation base, expendable in the
event of Allied attack. Troops continued to be withdrawn
from it, we said, despite Rommel's orders to meet invasion with counter-invasion.

Further task forces from the command of C.-in-C. West
[declaimed the Calais announcer in a typical news item of
this time] will shortly follow the S.S. Panzer divisions Hohen-
staufen and Frundsberg to the Eastern Front. Drafts are also
being sent from west units hitherto considered below the
standard needed for the Eastern Front. They are being sent
to reinforce the Romanian sector, where our long-distance air
reconnaissance reports heavy Russian troop concentrations, in-
dicating the imminence of a new Russian offensive here.

We also reported the withdrawal of troops from the
west for transport to the east in easily remembered "human stories." Here is an example:

A new swindle racket by platform vendors on Cologne main
station is claiming numerous victims among Wehrmacht personnel in the many transports now passing through Cologne
on their way from the west to the Eastern Front. Just before
the train is due to depart the vendors offer the comrades
bottles of eau de Cologne at much reduced prices. But though
these bottles contain genuine Cologne water it is not the
famous Cologne perfume but only Cologne tap water.

Our main attack, however, was still indirect. We reported events from the Russian and Italian fronts which
I hoped would stick in the minds of our Wehrmacht listeners in France when their turn arrived. One feature of
this attack was what I called our "briefing" items. I had
been greatly impressed by the admirably clear and ob-

jective briefings which General Brooks used to give the top executives of the department at our weekly conferences. So I now decided to have similar "briefings" for our Calais audience—but with a very different purpose.

The sudden collapse in Italy is ascribed to two main factors [said our military expert on June 4, 1944—just two days before the Allied landing was due]. Firstly to the overwhelming air superiority of the enemy. And secondly to our High Command's unjustified confidence in our defensive system of concrete strong points. As a result of this excessive confidence in their impregnability the redoubts were being manned in many instances by troops of inferior quality. . . .

Depressing listening, this, for the units in France who had been told by us again and again that they were second class. Furthermore, they were well aware of the Ukrainian and other foreign units in their ranks. Nor were these weaknesses we were suggesting in connection with the Italian campaign new to them. We had suggested much the same kind of thing in connection with the Russian campaigns.

When Sebastopol had fallen a month before, our military expert said that this fortress, which had been equipped with the latest and best fortification devices at the Führer's disposal, had been so unexpectedly captured by the enemy for four main reasons: (1) The penetrative power of the new armour-piercing bombs and phosphorous shells supplied to the Russians by the Americans. They broke through the toughest armour and ferro-concrete. (2) The remarkable knowledge which the Russians possessed of the weak points in the German defences. (3) The failure of the mine-fields to hold up the Russian attack. (4) The confusion in the ranks of our comrades caused by the folk-

Germans (naturalized Poles) and foreign troops in German uniforms. Some of the Vlasov soldiers turned out to be Russian partisans who attacked the German units from the rear. . . .

All of it was grand stuff to help the troops in France justify their own desire to surrender when the time came. And we spared no pains to suggest to our listeners that the British and the Americans were no less well informed than the Russians about the most closely guarded German secrets.

For instance, when my friends with U.S. Air Force Intelligence reported to me that a group of Mustang fighters had made a rocket attack on a château believed to have been a German staff headquarters, we put out this item within six hours of the attack:

Field Marshal Rommel has once more escaped an attempt to ambush and kill him. This morning he was due to visit Château Lebiex. At the last minute he changed his mind and cancelled the inspection. But at nine-thirty A.M., ten minutes after his party had been scheduled to arrive, a flight of enemy Mustangs dived out of the clouds on to the château and shot it up with rockets. The château and the entire staff headquarters were destroyed.

News items intended to stimulate surrender and desertion by drawing attention to their advantages and feasibility belonged to the routine bread and butter of the Calais bulletins and *Nachrichten*. Here is a favourite one exploiting "Operation Tuckbox":

The chief of the O.K.W. Wehrmacht Fürsorgeamt [Welfare Office] appeals once more to relatives of missing men receiving a first sign of life from a soldier previously reported missing to communicate this instantly to the nearest Wehrmacht Meldeamt [Reporting Office]. Frequently the first sign of life to be received from a missing man is a letter to his relatives showing that he is a prisoner of war. In isolated instances it takes the form of a food parcel which the prisoner caused to be purchased out of his dollar earnings and sent to his home address. It is in the relatives' own interest that they should immediately report such signs of life, as the authorities themselves are frequently only informed much later, and rapid notification facilitates the payment of family allowances and other monies.

With the exception of the bit about the food parcels the announcement was copied from a genuine communiqué which we had taken from the D.N.B. Hel-schreiber.

Typical of our attempts to stimulate desertion were items reporting the escape of Allied prisoners to neutral territory. To rationalize desertion and make it seem an every-day practice we even suggested that General Kreipe had not been captured in Crete but was a deserter. I herewith make belated apologies to my friend Patrick Leigh Fermor for casting this slur of doubt on his brilliant guerrilla operation!

The impotence of the police was illustrated in news items varying from the unsuccessful police search for the French mass murderer Dr. Petiot to straightforward reports of the increase in unsolved crimes. And as part of the same campaign—although the main purpose of the item was slightly different—we reported that French Resistance fighters were masquerading in S.S. uniforms with false papers, and getting away with it.

The increase in acts of sabotage committed by French guerrillas disguised in Waffen S.S. uniforms has led to the issue of a new order by the chief of the military government in France, Dr. Michel. It lays down that all directives must in future be signed with the full name. In several cases members of the French underground have succeeded in obtaining Waffen S.S. uniforms by producing orders with illegible signatures. The habit of signing orders illegibly has increased recently, since it became known that French secret organizations are collecting the names of officials of the occupying authorities and smuggling them abroad to have them added to the lists of war criminals.

An order had in fact been issued by Dr. Michel insisting on the greater legibility of signatures, though he did not motivate it with the reasons we gave here. Yes, with skillfully angled news items it was possible to put any amount of ideas into the heads of our listeners. We could even suggest ways of malingering, for instance, by reporting exactly how a Hitler Youth Führer had got himself sent home by temporarily laming his leg:

. . . Oberstammführer Schmutzler owes his temporary laming to an old and infallible prescription. He tied a rubber eraser to the hollow of his knee at night so that it pressed hard against the nerve until all the symptoms of genuine lameness were manifested, thus procuring him release from the Army.

Innumerable, of course, were the news items about party dignitaries and the efforts of the Party propaganda apparatus to eradicate from the German people what we called *Kriegs-und-Parteimüdigkeit*—"war-and-party weariness." We reported the failure of these efforts and attributed it to the "privileges which high Party officials enjoy and which continue to arouse bitterness among the people." Then we would list the privileges:

(1) The exemption of Party officials from the living-space ordinance [*Wohnraumlenkungsverordnung*], under which they

are not, like other folk-comrades, compelled to receive bomb victims or East refugees in their homes.

(2) The exemption of young political leaders from front-line service. Such political leaders either are exempted altogether from military service or serve for a short token period of war service as propaganda speakers behind the lines. Then they return as propaganda speakers to the home front.

(3) The exemption of the Party aristocracy from food rationing by granting them so-called Diplomatic Rations for purposes of entertaining and representation. By this means higher Party officials receive two and three times the amount of food allocated to ordinary folk-comrades.

(4) The exemption of Party officials from ordinary justice and their subjection to the special judicature of the Party. In this way Party officials escape prosecution for offences which, in the case of ordinary folk-comrades, would entail severe penalties.

And, of course, the speeches of the Party dignitaries—full of pathos, with unwavering confidence in the Führer and final victory—provided us not only with admirable cover but with a bottomless source of the kind of irony which finds a ready appreciation among the more sophisticated Germans.

Gauleiter Jordan forged a new slogan on the occasion of the conference of the Gau Labour Chamber in Magdeburg. "Our enemies may boast," he said, "that they have the largest number of aircraft, Panzer tanks, the most numerous Labour force and the most gold. For us National Socialists however, it is decisive that we possess the best philosophy [*Weltanschauung*]."

After which stirring pronouncement, Alex Maass, our chief disk jockey, would play a short tinkle on a piano record, just five or six seconds, to allow the point to sink in.

Taken in a continuous series as I have presented them here these items would of course have reeked of enemy propaganda. But they did not appear one after another like this. They appeared in between items taken from Dr. Goebbels' own D.N.B. service announcing decorations and birthdays, proclaiming ordinances, telling the listener about the new films being shown in Germany and the latest football results. In this mixture our "softening up" went down as smoothly as arsenic in a cup of cordial.

What was perhaps just as important in attracting listeners was that our programmes were always entertaining. They did not bore our German audience, jaded as it was by a surfeit of Dr. Goebbels' eternal optimism. We did not go in for pompous generalities. We reported detailed and telling facts and we took immense trouble to present our news wherever possible with the human and personal angles beloved of popular newspapers such as my own *Daily Express*. Where the B.B.C., for instance, would have said, "R.A.F. bombers last night dropped a heavy load of bombs on the marshalling yard at Metz . . ." the Soldatensender handled the news in this way:

Many comrades who had hoped to travel home this week-end on a short Whitsun leave from their billets in France are tonight held up in and around Metz. All railway traffic through Metz has been stopped as a result of last night's air raid. As we learn from the Railway Transport Office in Metz it will be another forty-eight hours before the damage can be repaired, and the leave trains can proceed. Cafés and night-spots still open in Metz which we can recommend are . . .

In neutral newspapers from Istanbul to Stockholm it was one of the minor sensations of D-day: the first news of the allied landing in Normandy, so they reported, had been given to the world by the German Soldiers' Radio Calais. At 4:50 A.M. on June 6, 1944, a Calais announcer had interrupted the station's dance music to flash a report that the invasion had begun. Fifteen minutes later the announcer had been back with a longer report. It was so graphic that Swedish monitors picking up the broadcast, said an *Aftonbladet* reporter, decided that the radio station itself must be either in the invasion area or close to it.

In fact, however, the distinction of having "scooped"

the invasion story did not belong to us at all. It belonged to our competitor Dr. Goebbels and his indefatigable news agency the D.N.B. We ourselves had picked up the invasion report from a flash on D.N.B. and had immediately put it on the air. But we knew a little bit more about the invasion than did Dr. G. and the D.N.B. And with "Aspidistra's" 600 kilowatts of power to boost our announcer's voice we made a great deal more noise.

Ten anxious hours I had waited at M.B. for that D.N.B. flash which gave us the signal to put out our carefully prepared invasion reports. Donald McLachlan, the only other member of the M.B. team to be in on the secret of D-day and H-hour, had spent most of Monday, June 5, at the SHAEF headquarters in Bushey Park, just in case there was another change in the plans. Shortly after seven in the evening he strode into my office at M.B., flung his naval officer's cap on my desk, and announced, "It's on! Ike is definitely going through with it."

"Are you sure he can't change his mind once again and call it off?" I asked gloomily. For we had been through this once before twenty-four hours earlier. "The weather is bloody awful," I added. "Just look at it."

"No," said Donald, "I am sure it's all right this time. And the 'Met' boys say the weather will improve."

So we decided to go ahead with our plans. I warned Harold Keeble, who was in the know, that I hoped to be changing the front page of *Nachrichten* with a "special" piece of late news. And then we went to dine at R.A.G. It was a trying meal, for we had strict instructions from the Security men to let no one in on the secret. Donald and I could think of nothing but what lay ahead. We would have given anything to talk about it, but we dared not. The trickiest part of the evening was getting Hans

Gutmann, my chief news writer, to come back to M.B. with me at midnight without anyone noticing that something was up. Hans had been with us for dinner. And when, just before midnight, he got up to go home I offered to drive him to the married couples' house where he stayed.

"I have to pop back to M.B. for a moment," I said. "There are one or two items I want to rewrite. I'll give you a lift on my way."

"Perhaps I can help?" Hans asked, as I had hoped he would.

"Well, that would of course be most useful," I said.

"I'll come too," said Donald, and off we went without my team suspecting anything.

At M.B. the three of us went through to my office.

"I am very relieved you have come, Hans," I now said. "Donald and I could not really have done this job without you. You see, what we want to do is to work out a top-secret draft in German of the kind of story we shall put out, if and when the invasion takes place. I want to have three stories on ice for the great moment: the first a brief flash announcement for Calais, the second a rather longer story for the first bulletin, and finally a much fuller piece for *Nachrichten*. The object will be to suggest to the garrisons of the Atlantic Wall defence works that their line has been breached, that they are cut off, and that they might as well give up. We don't want to say that, of course. All we do is give them a picture of the situation from which they can draw their own conclusions. The whole thing is only a mock-up, of course, Hans, but I would like to get on with the job full speed ahead, as one never knows when it will be needed."

Hans' liquid brown eyes shone with enthusiasm. I could

see from the grin twitching around his mouth that he had guessed what was up. This was the great moment he had been waiting for ever since that evening in November 1938 when the storm-troop mob had smashed the plate-glass windows of his antique shop in Berlin's Kurfürsten-damm and he had been forced to flee for his life. He yearned to know more. But Hans Gutmann did not em-barrass me by asking difficult questions.

"Just a mock-up to be kept on ice for the great day," he said in German, "and you want us to write it now, at one o'clock in the morning. I get it."

I grinned. "Fine! Here is the outline of the stories. Donald has cleared the stuff with SHAEF."

And that is how we came to capture what should have been Dr. Goebbels' great scoop. For when the D.N.B. flash came through on the Hell-schreiber tape, thanks to Gutmann and Donald, we had everything ready. Our announcer put out his flash: "The enemy is landing in force from the air and from the sea. The Atlantic Wall is penetrated in several places. The command has ordered alarm grade 3."

Without waiting for the main story in the Calais bulle-tin to be broadcast, I jumped into my car and raced off to Marylands with the new front page for *Nachrichten*. Harold Keeble was ready and waiting to replate.

It was a splendid front page that he and Dennis Clarke produced. And, despite its lateness, John Gibbs and his printers rushed it through in time for the American For-tresses to deliver *Nachrichten* to our readers in Normandy only a few hours later. "Atlantic Wall breached in several places," said the banner headline in German. "Armour penetrates deep into the interior: bitter fighting with parachute commandos."

I still have a copy of that number.* And when I read it again today and remember that this "report" was based exclusively on Donald's knowledge of the plans and his picture of what he hoped would happen, and that it was at least twelve hours in advance of any official news releases, I thrill once more with admiration for the masterly job done by Donald McLachlan and Hans Gutmann. But it is even more interesting as an historic document. For it shows how our reports were written to fit in with the Allied deception plan which was to mislead the Germans into the belief that the invaders were striking at the mouth of the Seine and at Calais.

To top the whole thing off, Donald and Hans had produced a box-insert under the heading "What is available" (*"Was bereit steht"*). It showed the tenuous German resources and gave a most alarming picture of the over-extended German defence front. I will quote just three sentences from it: "An average of 18 Luftwaffe aircraft go with each German division in the West. At the time of the battle of France in 1940 there were eighty Luftwaffe aircraft to each German division. During last week's battle of Rome the Anglo-Americans had 160 aircraft for each of their divisions."

We had begun to slap that biceps at last.

My German team were all men who had broken with Hitler's regime the hard way. They had sacrificed their homes and jobs in Germany for an unknown future abroad in order to fight against the evil that had seized their country in its grip. Prisoners like Virchow and Mander had come over to us knowing that even in Britain they risked assassination by the Nazi prisoners' underground

* See Appendix, page 297.

for doing so. Every man among them wanted Hitler's Germany to perish, and to perish as rapidly and as violently as possible, so that a new and better Germany could take its place. And yet with all that, I could feel the secret, often subconscious, sympathy and sadness with which these men now watched their countrymen across the channel being bludgeoned into extinction by the vast juggernaut of the Anglo-American armada. Not for nothing had we immersed ourselves so completely in the life and surroundings of our Wehrmacht listeners. We were able to feel those cannonades as though they were coming down on our own heads. And the talks which my speakers now put out reflected this. They had an undertone of personal tragedy which made these ephemeral pieces of psychological warfare as moving for me to listen to as if they had been the greatest literature.

There was René Halkett, for instance, an odd Bohemian of a German aristocrat, who derived his name from Scots ancestors. His uncle was General Werner von Fritsch, the former C.-in-C. of the German Army whom Hitler sacked for his opposition in 1938. Halkett had done just about everything in his life that a Prussian aristocrat was not supposed to do. He had served before the mast, danced in ballet, written a best seller, *Dear Monster*, played in a dance band, and acted in repertory. Now his job was to sound like a German officer of the old school. And he did. I can still hear the moving talk that he delivered five days after the invasion had begun, the quaver in his voice, the bitterness and the disgust. Part of it may have been conscious acting, but most of it was genuinely felt—the resentment and the sorrow of an officer seeing his fellow countrymen laying down their lives for a regime of criminals and cranks.

Halkett spoke in the short staccato sentences of the typical Prussian officer:

This is a report, an epitaph, and a warning. An epitaph for the comrades of the Kremlin Division, who were cut off on the beaches of Ouistrehan and Arromanches, who were left in the lurch and hammered to death. Only a few men of one regiment in this division remain. Of the 916th Grenadier Regiment. Only a couple of men from it have got back to tell the tale. What these comrades have to tell us must be a warning to everyone. It is a warning to all those who may be lying in an outpost somewhere on the beaches, or are stationed somewhere up on a hill, or on the coast. And as they lie there they may get the order, "Hold on, reinforcements are on their way to you."

The reinforcements will not come. They cannot come because nothing is being done about sending reinforcements, because all these men have been written off—written off as dead and lost.

Here is the warning story which the few survivors of the 716th Infantry Division, the Kremlin Division, have brought back with them.

On Tuesday came the first attack on the coast. The division got the order, "Hold on. Reinforcements are on their way." By Thursday for all practical purposes the division was already surrounded and over-run. In its rear were the enemy parachutists. In front of it lay the enemy battle cruisers firing at them, hacking their concrete dugouts to shreds. Overhead, in the sky, a thick curtain of enemy aircraft. They drop a never-ending barrage of bombs and explode what is left of the minefields. Far and wide not so much as a single German fighter. No communication to the right or to the left. All that they knew was: the Anglo-Americans are landing continuously to both sides of us. Landing troops and heavy materials. And those reinforcements for the 916th? Not the slightest sign of them! But an order did get through at last from the command. "Hold out," it said. "Hold out to the last round of ammunition."

Halkett paused for a moment for the senselessness of the order to sink in. Then he went on:

There they lay in their smashed and slit-open dugouts, naked, without cover. Grenadiers with machine pistols and Mgs. and anti-tank guns. Guns which they were never to get a chance to fire.

Then word came through once more from the rear: "Reinforcements," said the message, "are on the way—they will get through to you and help you fight your way out. Armour is on its way to you from Caen." Quite true, armour was on its way. One single section of the 21st Panzer Division with Mark Four tanks. One single section with Mark Fours! On the third day! It was to push through in the direction of Luc sur Mer. A friendly gesture, I grant you. But nothing more. Needless to say, the Mark Fours never got through. They were stopped long before that. For, by the time they were being sent up, the enemy had six times as many tanks ashore around there. What remained of the section of the 21st Panzer Division had to turn back, back to Douvre, and on the following morning back to Caen.

That was the promised relief operation. That was the promised reinforcement. That was literally all that was done for the Kremlin division by land and by air. The 916th Grenadier Regiment. They withdrew then at last to the hillocks behind. A few of the men got through. But left behind to be over-run and rubbed out were 4000 men. Four thousand comrades left in the trap, defenceless, deserted, without cover or help.

In front of them on the water lay the enemy battleships. Those enemy ships had fun with a little target practice against our fortifications and our boys. They took their time over it. They approached to within three miles of the shore and anchored there. No one interfered with them. And then the battleships opened fire with observer balloons up in the sky to score for them. They covered every square yard, systematically, with twelve-inch shells. And in among the shells fell bombs and more bombs.

And when the enemy tanks then followed up no defences were left, no obstacle, no barrier, nothing between Ouistrehan and Arromanches. Two-thirds of the Kremlin Division perished in three days at the Atlantic Wall. The few men that were still alive in this cemetery are now prisoners of war in England.

That was the end of a division. The end of comrades who held out and waited for reinforcements for relief. Who did not know that they had been written off—written off from the very beginning.

It was a brilliant performance. Again and again Halkett had put over his theme, and never once did it become boring: The division was written off, help was promised, but there was never any serious intention of sending help. The division had been written off.

But behind all this calculated impact I felt the misery and bitterness in Halkett's voice. That was real, not acted.

The breakdown in communications between the German units at this period was so grave that many German commanders were tuning in to Calais for our "situation reports." They used them to chalk in corrections to the constantly changing order of battle on their staff maps.

We certainly did our best for the customers. As a result of Donald McLachlan's work—during those first weeks he was almost permanently at SHAEF headquarters getting us the latest and fullest operational information— our reports were far more up to the minute and far more detailed than any published elsewhere at that time. One

German-speaking reporter, John Kimche of the *Evening Standard*, discovered that we were getting advanced reports. He listened to the Soldatensender and, by taking our news without quoting us, laid the foundations of a well-deserved reputation for being better informed than his competitors.

Our reports were accurate, too—ninety-nine times out of a hundred. The hundredth time came when we put in some false information at the request of the tactical deception experts to mislead our trusting clients and send them headlong into a trap.

For the past fifteen months Hitler and Goebbels had been seeking to buoy up the German public's waning hopes of victory with allusions to a miracle weapon which was going to change the whole course of the war at one decisive blow. It was going to punish with a holocaust of destruction the criminal British who had dared to repay war with war and bombing with bombing.

An interesting feature of these allusions to the new V-weapon, as it was called—V for *Vergeltung* (i.e., retribution)—was that they varied in frequency and ferocity. Over one period the newspapers and the speeches of the Party orators would be full of V-threats. Then the campaign would die down again and such references as were made to the V-weapon did not speak of its use as imminent. This interesting variation did not escape my colleague Robert Walmsley.

Walmsley's job was, among other things, to analyse German propaganda for any clues it might give to Hitler's strategic intentions. He had been doing this succesfully ever since 1940, when from a careful study of the Goebbels' radio and the German newspapers he had managed to deduce that Hitler had called off the invasion of Britain.

What was more—as we discovered when Hitler's secret plans and orders fell into our hands at the end of the war—his guess at the date of Hitler's decision was only forty-eight hours off.

Not only my department found Walmsley's reports invaluable. The Joint Intelligence Committee and the Chiefs of Staff also paid attention to his analysis. They were right to do so, for Walmsley had discovered an important basic principle about the Goebbels propaganda. This was that, although the Germans did not mind how much they boasted in their output to foreign countries, they did their best not to promise victories to their own public unless they were fully confident of being able to bring them about.* (Dick Crossman's most brilliant contribution to "white" propaganda was his exploitation of Goebbels' caution by getting the B.B.C. to "commit" Hitler to promises of victories he could not bring off.)

Since the summer of 1943 Walmsley's propaganda analysis had been concentrating almost entirely on Goebbels' V-threats and their varying frequency. His section counted, analysed, and weighed the threats. And from their incidence and their ups and downs Walmsley produced his weekly analysis of how near Goebbels believed the realization of "retribution" to be.

---

* The accuracy of Walmsley's theory is also confirmed by this passage from the diary of Goebbels' press chief Rudolf Semmler for June 17, 1944. "Goebbels has personal reasons for being glad the V-weapon has appeared. On March 23, 1943, Hitler had told him for the first time of the plans for these weapons. At his request Speer had sent him regular information about the progress being made with them. . . . For a year now Goebbels has been promising the coming retaliation in articles and speeches. . . . One month after another passed without the weapon appearing, and Goebbels' prestige fell lower and lower. . . . Now he feels he has been rehabilitated. He has turned out right. He has triumphed."

For months now we had been reading his reports as
Bomber Command's raids on V-bomb arsenals in Germany
and the launching sites forced postponement after postponement. It was like sitting in a submarine at the bottom
of the ocean with the bleep-bleep of the asdic growing
now stronger, now fainter as the enemy destroyer approached and then drew away.

But in this D-day week Walmsley was saying that the
Germans were likely to launch their V-bomb as a counter-
invasion measure even though they were not ready for a
full-scale bombardment.

As I read Walmsley's paper, it seemed clear enough to
me that the Germans were determined to launch their
wonder weapon for political reasons, to shore up their own
invasion-shattered morale and do what they could to smash
ours. That bleep-bleep-bleep had risen to a crescendo.

And then, sure enough, there it was. On June 13, just a
week after D-day, the first German V-weapon, or buzz-
bomb, crossed the channel coast, flew to London, and burst
in London's Bethnal Green. On June 15 the *Vergeltung*
offensive started in earnest. Two hundred buzz-bombs
flew in during the first twenty-four hours, and it looked
as though Hitler had found a wonderful morale-booster
for his shaken and dispirited troops, even if it was not a
war-winning weapon. The Soldatensender and *Nachrichten* were asked to go into the counter-attack.

We had discovered from prisoners that the German
Army nickname for the V-1 was strangely similar to the
name the Londoners had given it. London called it the
"Doodle-bug"; the German soldiers called it *"Der Dödel."*
We therefore also called it *"Der Dödel"* when the Corporal launched into our first attack on the new morale-
booster.

His attack took the form of three questions: "What has the weapon achieved in its first attack? What can one realistically expect of it? Does the new weapon provide a solution for our most urgent military problems?"

To the first he answered: "We don't know, and we cannot know because our reconnaissance aircraft are unable to reach England. Or if they do reach England they cannot get back." On the second, his comment was that whether the Dödel hit an object that was militarily worth while was purely a matter of luck, because owing to the absence of any observation it was impossible to correct the range and direction of this missile, which in any case had a high factor of deviation (*Streuung*). And then he got to his third point—"Can the Dödel solve our most urgent military problem? Can it stop the Anglo-American supplies from being delivered across the channel? The Navy and the Luftwaffe have been unable to do so. Can the Dödel do it?" And again his answer, delivered in the style of a staff officer frankly assessing the military situation was, "No, it cannot."

The B.B.C. under Crossman's directive took exactly the opposite line. Instead of playing the buzz-bomb down, as we were doing, they played it up and pretended to respect its effectiveness. Crossman's intention was that the Dödel should as a result cause all the greater disappointment when it failed to produce a result. But for us as "critical Germans" the Soldatensender line was right and a useful antiphony to the "white."

So we repeated the same themes in other talks on the Dödel and in news items. And then when I felt these themes had been successfully planted, we went a step further and attacked the Dödel as a miserable waste of precious fuel—fuel which we claimed could have been more profitably used for Rommel's petrol-starved armour and transport or for fuelling the fighters of the Luftwaffe. *"Da fliegt der Sprit!"* was the disgusted comment we tried to suggest to our German soldier listeners, as they watched the Dödel fly through the air—"There goes our fuel!"

The "Gen.d.Mot" (a cabalistic German army term designating the general commanding the motorized units), so the Soldatensender alleged in its news bulletins, had written a memorandum on the Dödel for the O.K.W. In it the Gen.d.Mot estimated that the Dödel was using as much fuel in a day as 100 Panther tanks, 50 bombers, or 100 fighters.

. . . Shooting these Dödels would have been good fun at some other period of the war when there was still plenty of fuel . . . [commented Halkett, taking his turn as our military expert] but to perish at the front now for lack of fuel only in order that these fellows can shoot some Dödels into the air for the satisfaction of the propaganda wallahs—I ask you! . . . But that is exactly the way certain people in the Führer headquarters imagine a war should be conducted. "All right," they say. "When there are no real weapons, then you must rely on the Führer's will to victory and his *Weltanschauung* and to hell with the grenadier at the front. . . .

As usual, we illustrated the same theme with news items. Among other Dödel items, we reported that Albert Speer, the armaments chief, had complained that the factory space, manpower, and material he had been forced to allot for production of the Dödel would have been better used in producing fighter planes and tanks.

That item, as far as we were aware, was just a plausible invention. We had no intelligence backing it up. But in 1946 when Speer was sitting in the prison at Nuremberg waiting to be tried as a war criminal he said, "Of course

I was always against the Dödel. It was a damned waste of fuel and of technical resources that should have gone into more worthwhile weapons—fighters, for instance."

Was this a coincidence? Had Albert Speer really protested to the Führer about the Dödel? Or had he listened to the Soldatensender, and allowed our "poison," as Goebbels called it, to seep into his subconscious?

I hope that some day soon Speer will be released from the prison at Spandau and tell us.

16

At ten minutes past eight on the evening of July 20, 1944, the D.N.B. Hell-schreiber in the M.B. news-room began clicking out with tantalizing deliberation the first news of what, for all of us, was to become the greatest story of the war.

The ribbon of tape from the Hell-schreiber ran straight through to the typewriter of blond and buxom Mimi Molnar, a German-speaking Czech girl, whose duty it was to read the spidery tracings and type them straight into her machine. Ordinarily Mimi Molnar merely typed the D.N.B. stuff without taking it in. Typing D.N.B. bored her. She wanted to write herself, not type. But what she was taking down now made her sit up with excitement.

"Dr. Gutmann," she called, "please come over here and look at this. It looks important." Hans Gutmann got up from his desk, walked over to the Hell machine, and read the copy over her shoulder, as she was typing it. His eyes goggled.

"Give me that," he roared as he tore the page out of her machine and rushed away to call first Karl Robson, who was on duty, and then me. Dick Crossman, who was writing the directives for the "white" psychological-warfare attack at SHAEF, had come down to visit me at R.A.G. and talk over plans. We were at dinner savouring the penultimate bottle of a most perfect Graacher Himmelreich 1934 when Gutmann got through to me.

"It has happened," Hans exulted over the telephone.

"What has?" I asked irritably.

"The Army has risen against the Party. They have tried to murder Hitler."

For a moment I thought it was a leg-pull, that Frank Lynder or the Corporal had been trying to play one of their silly tricks on poor old Hans. Enmity between the Army and the Nazi Party—which the Army had itself created, financed and fostered as its political instrument —was what we had been trying to stimulate, exploit, and aggravate ever since Corporal Sanders and I had first launched Gustav Siegfried Eins three and a half years before. We had been constantly reporting and rumouring a growing cleavage between the generals and the Führer with all the means at our disposal. Only recently I had learned of the infuriated reaction of the Party authorities to a circular letter posted for us by our Polish friends, in which the East Prussian Gauleiter Erich Koch warned that the Führer was in danger, that "certain circles which pay lip service to the sacred name of Prussianism but show

none of the heroic spirit of the Seven Years War . . ."
were preparing a *Putsch* to remove the Führer from the
command of the Wehrmacht and replace him with a traitor, an oath-breaking General.*

"Are you sure no one is trying a stupid hoax?" I asked
Gutmann.

"Of course it's no hoax. Here, listen in for yourself. The
story is now coming over the Deutschlandsender." And
Gutmann held the receiver to his radio so that I could
hear the Berlin announcement. Sure enough, there it was,
in the cultivated fluting voice of the Deutschlandsender's
news reader: ". . . a criminal attempt on the life of
the Führer . . . time bomb . . . miraculous escape . . .
preserved by providence for his great task . . . small
group of irresponsible reactionaries . . . hue and cry . . .
Führer himself will speak over radio and disprove all
rumours. . . ."

Dick Crossman and I abandoned Mrs. Maddy's venison,
as if we had been stung by another of Crossman's wasps.
We jumped into a car and raced over to M.B. Karl Robson
had already put out the first flash announcements. Child,
Karl, Gutmann, Virchow, and I, with Crossman sitting in
as a welcome adviser, now quickly decided what we would
say. After ten minutes of discussion I laid down that our
main line would be that this was a "peace putsch"; that
high staff officers of all three services were behind it because they knew the war was lost and wanted to save
Germany; that they had issued a proclamation to the German people and the Wehrmacht announcing that Hitler
had been deposed and a new government formed which
was to begin immediate peace negotiations; and that the
"peace putsch" had not been put down, despite what the

* For text of this counterfeit, see Appendix, page 285.

government would now be saying. The fight was still on.

"We must make it clear," I said, "that this conspiracy had very important leaders and that it was widespread. It had accomplices everywhere, even in the *Führerhaupt-quartier* itself. We must paint a picture of confusion. Some Army units are following the orders of the 'peace generals' by disarming and imprisoning S.S. guards and Gestapo, and by seizing munition dumps. Elsewhere Nazi officers have the upper hand. And don't forget—we must implicate as many officers as we can without losing credibility."

As the story grew and more details came through on the Hell-schreiber and the Goebbels radio, Dick Crossman felt that our ministerial masters should be informed. He hoped they might be induced to take cognizance of the rebellion and authorize some statement to encourage the generals in their hopes. But in any case they should be informed what had happened. So he telephoned Bruce Lockhart.

Poor Bruce was in bed with a painful attack of shingles. He was not at all anxious to call up the ministers. But Dick persuaded him. It was after midnight when Bruce rang back.

"It was as I feared," he said, "and I have a message for you, Dick, from Brendan Bracken,* who is dining with the P.M. Bracken says he is amazed that you should have fallen for this all too obvious Goebbels canard, and will you please never disturb him with such nonsense again. Please tell the B.B.C. to refrain from saying anything that could suggest we accept the story that there has been a revolt by the generals."

Even worse was to befall our political warriors of the official voice of Britain the following morning. Any hopes they might have cherished of splitting the Germans and

* The Minister of Information.

inciting the generals to further rebellion were crushed. For not only were Crossman and Carleton Greene stopped from saying anything to encourage the rebels, but they were specifically ordered to announce that His Majesty's Government was not prepared to absolve the Army from its responsibility for the war or to differentiate in any way between Germans and Germans. All were responsible. The only terms on which Germany could have peace were— as before—unconditional capitulation.

The task of dividing the Germans was therefore right back in the laps of the "black" men. And we had got down to it, uninhibited as we were by ministerial complexes about estranging the Russians by "softness" towards the Germans. All that first night and throughout the next days we were busy clothing the bare skeleton of news Goebbels had given with details of our own invention which would implement the general picture we wished to present. My memories proved useful—particularly those of what had happened on the night of the long knives on June 30, 1934, and in the days that then followed Hitler's purge of the Storm Troops. By the time our story was fully launched we had involved almost as many members of the German Wehrmacht, the Foreign Office, and the administration generally in the "peace putsch" as ultimately claimed to have been conspirators when the Allies took over from Hitler in 1945!

One of our aims was to involve German officers in the conspiracy whom we wanted the Gestapo and the S.D. to suspect of complicity. Among those whom we successfully implicated in this way was the German naval attaché in Stockholm. He was recalled from his post and arrested— much to the annoyance of his British opposite number, who had found him useful! When the German officer subsequently returned to Stockholm, he complained bitterly of the shabby trick the Soldatensender had played on him.

What we did not know, however, or even suspect at this time was that in our own immediate target area of the Western Command the revolt had been carried further than anywhere else. In Paris the Gestapo and S.S. men were, in fact, arrested and disarmed by the Army, and kept that way for a night. I would like to think that our reports on what was happening in the rest of Germany and on the Eastern Front had something to do with this. It is certainly true that the rebels in Paris believed the putsch was a success long after the other plotters had discovered it was not.

To me, the most astonishing and gratifying aspect of the generals' coup was the way Hitler's Third Reich appeared to be doing its best to live up to the picture we had been presenting of it, a picture which I myself had always regarded as a propaganda caricature. Here were genuine German generals rising in rebellion against Hitler just as though Der Chef of Gustav Siegfried Eins were directing them. And the Gestapo and the S.D. had been shown up as the fumblers we had always said they were. It was incredible.

Even today I am still baffled by the failure of the Gestapo to discover the plot and nip it in the bud. For, far removed from the scene of the drama as I was at M.B., I could have warned Himmler what Count Stauffenberg was up to. I knew that Stauffenberg was in a plot against Hitler at least two months before he pushed his briefcase, with the time-bomb in it, under Hitler's conference table. German officer prisoners gossiping together under the microphones of their country-house prison camp in England had mentioned Stauffenberg as belonging to a group which intended to get rid of the Führer. If the officers gossiped like this in England, it seemed to me they must also have gossiped in Germany. But the Gestapo's big ears did not hear them. Or, if they did, they did not understand what they heard. Which was as bad, if not worse.

With all this to encourage us, the Soldatensender now demanded that an end be put to the war in order to save Germany. And in our self-appointed capacity as spokesmen of the "decent fighting front-line soldier" we turned the heat on Hitler himself, whom hitherto we had never attacked directly and in person. In a talk by René Halkett the day after the abortive assassination attempt we ridiculed the allegation that the time-bomb was of British manufacture and that the whole attempt was a British plot.

René Halkett (reading his script, a monocle jammed into his left eye): "The British and the Americans and the Russians are the last people to want to rid us of the Führer. On the contrary. The enemy can wish for nothing better than to have us led by a man who has never learned the soldier's trade, who relies on mystic inspiration, who, in his conceit and ignorance interferes in everything and everywhere. Why, a fellow like that is, for the Allies, an ally!"

We defended the Officers' Corps, that sacrosanct Prussian caste, against the attack which the Nazi labour leader Dr. Robert Ley had made on it in his sycophantic ecstasy over the tyrant's preservation. The Corporal, speaking in his best Der Chef style, tore into Ley to avenge the German "peace generals."

"Herr Robert Ley is of the opinion," he drawled haughtily through his hawk-like nose, "that German officers are a lot of ungrateful, blue-blooded pigdogs to whom the

Führer gave back their uniforms only to have them come along and shove a bomb under his desk. High time, says Ley, that the National Socialist Revolution does the job it should have done earlier and exterminates the entire lot of them. Well, let us take a look at the fellow who says all this and the men he is saying it about." After which introduction the Corporal proceeded to lambast Ley as a callous war profiteer who had grown rich and fat while children starved, who owned a whole string of town and country houses (addresses given), into none of which he had allowed so much as one bomb refugee.

"And men like Colonel Count Claus Schenk von Stauffenberg"—he mouthed the title with just the right amount of unctuous *Offizierskorps* deference for the nobility—"whom Ley calls a cowardly idiot—after he is dead—such men have been out at the front fighting the war which has made this Ley a multimillionaire." There followed praise of Stauffenberg as a staff officer plus a brief history of his career. The Corporal stressed that Stauffenberg's promotion to the High Command of the Army had given him insight into "what was really going on," and that it was this which prompted him to take the action he had taken.

"If anyone is to be called ungrateful it is not such brave men as Stauffenberg, who had the courage to speak out and act for the good of the fatherland, but the lickspittle lackeys in the Führer-headquarters who have been hushing up the facts in an artificial fog of sycophantic optimism."

It was a fine virile talk put over with force and emotion. Many more like it followed. And each contained not just a rodomontade of invective and denunciation, but plenty of inside information and "news" to widen the cleavage and feed the new "peace movement."

Not many weeks had gone by after the generals' putsch when I received even more dramatic confirmation that the Gestapo and S.D. were not up to their job. They had not even been able to close the stable door after the bomb had burst. As a new recruit for my team I was being offered one of the men who had taken part in the coup. He had managed to escape from Germany to Spain and had now come to England anxious to continue from here the fight in which he and his friends had failed in Germany.

Bruce Lockhart rang me on the green-painted secret telephone in my office. "Are you with me?" came his husky eternally anxious voice when we had "scrambled." "C. has just been through to me," he said, using the cipher by which the chief of the Secret Intelligence Service is known.* He wants to know whether you would be interested in having one of the Twentieth-of-July fellows on your team. The man has just arrived in Britain. Might be able to give you some useful background. You're not to use him as a voice, though."

"Sounds fine to me, Bruce," I said, "but I would like to take a look at him before I commit myself."

"Of course, of course. I'll fix it. When can you go?"

And that is how I first came to meet Dr. Otto John, that

---

* In Britain the identity of the head of the Secret Intelligence Service is kept a strict secret. Never is he referred to by his name, and even the cipher until recently was only known to a few. Not for him the personal publicity which Allen W. Dulles, or J. Edgar Hoover get in the United States or General Reinhard Gehlen in present-day Germany—or, for that matter, such as I accorded to the late Admiral Canaris in Germany during the war—much to the amusement and satisfaction of C., as he himself once told me.

tragic victim of post-war Germany's vendetta against the "traitors and collaborators" and of Whitehall's eternal readiness to sacrifice the friends of Britain. I found John in one of the innumerable London school buildings that had been turned over to the government for the duration of the war. My own school, St. Paul's, had been serving my fellow Old Pauline Field-Marshal Montgomery as his planning headquarters for the invasion. The school which I was visiting now had been turned into an interrogation and detention centre for incoming aliens.

Dr. Otto John was occupying, all by himself, what must before the war have been one of the assistant masters' private studies. It was a dark and gloomy room. But even in its darkness one thing shone out—the peroxide brightness and blondness of Otto John's hair.

"Good God," I thought, "I do hope he is not another one of those." C. had already supplied me with a German diplomat who wore long silk stockings, and I did not wish to complicate the life of my little community at M.B. by adding to it yet another member of exotic tastes. My first words, therefore, when we had been introduced and left alone to talk, formed a highly personal question.

"Do you peroxide your hair regularly, Herr Doktor? It is a becoming colour."

Otto John laughed. I was relieved to note that he laughed freely and easily.

"I dyed my hair and eyebrows black while I was hiding from the Gestapo in Spain," he said. "Now I have used a little artificial aid to start my hair on the road back to its normal fairness. I did not relish looking like a zebra while the black dye grows out."

As we talked I looked him over. It was clear that he was still suffering from the mental strain of his narrow escape. His blue eyes were fixed on mine with an unnecessarily concentrated stare. Beneath his rather short and stubby nose he was drawing down his upper lip as though to prevent it from twitching. But when he spoke he was clear and articulate.

The first thing I wanted to hear from John was how he had got away. It seemed almost too good to be true, I told him, that one of the most important plotters of the conspiracy should have escaped the Gestapo so easily. After all, he had been moving around quite openly among men who, because of their known attitude to the Third Reich, had been immediately arrested when the great round-up began after the putsch. His own brother had been arrested —and condemned to death. How was it possible for Otto John to have escaped abroad? At M.B. we had assumed that flights to foreign destinations would have been automatically stopped, just as all flights out of Britain had been stopped in the weeks that preceded D-day. It seemed a routine precaution for a Security Service to take.

"No," said Otto John, "you were wrong in assuming that. The Lufthansa flight to Spain on the morning of July the 24th was allowed to leave as usual. The Gestapo bosses are not as imaginative as all that. For them it was good enough that only passengers with exit visas could leave. I had my permanent exit visa as a Lufthansa official who had to travel frequently to Madrid on Lufthansa business. I presented it at Tempelhof airfield, and they let me through."

"Did you say you only left Berlin on the 24th?"

It seemed unbelievable. But even more incredible, if one had any sort of respect for the efficiency of the Gestapo, was that John in the time before he left, as he now told me, had openly moved around Berlin visiting a number of his fellow plotters. He telephoned to Stauffenberg's secretary in Stettin to inquire after Stauffenberg. "He is travelling" was her answer. And he called at the homes of two other conspirators to find one of them arrested while the second, the Foreign Office man and former Oxford Rhodes Scholar Trott zu Solz (also arrested later and executed) said to him, "Get out, Otto. You're the only one of us who can get abroad. Hurry!"

He made it, all right. The Lufthansa plane flew straight through to Barcelona and thence on to Madrid. Once in Madrid, John immediately got in touch with the British.

Under orders from his associates in the opposition group he had been secretly meeting members of the British and American Intelligence ever since 1942, giving them the picture concerning the plans and expectations of the conspirators, and giving them also any bits of information that came his way. For Otto John and his friends believed that the only way in which Germany could be saved physically and morally from the evil that Hitler embodied was for them to fight him in every possible way.

As soon as the British in Madrid learned of the danger John was in, they smuggled him out of Spain into Portugal. Even in Lisbon the Gestapo and S.D. were still after him. But our people got him safely aboard a British aircraft and brought him to England—only to shut him up in London in this not very congenial interrogation and detention centre.

I had seen enough of Otto John during our talk, and heard enough from him of his underground work and friends to make up my mind that I certainly wanted to have him in my team, if he would join it. He knew the people around Hitler, and a good many others too. He would be invaluable in bringing us up to date and filling in those bits of detail and local colour essential to our operations. Even if he did not turn out to be a writer, he would still be immensely useful. So I now went into the routine which, with only slight variations, I used with all prospective recruits once I knew I wanted them.

"I am in charge of a unit," I said, "about which I can only tell you very little at this stage. But I will tell you this—we are waging against Hitler a kind of total war of wits. Anything goes, so long as it serves to bring nearer the end of the war and Hitler's defeat. If you are at all squeamish about what you may be called upon to do against your own countrymen you must say so now. I shall understand it. In that case, however, you will be no good to us and no doubt some other job will be found for you. But if you feel like joining me, I must warn you that in my unit we are up to all the dirty tricks we can devise. No holds barred. The dirtier the better. Lies, treachery, everything. Your experience in Germany, your acquaintance with leading Germans—which you would of course have to place unreservedly at our disposal—would I think make you very useful. What do you say?"

I had deliberately overstated the rascality of our operations. I did not want John to develop pangs of conscience once he had joined the unit.

John looked me in the eyes for a moment. "Mr. Delmer," he said, "my friends have given their lives in the attempt to rid Germany of Hitler. They believed that we Germans must ourselves liberate the world from this Satan. I understand your unit consists largely of Germans"—I nodded in confirmation—"although it is of course under your direction. I shall be happy to join my fellow countrymen in their work. Anything that you ask me to do, whatever it may be, I shall consider a continuation of the war my friends and I have been waging against Hitler. May I ask you to do the same?"

"Of course. I will most certainly do that, Dr. John. I must say that you will find that your attitude coincides exactly with that of the other German members of my team." We shook hands. "But now there is the little matter of your name," I said. "I usually give my associates English names in place of their German ones, you know. But as "John" sounds so English I think I'll give you a German name for a change! How would you like to be called Oskar Jürgens?"

Otto John stood up, made a little mock bow and clicked his heels. "Oskar Jürgens," he said, introducing himself in German style, and then roared with laughter.

When he was brought down to me in the country a couple of days later, I immediately made him a member of my own "household brigade" at R.A.G. and I did not regret it.

Quite apart from the many excellent suggestions with which "Oskar Jürgens" came up at our mealtime conferences in R.A.G., the psychological impact of his presence among us was immensely stimulating. For he, in his person, provided living evidence that, suppressed and submerged, another Germany still survived which it was well worth trying to excavate from under the debris—a Germany which recognized its collective responsibility for Hitler and the need to expiate the infamies committed under the Führer.

For me in particular this was an encouraging discovery. I had of course long been aware of the peace feelers put out from time to time by German diplomats and others who claimed to be speaking and acting on behalf of Germany's "inner opposition." But while I considered that this opposition was well worth fostering, particularly where Army leaders were involved, I refused to accept it as a sincere moral force. I was convinced that these overtures sprang not from a genuine repudiation of Hitler's war of conquest but from an opportunist desire to insure against its possible failure. Moreover, I had been impressed with the all too transparent strategic intentions behind many of the peace feelers. They were simply aimed at splitting the alliance. One group of emissaries from the so-called "Resistance" wanted to make a deal with the Anglo-American West, while the German armies continued the fight against the Russians with Anglo-American backing. The other wanted to make peace with the Russians and renew the old Wehrmacht alliance with the Red Army. So I approved the joking brush-off that our Stockholm embassy's cultural attaché Roger Hinks had been giving German opposition approaches with his immortal "If you'll feel my peace, gentlemen, I'll feel yours."

In Otto John, however, I was getting to know a very different type of German Resistance leader. From him I was hearing too about such fellow plotters of his as Dietrich and Claus Bonhöfer, whom I had, of course, heard of long before but who, it now became clear to me, were not just trying to lay off a bad bet. They were inspired to action by a deep Christian conviction of the need to expiate their nation's crimes. I now was convinced of their complete sincerity, even though they had accepted as fellow conspirators men whom I still dismissed as mere opportunists.

Otto John told me how he had joined the opposition to Hitler through his friend Claus Bonhöfer, under whom he was working in the legal department of Lufthansa Airways. John's blond hair, blue eyes, and pink cheeks, with their air of super-Nordic health and zest, coupled with his Lufthansa job, had given him the entrée to the pilots' mess of the Führer's personal courier and transport squadron. From these pilots he had learned the secret of Hitler's impending march into Prague in 1939 and had been able to warn Admiral Canaris, who was the head of Germany's *Abwehr* espionage and used his position to provide cover for more active plotters of the resistance inside his organization. That had been his first Intelligence coup for the "inner opposition."

Most productive of all the information which John gave me was his account of Himmler's flirtation with the Resistance. As a result, I set up an operation which I called "Himmler for President." This was a rumour campaign to suggest that the ambitious Himmler was out to double-cross his wounded Führer, remove him from power, and take his place himself. The story that John had told me made me feel that such a campaign might not be too far from the truth.

In August 1943, John said, Himmler had received Professor Johannes Popitz, a conservative politician who, just after Hitler took power, had served as a minister in Göring's Prussian cabinet but was now one of the leaders of the "inner opposition." Popitz had expounded to Himmler the hopelessness of Germany's position, the urgent need of peace with the West, and had given it as his considered opinion that a separate peace with the West was possible, if Hitler was removed and Himmler ruled in his stead. The Western powers, Popitz had argued, were afraid of letting the Russians get too strong. They would be only too pleased to shore up Germany as a bulwark against Bolshevism providing the Germans ridded themselves of their unfortunate Führer and the unspeakable Ribbentrop.

What was needed in Hitler's place was a man who was strong but humane and reasonable.

Himmler was impressed. He was even more impressed when he received a similar lecture from another Nazi turned Resistance leader. This was Himmler's personal friend, the lawyer Dr. Karl Langbehn. He authorized Langbehn to travel to Switzerland to find out from his contacts there how the Western Allies would react to the suggestion of a separate peace with a Himmler Germany. So Langbehn duly travelled to Switzerland on the same mission with which Himmler in the last weeks of the war was to entrust the Swedish Count Folke Bernadotte.

Langbehn's mission, however, had leaked out, and to save himself from the wrath of Hitler, Himmler had him arrested shortly after his return to Germany in September 1943.

I was, of course, sorely tempted to put out the story just as John had told it to me with only a few embellishments to bring it up to date. But I refrained. For I had no desire to excite the suspicions of Stalin with stories of German proposals of a separate peace with the West. Instead, I set up the "Himmler for President" campaign. It is not one on which I look back with pride and satisfaction, for in at least one of its features it was far too light-hearted and flippant and made a silly prank out of something that should have been a serious subversive operation.

We started off well enough, however, with reports of preparations by the S.S. to seize munition stores belonging to the Army as well as other strategic points in the Reich. We quoted speeches and articles about Heinrich Himmler which we said were part of a new propaganda drive to popularize and glamourize the Reichsführer S.S. as the "people's friend." We revealed alleged instructions to press

photographers issued in connection with the "populariza-
tion campaign."

The personal photo-reporter attached to the Reichsführer
S.S., S.S. Sturmbannführer Paul Kurbjuhn, after careful study
of the physiognomy of Heinrich Himmler, has come to the
conclusion that the left side of the Reichsführer's face has a
kindlier expression while his right profile gives a more mascu-
line and martial impression. S.S. Sturmbannführer Kurbjuhn
has accordingly decreed that for internal service use in the
S.S. pictures are to be issued showing predominantly the right
side of the Reichsführer's face while the left side is to be
preferred for shots showing the Reichsführer S.S. in friendly
conversation with folk-comrades or with children.

Next we reported that Field Marshal von Rundstedt
had complained at the way the S.S. Hauptamt (Headquarters office) was issuing directives to the National Socialist leadership officers (the Nazi equivalent of the Communist Political Commissars) at divisional level without
going through the normal channels of the Army High
Command. Rundstedt feared, we said, that the next move
would be for Himmler to issue strategic and tactical orders
direct to Army units. In yet other items we revealed the
grave concern of the Reichsführer S.S. concerning the
wounded Führer's failing health, both physical and mental,
and his preparations to replace him should the need arise.
We reported too the counter-intrigues of Bormann and
S.S. Obergruppenführer Müller. All this was fine. It presented an entirely credible picture of a dying despotism in
its last agonies of disintegration. Alas, in my eagerness to
support this picture with documentary "evidence" I went
much too far—well beyond the bounds of what was plausible.

As a first document I got Armin Hull to produce for us

an exact replica of the printed forms of the "Oath of Loyalty to the Führer" sworn by German soldiers on joining the Wehrmacht. We had found a number of copies of this print among the documents captured at German staff headquarters in France, and the counterfeiting presented no difficulty. But I made one change. For the name of Adolf Hitler I substituted that of Heinrich Himmler.

These forms with a new version of the Wehrmacht oath we then said had been prepared by Himmler in readiness for his assumption of power. In addition to having copies of it left around by underground agents in places frequented by Wehrmacht personnel, we published a photograph of the document in *Nachrichten für die Truppe* with a suitable elucidation by our omniscient military commentator Oblt. J. von Ö. Even this document I am willing to accept today as not too far-fetched.

But the next document I asked Hull to produce for me was utterly beyond the bounds of possibility, and I ought never to have ordered it. This was a set of German postage stamps showing, instead of the head of Hitler, that of Himmler. From the counterfeiting point of view it was a masterpiece. The Himmler head was engraved in exactly the same style as that of Hitler on the ordinary German postage stamps. This was not at all surprising, for Hull had been producing scores of thousands of Hitler postage stamps over the past three years. We used them for our posting jobs in the Reich because our agents quite understandably felt it beneath their dignity to subsidize the German war effort with even the price of a postage stamp.

Unlike the stamp itself, however, the story that went with it was entirely unconvincing. Philatelist Himmler, it said, eager in his vanity to taste in advance the pleasures of Führerdom, had secretly ordered these stamps to be made in readiness for the day of his accession. He loved looking at them. But owing to the mistake of a subordinate official a few sheets had been prematurely issued to the Post Office and the public, and, despite the frantic efforts of trusted Gestapo and S.D. agents to hunt them down and retrieve them, quite a few were still in circulation.

My friends of the underground went into operation with considerable enthusiasm for this silly Delmer stunt and posted letters and newspapers bearing the Himmler stamp in letter-boxes all over Germany. S.O.E. agents delivered German newspapers with wrappers bearing the stamps with counterfeited cancellation marks to subscribers in Sweden and Switzerland who we knew were regular recipients of German newspapers.

But no one noticed the stamps. Not even when in my gloom at the lack of an echo to the operation I asked that the newspaper wrappers with the Himmler stamps should be delivered to known philatelists. The trouble was that Hull's counterfeit was far too good, the Himmler stamp much too similar to the Hitler stamp, and the public—including the philatelists—far too unobservant. Finally in sheer despair my friends in S.O.E. sold some wrappers to stamp dealers in Stockholm and Zurich, and that way the story of the Heinrich Himmler stamp did at last percolate into the neutral press. But as an operation that campaign had mostly sadly misfired.

Not, however, for the stamp dealers. A set of these Himmler stamps commands a high price in philatelistic auction rooms today. I wish I had some.

I had, however, another and more effective shot in my locker for the discomfiture of the "humane and kindly people's friend" Herr Heinrich Himmler. This was a secret transmitter operated on short wave, ostensibly from somewhere behind the Eastern Front, by an anti-Hitler group of the Waffen S.S. It fitted in neatly enough with our campaign of the Himmler double-cross.

Yes, in these last ten months of the war even the loyal and devoted Waffen S.S. had to be allocated its special Resistance cell and Resistance broadcast in the imaginary German world of M.B. The beauty of it was that the man who acted as speaker of "Hagedorn"—that was how the station announced itself—was a genuine officer-deserter of the Waffen S.S. He spoke the genuine S.S. jargon and claimed to be the genuine emissary of a genuine Resistance group of the Waffen S.S. In fact, he was so genuine that I disliked and distrusted him from the first moment one of C.'s officers presented him to me. Rightly so, as it was to turn out after the war.

"Dr. Nansen"—his real name was Zech-Nenntwich— was a bright-eyed, bouncey, rosy-cheeked young cavalryman who even in Austin Reed's grey flannel slacks looked as if he were wearing riding breeches. His S.S. Resistance group, he claimed, had its nucleus in the S.S. cavalry of which he himself had been an Obersturmführer. Its secret leader, he said, was none other than the S.S. Cavalry Commander Brigadier Hermann Fegelein, brother-in-law of Hitler's mistress Eva Braun and representative of the Waffen S.S. at the Führer Headquarters. Nansen himself as adjutant to Fegelein had been the second in command of the Resistance group. "Our men," he boasted to me, "will recognize my voice and obey my orders."

For my purposes it did not matter much whether Nansen's claims were false or true, so long as he made his clandestine S.S. station sound convincing and the message his broadcasts conveyed worth while. I think he succeeded in both, for his main theme was the favourite saga of all true German soldier-patriots—"We have been betrayed. We must rid ourselves of those who have betrayed us. . . ."

The patriotic ideals of the fighting heroes of the S.S., Nansen declaimed, had been betrayed by the unworthy Führer, who had clothed his worst hangmen, sadists, and concentration-camp jailers in the *Waffenrock* (uniform) of the noblest élite of German youth, thereby soiling their good name throughout the world. The Hagedorn group was going to wipe out this stain while there was still time. And, true to our old Gustav Siegfried recipe, we gave him enough inside news to accompany these tirades to make Herr Himmler highly suspect and ensure the unfortunate Fegelein's disgrace. Fegelein did indeed fall under the Führer's displeasure—allegedly for his cowardice—and was shot. Himmler was ultimately deprived by Hitler of all his offices. I do not, of course, claim this was our doing, though we may have helped to create the right atmosphere.

But although he was reasonably effective as a broadcaster I refused to treat our S.S. recruit as an ordinary member of the M.B. team. I did not allow him inside the compound. Instead I hived him off with the officer who had to watch over him in a special abode of his own. This was Paris House, a *"nouveau* Tudor" mansion which one of the Dukes of Bedford had bought—beams, bricks, plaster and all—at a Paris exhibition of the seventies, and re-erected in Woburn Park. Here Child, Stevens, and I—and occasionally the Corporal and Max Braun—called on Nansen to discuss with him points of S.S. intelligence we wanted to elucidate. Most useful he was, too. And in between answering our questions, Nansen recounted something of his own fantastic story.

"I worked with the Polish underground," Nansen told me in his high-pitched tenor voice. "I procured Red Army guns for the guerrilla army of General Bor Komerovski and ammunition too to go with them."

"But why Soviet guns, Nansen?" I asked, suspicious that he was romancing.

"Because the S.S. had large dumps of captured Soviet guns and munition in Poland, and I could get hold of the stuff without it being missed." Yes, I thought, that sounded likely enough.

"I also helped the Poles free Polish Resistance men from an S.S. prison," Nansen went on. "Other Poles I smuggled to Sweden by pretending they were agents of the S.D. Later, when I was arrested and imprisoned by the S.D. myself, my S.S. group got me out and the Poles in their turn smuggled me to Sweden by their own special escape route. That is why I am here. In Stockholm the Poles introduced me to your intelligence and they flew me over here."

I checked his story with my Polish friends. It was perfectly true. He *had* sold them Soviet guns and ammunition. He *had* helped their men escape and they *had* passed him over to Sweden. But I still did not feel like bringing him to M.B. For one thing, I did not know what effect contact with an S.S. man, even an allegedly repentant one, would have on some of my more emotional Jewish collaborators.

But I did take pity on Nansen sufficiently to give him a companion. I arranged for him to be joined at Paris

House by Wolfgang von Putlitz, a German diplomat friend of mine from my Berlin days. "Mr. Potts," as we called him, was not of much use to me at M.B. He had been out of touch with Germany too long, for the S.D. had got wise to him in the earliest days of the war. Putlitz, who had been passing information and documents to the British over a number of years, had been forced to flee helter-skelter from his post at the German embassy in the Hague and take refuge in Britain. C. had passed him on to me. At M.B. he contributed an occasional item to Max Braun's daily list of suggestions for the Soldatensender. The rest of the time he lounged elegantly around the compound, cheering up the secretaries with the happy smile which at Berlin cocktail parties in the golden twenties had earned him that highest of Berlin's social accolades: "*Er hat ein gutes Auftreten*" (He has a good presence).

So to put his charm to better use I now sent Putlitz along to cheer up our S.S. man. Before he went I made him promise me not to talk about M.B. to Nansen, and not about Nansen to M.B. That was a waste of breath for both of us. Putlitz gossiped to Nansen about everyone and everything he knew. Fortunately, his knowledge was far from exhaustive. But it was enough for Nansen, when he returned to Germany after the war, to try to "rehabilitate" himself, as he put it, by turning informer against the "worthless traitors and collaborators at M.B."

In January 1950 Zech Nentwig, alias Dr. Nansen, was received by Chancellor Adenauer in a tête-à-tête audience at his Rhineside home in Rhöndorf. For two hours Nentwig sat with the old Chancellor, so he boasted later, telling what he knew of the men who had worked with me, particularly of those who, like the Social Democrats, had become active in post-war Germany's political life and were now opposing Adenauer. Among the men whom this apple-cheeked S.S. renegade denounced was Otto John, who was nominated Security Chief of the Federal Republic later that year.

I am not really surprised that Nansen's S.S. conscience should have begun to prick him after the war. It must have been most galling for him to find his old S.S. comrades from the Gestapo and the S.D. trickling back into fat jobs with the new West German police and the multiplicity of security and espionage services that were springing up again in 1950. It is never pleasant for an opportunist to find he has backed the wrong side after all.

But while he was at Paris House he collaborated most nobly and helped us, not only with his own broadcasts, but as a consultant on everything pertaining to the S.S.

One day I was visited by two American Intelligence officers from General Sibert's staff. They asked me whether they could borrow Virchow from me for a few days for a most important operation. The German commander opposite one of the American units had signified his readiness to negotiate a surrender if the Americans would send him as a negotiator an American officer accompanied by a German. Apologetically I told my American visitors that I could not jeopardize anyone so deep in our secrets as Virchow.

What a pity I did not offer them "Nansen." The German commander's readiness to negotiate surrender was, of course, just a variation on the "Venlo" trick,* designed to

---

* On November 8, 1939, the German S.D. man Walter Schellenberg, masquerading as an emissary of the German "Resistance," lured the British Intelligence agents Captain Payne Best and Major R. H. Stevens to the German-Dutch frontier at Venlo and with the aid of a commando of S.S. troops shanghaied them across the border.

lull the Americans into false confidence before the Ardennes offensive.

Poor Nansen. I am being a little unkind. After all, he is not such an unusual phenomenon as all that—though I must confess he is the only one among the Germans that worked with me.

17

"Aspidistra," our powerful 600-kilowatt medium-wave transmitter, was not only the biggest and loudest radio in Europe at that time, it was also the nippiest. It had been specially designed for us by the Radio Corporation of America so as to be able to make lightning changes of frequency. As Goebbels had noted in his *Diary,** it hopped all over the wave band. First it broadcast on its own regular frequency; then it switched suddenly to that of the Deutschlandsender, when the Deutschlandsender went off the air, or to that of Radio Frankfort or Radio Munich. Agile "Aspidistra," served with a priest-like devotion by

* See page 123 of this volume.

Harold Robin and his team of radio engineers, could accomplish a frequency switch in under half a minute—something which it would take an ordinary transmitter hours to make, if not days. This faculty came in handy when we wanted to shake off the German jammers which were now devoting more and more of their strength to howling down the Soldatensender.

We made full and frequent use of it.

It was not, however, merely in order to play hide and seek with the German jammers that "Aspidistra" had been endowed with this capacity for switching frequencies. That had its origin in a far more sinister and ambitious design. Quite simply this was that we should "capture" a station in the Goebbels network for a few minutes and use it to put out misleading announcements and instructions to the German public in the name of the German authorities. Bruce Lockhart had given me his formal approval of this plan * as long ago as Christmas 1942—at the same time, in fact, that he had granted my request for the use of the M.B. studios for the Atlantiksender.

"I approve in principle," Bruce had said then in that husky voice which seemed to suck back every word the moment he had incautiously uttered it. "But please note that 'in principle.' Get everything ready for this operation so that you can lay it on at a moment's notice when opportunity offers. But always remember this"—and he had cocked his head to one side as he always did when he wanted to emphasize a point. "This is our Big Bertha. We

* The original plan for "Aspidistra" when it was ordered from America was that its voice should be superimposed on an enemy broadcast and outshout it. I managed to get this idea shot down on the grounds that it was not a "black" operation and would deceive no one. Dr. Goebbels' men at one time in 1941 superimposed a German voice on the B.B.C. Home Service. It cried, "We want milk." The answer of the public was, "Poor fellows. Let them come and get it."

can't go pooping it off on just any playful stunt you or Donald McLachlan may dream up! This has got to be a real war-winner."

Almost two years had gone by since then without our using our Big Bertha, and I was beginning to fear that if we did not do something soon the war would be over without her having fired a shot. The question was, what sort of a shot could she fire that was sufficiently devastating to be called a "winner," let alone a "war-winner"?

The operation which Bruce Lockhart had approved "in principle" was straightforward enough. It was that we should attack what had always seemed to me the Achilles' heel of the German radio system. Unlike the B.B.C., the Goebbels radio had a separate frequency for every station in its network—a sop to the regional particularism of the Germans which one would not have expected from the henchmen of that fanatic for centralization and *Gleichschaltung*, Adolf Hitler. This had the result that when the bombers of the R.A.F. and the U.S.A.F. flew into Germany and some of the German transmitters went off the air so as not to serve as beacons for the raiders, a number of German regional radios closed down with them and their frequencies were left vacant—a practice which we had already been exploiting in our war with the jammers.

Our plan, therefore, was for "Aspidistra" to lie in ambush on the frequency of a German station we expected to go off the air and take over the moment it did. Harold Robin had perfected an electronic device specially designed for the purpose. It enabled "Aspidistra" to take over the German target frequency within one two-hundredth of a second after a German station closed down. On it we then planned to broadcast the identical programme the Germans had been broadcasting. For the German listeners, therefore, there would be no break in continuity. They would be completely unaware that the big bad British wolf had put on Grandma Goebbels' nightcap and spectacles and crept into bed in her place.

How did we mean to accomplish this? I had found that when Leipzig or Frankfort, whichever it was, closed down there were always a number of other stations left on the air broadcasting the programme which the dear departed had been carrying. All we had to do, therefore, was to take over this programme from, let us say, Hamburg or Berlin, on our antennae and relay it on to the frequency of our German target station through "Aspidistra," in much the same way as we occasionally relayed the radio speeches of Hitler and Goebbels on to the Calais programme. We only needed to carry on with the relay for a fraction of a minute. Then, having established the continuity, we would interrupt the programme with one of those special announcements which the German authorities, now that other means of communication had broken down as a result of systematic bombing, were increasingly fond of making over the radio. The announcement finished, we would carry on with the Goebbels programme for a minute or so. Then we too would fade out as "enemy terror raiders approached."

Two problems remained. How could we anticipate which frequency would be off the air at a given time, and what were we to tell the Germans that would do real damage to Hitler?

The first we solved without too much difficulty. Squadron Leader Edward Halliday, at that time the administrative boss of the M.B. compound and the R.U.'s, and today president of the Royal Society of British Artists, was the hero who did so. With the aid of some personnel re-

cruited from our bottomless source of staff, the German
Wehrmacht, and a small team of British girl researchers
to supervise them—the P.O.W.'s loved that—he set up a
twenty-four-hour radio watch.

Day after day, night after night, Ted Halliday's team
recorded which German stations closed down at what
time. Ted then compared the behaviour of the German
stations with the route followed by the Allied bombers.
Gradually he established a pattern. And when at last the
time came for us to "poop off" Big Bertha, Ted, who for
this purpose had been given the top-secret flight plan of
the bombers for the night, was able to predict with one-
hundred-per-cent accuracy who was going to be off the
air and when. But I feared there would be a mutiny by
the team long before the great day came. For they had
had to keep up this watch for the best part of two years
before we went into action, and I can think of few jobs
more uninteresting than listening continuously to the
Goebbels radio.

The second problem, however, remained a bother to us.
Maybe such imagination as I possessed had been ex-
hausted. Maybe my brain had become fatigued. The only
decisive operation I was able to dream up for our Big
Bertha was that at a moment to be chosen by the Chiefs
of Staff she should announce the deposition of Hitler and
the capitulation of the German armies. The announcement would be made in the name of the O.K.W., the
Commander-in-Chief West, or some other high German
authority—perhaps even Himmler. That, I believed,
would cause plenty of confusion in the German ranks,
military and civilian, and would give the German units
still facing our advance a valid excuse for quick surrender.
I was confident that we could put it across, especially if

the Chiefs of Staff approved the operation and we did not confine it to the voice of "Aspidistra," but borrowed two B.B.C. transmitters to reinforce ours on other German frequencies.

Neither Bruce Lockhart nor Dallas Brooks thought the operation stood much chance of being approved, but they were willing to let me have a try. So Donald McLachlan and I—Donald had returned to M.B. for a brief visit— drew up one of those paper plans beloved of Whitehall, stating objectives, proposed methods, and analysis of situation, all divided and sub-divided into sections and subsections with numbers and letters and an army of semi-colons. Donald, with his Admiralty training, had become an expert at this kind of thing, and when Dallas Brooks had put his final touches to it our paper, far from turning out as an article for the editorial page of the *Daily Express*, which directives penned by me had a way of doing, not only looked like a genuine staff paper but was one.

Not that this prevented it from being shot down in the end. Week after week I attended committee meetings in the underground caverns where the brains of Britain's war machine worked under the blinding glare of long strips of fluorescent lighting and in a fug which reminded me of my Paris concierge's lodge. Dallas Brooks and Bruce Lockhart took turns in presenting the bearded Delmer to the mighty—a little shamefacedly, I sometimes felt—so that he might argue his case. And then, at the last and mightiest meeting of all, Big Bertha's "war-winner" was firmly, finally, and irrevocably ruled out.

Two reasons were given for the hostile decision. The first was in my view pertinent and probably sound enough: "The disadvantage of the proposed operation is that it will cause almost as much confusion in the ranks of the Allied forces as in those of the enemy. To warn our own forces against it in advance would prejudice the security and surprise of the operation and in all probability jeopardize its effectiveness with the enemy." I did not quarrel too much with that view. I had too often seen "black" operations deceive our own side. But the second objection, inspired, I suspected by memories of German between-the-wars propaganda that President Wilson's fourteen points had tricked an undefeated Germany into surrender in 1918, seemed to my insubordinate Fleet Street mind just silly. "It would not be a good thing," it said, "for the Germans to be able to declare after the war that they had been defeated by a trick."

As Bruce and I drove back to Bush House from the War Cabinet offices where the meeting had been held, Bruce, in his kindness, tried to cheer me up. "Whitehall," he said, "is the real Heartbreak House. If you get twenty-five per cent of any scheme you put up accepted and ten per cent carried out you can consider yourself very fortunate indeed; normally schemes are just turned down."

The truth, however, was that I needed no comforting. For together with the rejection of Big Bertha's "war-winner" I had been given *carte blanche* to go ahead with any minor operations for which I might like to use "Aspidistra's" capabilities as an intruder—the "playful stunts" which had hitherto been strictly taboo.

The fun was about to begin.

We did not have long to wait for an opportunity to try out Big Bertha. Winston Churchill saw to that.

As the British and American armies began their advance into Germany, the B.B.C., the Voice of America, and the 12th Army group broadcasters of Radio Luxemburg had all been telling the German civilian population, "Stay where you are. Don't move." They had done so under a carefully considered directive from SHAEF. But when Winston learned of this advice—quite fortuitously —he blew up in hot outrage.

Churchill was spending the week-end at Eisenhower's headquarters outside Rheims. At breakfast on the Sunday morning he was leafing through the only newspaper available, the American forces' *Stars and Stripes*. There his incredulous eyes lit on an item proudly reporting that Radio Luxemburg and the B.B.C. were telling the German civilians to "stay put."

"Pray, General, what sort of nonsense is this?" the old man growled at host Eisenhower, and pointed an accusing finger at the news item. "Surely we should not be telling the German civilians to stay where they are? We should be driving them out into the highways and byways so that they impede the strategic communications of the Hun armies, just as the French civilians impeded the communications of the French Armies in 1940!"

It was not, of course, a new thought this for the SHAEF planners. It had been carefully considered by them and rejected before the "stay-put" directive was issued. Eisenhower's British and American experts had decided against driving the German civilians into the roads because they feared they would be just as much hindrance there for the advancing Allies as for the retreating Germans. Also, it was a good way of indirectly assuring the Germans that they would be well treated by the Allies without making any direct promises. It countered Goebbels' prophesies of Allied frightfulness. In fact, it was a very good line indeed.

But Eisenhower was a politician and a diplomat as well

as a soldier. He was anxious to please Churchill. He had angered the old man by turning down his strategic recommendations for the final push across Germany, and the sacrifice of a psychological-warfare directive seemed the easiest and cheapest way to placate him. So General Mc-Clure, Dick Crossman, and the American planner C. D. Jackson * were hastily summoned to Rheims—each flew in his own little Piper Cub—and there Eisenhower's chief of staff bitterly informed them of the change in orders. The Germans, said General Walter Bedell Smith, were *not*—repeat *not*—to be told to remain in their cellars to await the Allies. Instead they were to be panicked out on to the roads. Period.

That, however, was much more easily stencilled into a directive than done. Neither the B.B.C. nor the Voice of America nor even Radio Luxemburg could openly go back on what they had been saying without losing all authority and good will. In their dilemma General McClure and Bruce Lockhart turned to us, the ruffians of the "black," the disavowable scallywags who did the dirty work.

Bruce Lockhart called me up on the scrambler and explained the situation.

"Tom," he then said, "I want you to run a campaign on the Soldatensender that will drive the German civilians on to the roads. Can you do that?"

"We can have a shot at it on the Soldatensender," I replied, "but surely this is just the job for Big Bertha. If you agree, I think we could issue some pretty drastic evacuation instructions to the population in the name of the German authorities. And perhaps we could hold out some other inducements as well," I added, as I suddenly remembered the "bomb-free safety zone" we had tried out

* Now a vice-president with Time Inc.

on the Italians. "Do you want me to send you a short list of suggested announcements?"

"Yes, do that, so that I can report what you are doing. But don't wait for me to give you my formal approval. Get cracking. I am sure you will think up something good." Which was very generous of him after the crashing failure of our "war-winner."

We were in luck. Everything was set fair for our first Big Bertha operation. Radio Cologne, our target, had been behaving just the way we wanted it to behave. During the past couple of weeks it had been frequently interrupting its programme to give its listeners situation reports and instructions. We had been making special recordings of these emergency broadcasts and had filed them in our record archives together with the "air situation reports" and instructions we had recorded from other radios in the German network. Now we brought them out and listened to them again.

A man and a woman had been the voices broadcasting the instructions from Cologne. Fine. I had a man and a woman ready to take their places. The man was Moritz Wetzold, a German prisoner who had been a trainee announcer on the German radio before he was called up. I had been keeping him on ice for just such an operation as this, ever since he had joined my team six months before. The woman was Margit Maass, the actress wife of Alex. She could imitate anything.

Next we had some captured documents showing that the area on both banks of the Rhine had been divided into zones under special Nazi commissars. We even had the code name for the operation. It was "Siegfried." The operation itself was called an R-operation—R. for *Rück-*

führung (evacuation). That was just the jargon to make our instructions sound convincing. Clifton Child, Stevens, and Hans Gutmann now set to work to prepare the actual text of our announcement. I gave them the rough outline.

"The orders will be issued in the name of the Gauleiter" I said, "and they will say that enemy armour is approaching and that women and children must leave their homes at once, this very night, taking only fifteen kilograms in weight of their most essential belongings with them. Wherever possible the local Nazi group leader is to form them up in columns and lead them. The men must of course stay behind with the Volkssturm and defend their villages. The women and children are to take handcarts, perambulators, bicycles, and anything else they have on wheels. We must give them some Rhine crossings and assembly points on the other side—well inland, I suggest, where special trains are waiting to take them to the evacuation centres of the National Socialist Welfare Organizations in Bavaria. The families must be sure to take their documentation with them. Identity cards should be tied round the children's necks in special bags."

I felt just like a Gauleiter myself by the time I had finished.

Child, Gutmann, and Stevens got down to the job of preparing the announcement; Margit Maass and Moritz Wetzold began their rehearsal in the Operation studio. We had typed out the text of one of the genuine Cologne announcements, and now Margit and Moritz read it over, copying the inflection of the Cologne announcers which they had heard on our recordings.

Only one question remained: was Cologne going to be off the air that night? And then, just as Harold Robin and I were beginning to get worried about this, Ted Halliday rushed in. He had been getting the night's operational plan from the R.A.F. "Cologne" he announced theatrically, "will go off the air at nine-fifteen tonight—or just after."

Without another word Harold Robin picked up the telephone and called his chief engineer at the transmitter's underground home near Crowborough and told him to get "Aspidistra" ready for action. Then he added one final touch. He produced some tinfoil sound reflectors and put them up behind the microphones.

"That will give your voices the peculiar metallic timbre of these Cologne announcers," he said to Margit and Moritz.

He was quite right. Margit and Moritz were practising our announcement now, and with the reflectors added, they sounded entirely genuine.

All there was left for us to do was to wait for Cologne to be driven off the air. Nine-fifteen came and Cologne was still broadcasting. Nine-twenty, and Cologne was still there. I looked a little reproachfully at Ted Halliday.

"Your schedule seems a bit out, Ted," I said. Before Halliday could answer, the telephone rang. Harold Robin was on the line.

"What do you think of the signal you're getting now from Cologne?"

"It's good and strong. Time they were off the air though, isn't it?"

"They are off the air. That's us you're hearing. We took over from the Germans exactly twenty seconds ago. So when you're ready . . ."

I looked across at my announcers. Both of them gave me a grinning thumbs-up. "Okay Harold. Fifteen seconds from . . . now."

The whole thing worked perfectly. Nervous as they

were, Moritz and Margit put out their text without a
fluff and in the exact rhythm and intonation of the genuine Cologne team. When they had finished Harold
switched back on to the German programme he had been
relaying. We carried on for about an hour, repeating our
bogus announcement at intervals. Then at last "Aspidistra" faded out. "Cologne" stayed off the air for the rest of
the evening.

We followed up our guest performance on Cologne
radio with similar visits to Frankfort and Leipzig on the
following nights. The citizens of the Frankfort and Darm-
stadt areas we tried to entice from their homes with reports of special Red Cross welfare trains, distributing food,
hot drinks, and clothing, which we said were calling at
certain stations at certain times. The railway section of
M.E.W. and Stevens had worked out a most convincing
train schedule with the stations just far enough away to
make it a real trip to get there. We announced special
orders from Gauleiter Florian to the local cadres of Nazi
Party functionaries. As "the most valuable element of the
nation" they were to retire (*sich absetzen*) from the threatened areas in order that they might survive and "hand on
the torch of the National Socialist faith."

On the Soldatensender, and in *Nachrichten,* we plugged
a story of seven bomb-free zones in central and south Germany where refugees would be safe from further enemy
air attacks. Neutral Red Cross representatives in Berlin,
we reported, had informed the Reich authorities that
Eisenhower was going to declare these zones as safety
areas. Banks were already moving their securities into
them.

These "safety zones" were all the more effective as almost at the same time as we were announcing them Eisen-

hower began to proclaim as "targets for tonight" the total destruction of such city areas as Cologne, Düsseldorf, Frankfort, and Mannheim. Ike, too, was following the Churchill directive.

Were Big Bertha's instructions obeyed? Did the population leave the towns and villages, and crowd the roads, as Churchill had wished? The confidential "weekly report" of the Gauamtsleiter of Lemgo, which I reproduce in the appendix,* suggests that they did. But I never checked any further.

When I got to Germany at the end of March, the roads were indeed crowded with refugees—miserable ragged families, trudging wearily along the Autobahn and through debris-cluttered streets of bomb ruins. Behind them they dragged carts, buses that had no fuel for their engines, and even hearses. All were loaded with bedding and babies. It was the epitome of everything I had seen in Spain, Poland, and France.

I did not stop to ask any of them whether it was a message on Radio Cologne or Radio Frankfort that had first started them on their trek. I did not want to know. I feared the answer might be yes.

What I do know is that by our intrusion with counterfeit instructions we finally deprived the German authorities of the use of the radio for issuing orders to the German population. For when Hitler's men woke up to what was happening they howled in protest. "The enemy is broadcasting counterfeit instructions on our frequencies," the Nazi announcers cried. "Don't be misled by them. Here is an official announcement of the Reich authority for . . ." That was just what we wanted.

"The enemy," said our own announcer in Big Bertha's

* Page 274.

next intrusion, "is broadcasting counterfeit instructions on our frequencies. Don't be misled by them. Here is an official announcement of the Reich authority for . . ."

It was such a pushover for us that Goebbels abandoned the battle. He gave up just as he had given up once before when we counterfeited Mussolini's Fascist Republican Radio from Munich. No more orders and announcements went out over the ether. Instead, the Reich government confined itself from then on to giving out its announcements and instructions over the *Drahtfunk,* a wired diffusion network on which we could not intrude but which was greatly restricted in its scope.

And of course we did not limit our big Bertha counterfeit to messages designed to get the German population moving out on the roads. I also did my best to further our oldest psychological-warfare aim of setting Nazi against Nazi. Here an experience proved useful which I recalled from the time when as a ten-year-old schoolboy I was in Berlin at the beginning of World War I. In those earliest days of August 1914 the whole of Germany had resounded with rumours of a motor car, filled with a freight of gold bars, which its crew of Russian officers were trying to race across Germany from France to Russia. Motor cars were being stopped by zealous German guards at all conceivable and inconceivable barriers in the fatherland. On two or three occasions there was shooting. That story of the Russian gold-auto had deeply impressed me in 1914. Now I determined to give the Germans of 1945 a similar thrill.

"*Achtung! Achtung!*" called Moritz Wetzold on our next intrusion. "At the request of the R.S.H.A.* we make the following special announcement. Enemy saboteurs dis-

* *Reichssicherheitshauptamt*—Chief Reich Security Office.

guised as German officers in Wehrmacht uniform have stolen a field-grey Wehrmacht car Number W.M. 356–673, and are now proceeding from Karlsruhe in the general direction of North Holland. The enemy agents have been seen on the following roads . . ." and there followed a list of German highways. "But they may well have changed direction and be on another highway by now. They may also have changed the number plate of the car. These men are armed and desperate. They have already killed police who tried to stop them. German Volksgenossen, Comrades of the Wehrmacht and of the Volkssturm, these dangerous enemy saboteurs must be stopped at all costs. The chief of the R.S.H.A. calls upon you to erect road barriers to stop the enemy car. Those of you with arms are hereby ordered to shoot if you see the car. I repeat—a field-grey Wehrmacht car occupied by enemy agents in Wehrmacht officers' uniforms."

In my mind's eye, I fondly imagined Wehrmacht officers in speeding cars being held up all over the place and some of them being shot.

Sorry as I was for the refugee families, when I saw them later on the roads of Germany, I had only one real regret about Big Bertha. We should have "pooped her off" much sooner. For by the time the old girl went into action there was not much left for her to hit.

18

In the early autumn of 1944 my friends in S.O.E. began toying with the idea of a Skorzeny-style commando raid on the Führer's headquarters. They thought it would be a neat way of shortening the war if they could bump off Hitler and Himmler. And so too it would have been. I say *would* have been, because in the end this plan, like so many others before it, was rejected—not, however, before a most meticulous intelligence survey had been made recording every relevant and irrelevant detail that could be collected about the set-up in the Führer's headquarters and the ancillary headquarters of Himmler and Ribbentrop.

Captured German generals and staff officers were carefully interrogated about what they remembered from their visits to the headquarters, maps were drawn of the various Führer and Reichsführer S.S. camps and of the trains of Pullman cars in which Germany's leaders ate, slept, worked, and travelled. The security system with its rings of guards and strong points was described and analysed. Lists were made of the permanent denizens of the headquarters, and they were sketched with a detail which would have enraptured a gossip columnist. Then, as I have said, the project was abandoned.

But the intelligence that had been collected was not wasted. The monitored conversations between the generals, the interrogations, the maps—all travelled down to M.B. There they were built up into news stories about the hitherto top-secret private life of Hitler and his suite that tortured the ailing Führer with the suspicion that the British had their spies right inside his H.Q. Clifton Child was a genius at freshening up a piece of intelligence with a new development that made it sound like something that had happened the night before. We told of the adventures of the popsies brought in to amuse the tired Führer, of the boisterous high jinks of blonde Blanda-Elisabeth, the young wife of Dr. Walter Hewel, who represented the German Foreign Office at the H.Q. How, for instance, at a party in the Berchtesgadener Hof on the Führer's Obersalzberg she had shown off her prowess as a barber by soaping and shaving Herrmann Fegelein, the S.S. general who had become the Führer's unofficial brother-in-law by marrying the sister of his mistress Eva Braun.

We told stories about the drugs with which the Führer's court physician Professor Morell had been injecting him, and how these had turned Hitler into a half-paralysed trembling dotard. Shady deals in gold watches and human lives pulled off by Himmler's masseur, the plump and ever-hungry Felix Kersten, came under the merciless publicity of the Soldatensender's news bulletins. Kersten, we said, had gained such an ascendancy over Himmler by massaging away his stomach cramps that the *Reichsheini* could refuse him nothing. Himmler, according to the Soldatensender, even let Kersten have slave labour from concentration camps for his estate at Harzwalde.

We reported the jealousies and bickering between Hitler's sycophant courtiers. And nearly all of it was true, or was so close to the truth as to be most disturbing to the great man who had ordered a special monitoring watch of the Soldatensender. Quite early we got Hitler to the point where he commanded Goebbels and Schellenberg to check our news items to find out whether they were true, and, if they were, to try and hunt down our source.

Hitler's suspicions reached their climax when the Soldatensender, using the same technique of intelligent deduction and anticipation which had served us so well in the past, reported an order issued by the Führer at a conference in his headquarters, and did so only twenty-four hours after he gave it and before it had been carried out.

On March 7, 1945, the Americans, by an historic piece of dash and improvization, managed to capture the great railway bridge across the Rhine at Remagen before the Germans had time to blow it up. Donald and I were discussing the talk in which Sepp Obermeyer had said the Luftwaffe bombers had been ordered to make Japanese-style suicide dives on that bridge with block-buster bombs.

"Of course, the real people to have a go at the bridge should be the Navy with their frogmen," said Donald as much in joke as anything.

I immediately turned to Frankie Lynder. "Where are the nearest frogman units?" I asked.

"I think Admiral Heye's K-force has some at Nimwegen. We could easily move them upstream and have them make an under-water attack against the bridge with those special torpedo mines—the T.M.C., you know, sir."

Frankie had never lost his admirable habit of saying "Sir" to his superior officers which had won him three stripes in the Pioneer Corps.

"Oh, I don't think we want to report an actual attack, sergeant. We'll just say that the Führer had the brilliant idea of an under-water attack and that Admiral Heye, eager to add the diamonds to his oak leaves—or whatever else it is he covets in the way of decorations—has graciously consented to sacrifice his frogmen on 'Operation Lorelei.' I think you should make a great play of some chap arguing that the whole scheme is impossible rubbish owing to the incalculable under-water currents of the Rhine."

It was just a routine "black" story like hundreds of others we had thought up. But what a commotion it caused in Hitler's headquarters in the underground shelter at the Reich chancellery in Berlin, when we put it on the air on March 11! For, unknown to us at the time, the Führer had in fact ordered the German Navy's C.-in-C. Grand Admiral Doenitz to set up an under-water operation by naval frogmen against the bridge. The whole episode is most painstakingly recorded in the secret Minutes of the Führer's Conferences on Naval Affairs.*

Hitler, it appears from the Minutes, had ordered the operation on March 8, 1945. On March 9 at 17.00 hours Admiral Doenitz reported to his Führer that two detachments of frogmen had been selected for the operation and that they were being sent up-river as fast as possible. They would use torpedo mines attached to one another—exactly the technique Sergeant Lynder had recommended!

Then on March 11 the Soldatensender and its twin brother the short-wave Atlantiksender made our announcement.

And here is the minute taken at the Führer's conference of the following day.

Berlin, March 12, 1945, 16.00 hrs.
Remagen Bridge. The British Atlantiksender has announced German plans to use amphibious commandos to blow up the bridge at Remagen. The C.-in-C. Navy informs the Führer that he intends to carry out his plan regardless of this broadcast, because there is a possibility that the British made the announcement in order to bluff us.

Doenitz was trying to make light of the "leak" of his operational plans. Not so, however, Hitler or the unfortunate frogmen commandos. For Hitler, it was the supreme proof that he was surrounded by traitors. His secrets had become so cheap that the enemy broadcast them to the world. For the frogmen it was catastrophic. They felt like condemned men when they finally set out for their under-water swim to the bridge. Vicky had played them the Lorelei song by way of greeting, and as

* *Brassey's Naval Annual, 1948.*

they flippered their way through the swirling ice-cold currents with their unwieldy twin torpedoes they felt the eyes of the enemy upon them all the way. They surfaced and surrendered to the Americans before they got anywhere near the bridge.

Which did not, however, prevent Doenitz from claiming the destruction of the Remagen bridge as the work of his brave frogmen when at last it did collapse, not from any damage the Germans had managed to do, but from the after-effects of the pasting it had received from the R.A.F. and the U.S.A.F. while it was still in German hands. "I was right, *mein Führer*," he triumphed. "The Atlantiksender *was* bluffing. We have destroyed the bridge despite their claim to know our plans."

But Hitler just stared ahead of him without looking at his Grand Admiral.

"Perhaps . . ." he said, and that was all.

In these last few months of the war, the German section of S.O.E. had been given a new boss, a man of immense energy and drive who was determined to harass the Germans with every means at our disposal. He now co-opted me to sit in at a regular weekly meeting at which we discussed new plans and new ideas. And it was as a result of one of these meetings that my unit carried out its last and most bizarre counterfeiting operation of the war.

The new boss was Lieutenant General Gerald Templer.* He had been badly shattered during the campaign in southern Italy when his car collided with a retreating German army lorry, and a looted piano which the Ger-

---

* Field Marshal Sir Gerald Templer, G.C.B., Chief of the Imperial General Staff from 1955 to 1959.

mans were carrying off in the lorry fell on Templer and broke his back. Now Templer, effervescent and enthusiastic as ever, presided over our meetings, strapped in a corset of steel and plaster.

We had been discussing "Operation Periwig," a scheme for harassing the S.D. and Gestapo and submitting them to the utmost strain. The talk had got around to dropping fake agents by parachute—dummies that were got up in battle dress and fired off crackers which sounded like automatics—when young Squadron Leader Potter of S.O.E. mentioned carrier pigeons.

"I believe, sir," he said to Templer, "that we still have a considerable stock of carrier pigeons for which no one seems to have any use. The sort, sir, which we used to drop over the occupied territories for resistance-minded inhabitants to pick up and send back to us with intelligence about the Germans in their district."

Potter explained that the pigeons were parachuted to the ground in air-holed cartons which contained, in addition to the pigeon, a questionnaire concerning troop movements and other matters of interest to the Intelligence people. There was also a set of instructions on how to feed and water the birds and how to attach the filled-in questionnaire before setting the pigeon free to fly home to its S.O.E. loft.

Someone now suggested dropping these birds in Germany and giving the Germans a chance to repudiate Hitler by giving useful information. This was the cue for me.

"That is a splendid idea. But I think we might be able to do even better, sir," I said, speaking in my full dignity as the only psychological warrior on the committee. "I suggest that in addition to parachuting live birds with questionnaires in their boxes we should also drop a few dead ones without boxes but with questionnaires attached to their legs which have already been completed—by . . . er . . . ourselves."

Templer, who had—and still has—a schoolboy's delight in mischief, roared with laughter and immediately approved the scheme.

The object, of course, was that the birds and their completed questionnaires should fall into the hands of the Gestapo, who would try to detect from the answers what traitor had written them. We would phrase the answers in such a way, I suggested, that the Gestapo would be led into arresting some of their own trusted Party functionaries—men who they would be led to believe were now trying to buy themselves a little slice of last-minute re-insurance with the Allies. And if the dead bird was picked up by an ordinary civilian who did not hand it over to the police, it would still provide admirable evidence that well-informed and authoritative Party comrades were defecting. It would encourage him to do so himself.

"One snag, sir, occurs to me," I said to Templer. "Can we devise a way of landing a dead bird without it smashing to pulp when it strikes the ground? If it does, it will rather give the show away. For a tired pigeon or even one which had been killed in mid-air would surely not fall from such a height as to smash."

Squadron Leader Potter immediately promised to take care of this aspect, and I was authorized to go ahead and prepare the questionnaires—with and without answers.

The pigeons were duly dropped and duly picked up by the Germans. Quite a number arrived back with questionnaires that had been filled in by our German correspondents. But one pigeon scrambled into its loft with this polite message scrawled over an otherwise blank sheet: "I had the sister of this one for supper. Delicious. Please send us some more."

Whether the Gestapo fell for our deception, as I hoped they would, I never got a chance to check. But I think that anyone who knew that slow-witted and gullible Security Service and its methods will agree with me that it is a safe bet that they did.

19

One evening in April 1961 four of us were sitting around the fire in my club sipping the Hine 1904 and reminiscing about the war. Someone asked me, "Which single operation of your 'black' work during the war do you consider to have been the most ingenious and most effective?"

The veteran war historian who had put the question sat back and waited for an answer. I turned to Donald McLachlan, who was with me. But he, too, was at a loss for the kind of answer the old man wanted. For the truth was that there never was any one "black" operation that had been spectacularly effective all by itself. They were not designed that way. We never staged anything which could compare, for ingenuity and individual effectiveness, with deceptions such as Commander Montagu's "man who never was"—the operation by which the corpse of an unknown British officer carrying bogus plans for the invasion of North Africa was washed up on the Atlantic shore of Spain, so that German Intelligence should receive his plans and be deceived by them. We never attempted to concentrate on individual coups. Our task as I saw it was to corrode and erode with a steady drip of subversive news and "evidence" the iron system of control in which Hitler's police state had locked the body and soul of the German people. No one single campaign could be as effective on its own as "the man who never was" had been. All, however, from Gustav Siegfried to the Soldatensender and such operations as Tuckbox, Braddock, and Periwig, worked together to secure a dividend which, in the opinion of the Services Intelligence men watching the fall of the shot, was indeed helping to hasten the collapse of Hitler's military and social apparatus.

My American colleagues, however, had a different approach when they started up "black" on their own towards the end of the war. Not for them the concerted system of "black" campaigns which we had adopted. They were more ambitious, and perhaps also more sanguine than I ever was concerning the credulity of the German public. They launched several "black" operations which were intended to stand on their own just as "the man who never was" had stood on his own.

Two American operations in particular remain in my memory as typical of these American propaganda coups.

Howard Becker, a tall, slow-spoken, Gary Cooper-ish professor of sociology who was running "black" for O.S.S., was responsible for the first. Becker called on me one day at M.B. with a writer of film scripts named Polonski and asked me whether I would let him borrow "Aspidistra" for a one-shot broadcast which he and Polonski had worked out.

"Just one shot!" wheedled Howard Becker. "We're not trying to steal her from you, Tom!" Needless to say, I immediately agreed. It would have been churlish to refuse, specially in view of all the help Howard, and O.S.S. as a whole, had been giving me with intelligence, recordings of hit music, personnel, and so much else.

As a result, "Aspidistra" unhooked herself from the Soldatensender for a couple of hours one evening in September 1944 to put out over a temporarily vacant German frequency what must have been one of the most fantastic broadcasts of the war. It was nothing less than a speech by a man whom Hitler, the German Army, the German public, and all the rest of the world presumed to be dead—killed by his own hand and with his own pistol on the night of July 20, 1944, when his putsch against Hitler had collapsed.

"I am Colonel-General Ludwig Beck," intoned a deep resonant voice, coming seemingly from the bottom of the ocean. "I am not dead, as has been lyingly and all too prematurely reported by the spokesmen of our traitor rulers. When on the night of July 20th I was compelled to go through the act of shooting myself, I did not die—I was only wounded. Friends carried me away, pretending I was a corpse. They took me to a secret place, where I was nursed back to health. I would have remained in hiding there until the end of the war, but the plight of my fatherland compels me to come forward and speak." There followed an appeal to the Army to rise against Hitler in order to save Germany from total destruction and remove, by this gesture, the heavy burden of guilt resting collectively on the German people for its complicity in the Führer's crimes.

It was a beautifully written piece and beautifully spoken. Though I had never heard Beck when he was alive, I was quite prepared to believe that this was a more than fair imitation of him. None the less, I tried to propose some alterations in the script before the recording was put out.

"Why don't you change it just a little," I suggested to Howard, "so that we could claim that this is the speech that Beck had wanted to put out if the putsch had been successful. He had secretly prepared this recording. It was to be broadcast from Deutschlandsender. Somehow the Nazis and the Gestapo never found it. Now we have got hold of it. We could put it out over the Soldatensender, if you like."

But Howard and Polonski understandably did not like. They wanted to bring Beck back to life as a symbol of defiance and resistance. They wanted to stage a spectacular propaganda coup.

The other operation was put over under the auspices of Colonel Powell, who headed the "Sykewar" team in General Omar Bradley's 12th Army Group. Over one of the transmitters of Radio Luxemburg his men broadcast for a period of about a fortnight what was to all intents a "black" soap opera—the drama of a Rhineland town which had revolted against Hitler and the S.S. and was now appealing over an army radio to the Americans to come in and rescue them. The burgomaster of the town was the chief speaker. Every evening he went on the air to tell his fellow citizens what they should do and give them his daily progress report of the town's desperate battle against the Nazis. The whole show was staged complete with dialogue, sound effects, and messengers dramatically interrupting with bits of late news. Finally the city was liberated and in a moving final scene the burgomaster thanked his G.I. rescuers.

A blemish of this spectacular operation, in my eyes, was that the name of the city was never revealed. It was such a big story, this revolt of a German city against Hitler, that it should have been carried as news by radio networks everywhere. Listeners would have expected to find references to the town's ordeal and triumph on Radio Luxemburg and the B.B.C. But Luxemburg and the B.B.C. did not mention it.

I did my best to support my American "black" brothers by putting out a report on the Soldatensender that the O.K.H. had ordered the Army to take special precautions against allowing burgomasters and other civilians access to their radio equipment—especially officials of towns in the immediate vicinity of the Allied advance. "There must be no repetition of the recent incident at a Rhineland town where the burgomaster, in order to save his town from destruction, broadcast his capitulation to the advancing enemy."

That was the best we could do, lacking the name of the town. It was not much, but it was something.

At M.B. we never attempted to scale these American heights. Right up to the Soldatensender's last broadcast we remained a soldiers' radio, putting out news, speaking in the name of the ordinary browned-off fighting soldier, venting his hatred of the party profiteers who were sacrificing the fatherland to their selfish desire to hang on to power to the last possible minute. We voiced the tragic resignation and bitterness of a nation that had been betrayed.

"*Wer weiterkämpft, kämpft gegen* hi said—"Who fights on, fights against hi

But as the Allies swept deeper and d grating Germany I felt the Soldatensen an anachronism. It seemed to be almos the Third Reich functioning with cohe that it was time for us too to disband and go ....ground, as we reported everyone else was doing.

Both Robert Bruce Lockhart and Dallas Brooks had already retired from their posts in the department—Dallas Brooks to rejoin his Royal Marines and register his claim to become their Commandant General, Bruce Lockhart to nurse his failing health.

I therefore approached the new director general, Major General Alec Bishop, and suggested to him that the time had come for us to close the innings. He agreed. And accordingly at 5:59 A.M. on April 14, 1945, Soldatensender West—as it had been called since the fall of Calais— faded from the ether, never to be heard again. Almost at the same time the *Nachrichten* team put out their last news-sheet. We made no announcement that we were closing. We just disappeared.

This great moment, however, was not allowed to pass unsung and uncelebrated in our own units. Harold Keeble gave a fancy-dress party in the printing shop at Marylands. I gave another in the canteen at M.B. And for the first time security restrictions were relaxed sufficiently to allow the Marylands and M.B. teams to mix and visit each other's compounds. Charles Lambe, who had just been made an acting rear admiral, came down from the

...ralty with Ian Fleming to join in the festivities. ...onard Ingrams also dropped in, with his pretty driver, a demure young woman called Peggy Black. John Gibbs, the publisher who had rolled off 159,898,973 copies of *Nachrichten* from his printing presses at the Luton *News* during the paper's life, romped into the Marylands party in a suit made up of *Nachrichten* front pages printed on calico.

At M.B. I interrupted the Soldatensender swan song of dance music to make a special announcement—the only time I ever spoke over one of my "black" stations myself, and the only time I permitted a private joke.

"The Führer," I said in my best Berlinese, "has just radioed a message from his command post in the Führerbunker in Berlin to Grand Admiral Doenitz in Flensburg, authorizing him to promote the Bootsmaat Karl Lamm to Oberbootsmaat."

There followed a fanfare in the old Nazi victory-announcement style. Charles Lambe listened attentively and was duly gratified when the announcement was translated for him.

In the solitude of my bathroom at R.A.G. the next morning I performed another ritual ceremony to symbolize the end of "black." I removed my beard. I had to go to Germany on a special reconnaissance for the new job I had taken on. And this time I could not wear civilian clothes as on my last visit there in March. This time I had to wear uniform, and beards were not allowed with an officer's service dress.

As my razor shaved the soap-sodden whiskers from my face I gazed into the mirror with all the horror of Dorian

Gray confronting his tell-tale portrait. There staring at me was the pallid, flabby-mouthed face of a crook. Was this, I asked myself, what four years of "black" had done to Denis Sefton Delmer?

Beardless, I faced my team a few hours later that day to give them my farewell address as "director of special operations" and tell them about what now lay ahead of them.

I had called them all together in the canteen. And here they stood before me now—German and Austrian prisoners of war, German anti-Nazi exiles, British and American executives and editors, British girl secretaries and research workers.

By rights this should have been a solemn and emotional moment. But my team had not been brought up to be solemn and emotional. From somewhere at the back of the room came the Bremen voice of the sergeant, Frankie Lynder.

"Der Bart is ab! Der Krieg ist aus!"—"The beard is off, the war is over."

Everyone laughed, and they all took up the cry—*"Der Bart ist ab!"* which in German is the equivalent of "The cat is out of the bag."

They laughed some more when I told them of my Dorian Gray ordeal that morning in front of the bathroom mirror. It was as good an introduction as any to what I had to tell them about the new task which had been assigned to me, and to such of them as wished to stay with me. My main purpose, however, in calling this meeting was to issue a caution and a warning.

"Our security has been excellent up to now," I said. "You have not talked about our work with outsiders and nothing much is known about us or our technique. People may have their suspicions, but they don't know. I want you to keep it that way. Don't be misled into boasting about the jobs we have done, the tricks we have played on the enemy."

I praised them for their work, and went on to remind them that after World War I Lord Northcliffe's widespread revelations of the propaganda part he had played in the war had encouraged the Germans to say, "We were beaten not by the armies in the field, but by Northcliffe's propaganda."

"If we start boasting of the clever things we did," I went on, "who knows what the result of that will be. So mum's the word. Propaganda is something one keeps quiet about. Are you *einverstanden?*"

The team knew that *einverstanden* phrase, and many ironic quips had been made about it. But once more, with a great bellow of laughter they roared back, "*Einverstanden!*"

It was this same desire not to make any claims for our propaganda—combined with the journalist's innate desire to forget about yesterday's paper and get on with today's —that had impelled me to turn down the suggestion made a few days earlier by the new director general, Major General Alec ("Call me Bish, old boy") Bishop. He had proposed that I should send a team to Germany to check up on the effectiveness of our work.

"It is over now, and what's done is done," I told him. "While we were doing our stuff I was most anxious to find out whether we were having any effect, and what. That was useful. But with these other jobs you want us to take on I just cannot spare anyone for an inquiry which is now of purely academic interest."

Looking back on this decision today, I think that I was
wrong. I should have asked Clifton Child to go to Germany with a small team of interrogators and researchers
to find out what could be found out. For what I had not
expected was that P.W.D. (Psychological Warfare Department) SHAEF would include our "black" operations
in its official history and that as a result our work would
be dragged into the controversy between the two American "Sykewar" agencies, O.W.I. (Office of War Information), which was responsible for American "white" output, and O.S.S. (Office of Strategic Services), which was
responsible for American "black."

"Sykewar" historian Daniel Lerner of the O.W.I.* (who
announces somewhat astonishingly that his father's account of pogroms in tsarist Russia was his first lesson in
psychological warfare—I would have preferred to call
it a lesson in history) suggests that the "black" operations
were not only useless but harmful because they were
"blatant fakes" and undermined the reputation of Allied
propaganda for truthfulness.

He cites his British colleague, the poet Norman
Cameron, as a witness for the prosecution and quotes his
opinion that had our "black" stations been any good the
Luftwaffe would have bombed the transmitters! Lerner
further implies that "black" and "grey," by conducting
campaigns with such objectives as stimulating hostility
between the Army and the Nazi Party, were duplicating
a "white" campaign, and were at best superfluous. What
he overlooks is that "black" and "grey" spoke much more
convincingly on these internal German themes than

* *Sykewar: Psychological Warfare against Germany, D-day to VE-day*
(New York, George W. Stewart).

"white" could ever do, and that many of these campaigns had been first developed by "black" and "grey" and had then been taken over by "white."

Lerner even goes so far as to claim as "white" certain campaigns which were conducted exclusively on "black" —for instance, the Soldatensender operation intended to undermine the efficiency of the German Air Force by leading the Luftwaffe Command to believe that German flying personnel were deserting in their aircraft to the Allied side. Not the "white" broadcasts, as Lerner says, but the Soldatensender and *Nachrichten* carried the news items intended to make the German authorities believe they must tighten up their security watch to prevent those desertions—a tightening-up which (as in the case of the U-boat sabotage campaign) would, we hoped, have a deleterious effect on Luftwaffe morale.

This Luftwaffe "desertion" campaign, incidentally, was repeated by the Americans eight years later during the Korean war. In "Operation Moolah" they offered a reward of fifty thousand dollars plus asylum and freedom to any Communist pilot who would deliver a MIG fighter to the United Nations forces.

Unfortunately, however, the American psychological warriors of 1953, in their hunger for public recognition, announced to their own press that the object of this offer was not so much to induce Communists to surrender with their MIGs as to make the Chinese high-ups take morale-destroying measures against their flyers. That, alas, ruined what was otherwise an ingenious revamp of our operation.

I do not at this late stage intend to enter the dreary controversy between American "white" and American "black." Nor would I dream of countering the claim of

Dick Crossman that our psychological warfare would have been more effective if no talent had been wasted on "black" with a similarly totalitarian claim that British propaganda would have been better if left exclusively to "black" and "grey." In my view, all three colours were needed, and all three colours did well. Between them, their voices constituted an effective if somewhat cacophonous choir.

Nor am I in any way disparaging Carleton Greene and his men when I say that the spinsterish insistence of the B.B.C. on its freedom from government control made it inevitable that the Services would look around for an alternative medium without these virginal complexes. The whole of our "white" radio output suffered under the system of divided responsibility by which the B.B.C., an independent corporation, controlled what was broadcast to Germany in the name of Britain, while the government's planners and policy makers, sitting in my department, were merely consulted by the B.B.C. as advisers. This meant that it was never possible to gear B.B.C. output to operational requirements as perfectly as could be done with a unit where policy-making, planning, intelligence, and production were all under one hat. That alone made "black" and "grey" a necessity.

I will also say this to our post-war detractors: In their perfectionist attention to detail and their operational application of intelligence in co-operation with military planning, our "black" and "grey" provided a stimulating example to the B.B.C. Had they not done so I fear the B.B.C. might well have continued to plod along in the dreariness and pious unrealism which had so irritated Duff Cooper in 1940. Secondly, "black" and "grey," by their ability to speak from the German point of view, took on much of the task of internal agitation which the Russians performed with their "Free German Committee," a form of propaganda denied to us Westerners because of the refusal of our masters with their unconditional-surrender complex to tolerate even a "Free Austrian Committee," let alone a "Free German" one. That complex, I should add, made subversive propaganda by "white" virtually impossible.

Thirdly, we were able to help the Allied Intelligence and deception agencies. The Intelligence men we assisted by suggesting to Germans at all levels that nothing was secret from Allied Intelligence, and that they were therefore justified in speaking freely to their Allied interrogators when captured. The deception men we helped by our treatment of U-boat movements and the army order of battle, to mention but two categories of information we disseminated.

All these were legitimate and valuable psychological-warfare operations which, because of the quite proper restrictions of the official voices to truthfulness, could not be carried out by the B.B.C. or the other overt Allied media. "Black" and "grey" were necessities, not useless luxuries. I cannot, however, give any verdict, favourable or otherwise, on the success of our efforts to stimulate civil and military disobedience. In the aftermath of the war nearly every German I met put forward some example of his disobedience as evidence of his "resistance" to the Nazis. To vary the old Soldatensender refrain about police inability to check up on missing persons, it was impossible in 1945 and 1946 to check how far this disobedience had in fact taken place, and how far it was caused by propaganda and how far by bombs. Nor would I be prepared to claim that the German deserters who had made their way to Sweden and Switzerland by May 1945 were all clients of ours—even though in the last ten months of the war we had been distributing neat envelopes containing leave passes, travel vouchers, and furlough ration cards—all produced by courtesy of Armin Hull.

But I will concede this to Daniel Lerner. I too was distressed to find the "Let's do it all ourselves" ambitions of General Omar Bradley's 12th Army Group leading their psychological warriors into such second-rate duplications of *Nachrichten* and the Soldatensender as *Frontpost,* a daily soldiers' newspaper, and *"Radio 1212."*

I suppose I ought to have been flattered. "1212," however, just filled me with gloom. It was a caricature of the Soldatensender. Bradley's men had neither the resources nor the technique of my staff at M.B. By unnecessarily multiplying the "black" effort they weakened it.

Did my team do as I asked, and keep silent about our work after the war?

By and large I believe they did. The exception was our little S.S. man who, as I have related, thought it right to try to redeem himself in the eyes of Germany's new right-wing rulers by informing against the "traitors" of M.B. Nevertheless, a great deal has been printed in Germany about the mysterious Soldatensender and the men who produced it. It has appeared mostly in those illustrated magazines of which there has been such a flourishing crop in the new post-war Germany. Much of what has been published has been highly imaginative and wrong. But there have been layers of accuracy in this sugar cake baked up by the German "I am able to reveal" brigade.

One aspect that has interested me in particular is the change that the character of Delmer, the big, fat boss of M.B., has undergone in this Soldatensender fiction. After being a hero of light, a new Siegfried, fighting to free Germany from the yoke of an unrighteous despot—that is how I appeared in the *Frankfurter Illustrierte* version of 1949— I have now become an obese Fagin exploiting the idealism of young German anti-Nazi patriots, suborning them to foul misdeeds against their own kin and country. I have accepted the metamorphosis with resignation. For I regard it as an inevitable by-product of Germany's regained sense of national power and national grievance.

My decision to break my self-imposed silence about our work is due to my belated realization that, far from having prevented the evolution of a propaganda myth, we have by our silence contributed to the development of an equally dangerous legend in the new Germany—that of the good generals and the good Wehrmacht who were always against Hitler. By showing here one of the sources from which this legend sprang I hope I shall have done something towards banishing it. For it will be a sad day for Germany and for Europe if, disguised as anti-Nazis, the men who sponsored Hitler and Hitler's war are restored to power once more to undermine by their presence in our ranks the moral unity of the West in its resistance to Eastern aggression. Alas, it looks as if exactly that has been happening.

Postscript

Have there been any "black" operations since the war? I myself certainly have remained aloof from anything of the kind ever since I shaved off that beard in April 1945. Nor have I any first-hand knowledge of such enterprises entitling me to give evidence on the subject.

Travelling around the world, however, as I have been doing, and with the experience I gained during the war to keep my nose, eyes, and ears watchful, on a number of occasions I thought I sniffed the sulphurous odour of "black" men at work. As I write, there are reports of a "freedom radio" broadcasting nightly denunciations of the "oppressive" government of Nepal allegedly from somewhere inside that Himalayan state. Something tells me, however, that it is really speaking from the shelter of Mr. Nehru's India. When the troubles started between Katanga's Mr. Tshombe and Mr. Lumumba's Congo government, I was interested to notice that a fake Lumumbist radio went into action leading the Lumumba forces into ambush after ambush with instructions issued in the name of their official leaders.

At the time of Suez the British R.A.F. tried to knock out Cairo radio with a bomb attack. I am told that the plan behind this operation was for a British-controlled Arab radio operated from Cyprus to take over the Cairo frequency and broadcast anti-Nasser programmes on Nasser's wave length. The plan came to nought, however, for two excellent reasons: (1) the R.A.F. knocked out the wrong radio and (2) the Cyprus Arabs—apparently no one had thought to make sure of them in advance—led by their British director, went on strike when the British military took over their station.

Nearer home, the Soviet Germans in East Berlin have been broadcasting a counterfeit of the United States Forces' radio to the American troops involved in the dispute over Ulbricht's Berlin wall.

The Soviet Germans can even chalk up one small success for this operation. They forced the American troops to abandon the amiable habit of wearing their names on their uniforms. Communist spies copied the names and the radio men then used them to embellish stories in the broadcasts of their counterfeit radio, just as we would have used the names of German officers on Calais or Gustav Siegfried Eins during the war. They were less happy in their choice of a theme song for the station. Whether they knew it or not, the tune the Soviet Germans and their American Communist radio men were playing to introduce their broadcast was "Don't Fence Me In"—a somewhat double-edged jest for the defenders of Ulbricht's wall!

In both East and West Germany there has been a rash

of "black" practical jokes. West German "black" artists, for instance, posted invitations to Communist labour councils inviting them in the name of Ulbricht's government to attend a jamboree in East Berlin. When the delegates turned up they found no jamboree, no hotel accommodation, no food, no one to pay their return fare as had been promised —all of which, it was hoped, they would write down as evidence of typical Communist mismanagement.

The East Germans replied by sending out call-up notices to German doctors in the name of the federal defence authorities, ordering them to report forthwith at distant garrison depots and authorizing them to pay for their own transport. All expenses, said the forged notice, would be refunded. And so it has gone on.

Have I myself ever had an itch to get back into "black propaganda" and take a hand in the Cold War? I have not. For I speak no Russian, and a "black" man needs an intimate knowledge not only of the language of the country against which he proposes to operate but of its conditions and ideology as well. The "black" artist must have for his intended victim that strange quality which we call "empathy" and the Germans call *Einfühlungsvermögen*. And I have none of that, alas, for the Russians.

It has seemed to me, however, that the West has forgone some magnificent opportunities for creating havoc and confusion behind the lines of these Kremlin warriors who never miss a chance of stirring up trouble for us. The first opportunity came at the time of Stalin's death, the second during the fight for power between the Berias and Malenkovs, the Khrushchevs and Bulganins. The present quarrel between Peking and Moscow and that between

Stalinist Albania and Khrushchev provide yet another. Undoubtedly there will be more opportunities in the future.

I am watching to see who will exploit them, and how, with all the relish of a retired sea-captain watching ships manœuvring in the English Channel from his villa on the cliffs of Dover.

Appendix

Soon after the war was over the files of M.B. were consigned to the incinerators and destroyed. With them vanished two folders which I would dearly like to have possessed when writing this account—the one containing captured documents which showed the reaction of German civil and military authorities to "black" and "grey" operations, and the file of "black" and "grey" leaflets. Only the chance that several of my colleagues kept souvenirs of our work and preserved them to this day enables me to reproduce a few of these documents. Some illustrate the sensitivity of the German authorities to our operations; others are specimens of "black" printing. I reproduce them here.

The first German document which I reproduce is a warning against our "poison" from General von Schlieben, the defender of Cherbourg, who was later to avail himself of the Soldatensender's "phosphorous shells" * to cover his surrender.

* See page 136.

Commanding General   Headquarters, 5 Feb.44.
709th Inf. Div.

SUBJECT: Questions of leadership and Morale Defensive
           Measures against Enemy Propaganda.

TO: Commanding Officers of Regiments and Battalions.

1. The enemy is trying, with unheard-of hatred, with ever-changing tricks and ruses, with lies and falsehood and with everything however mean, to undermine the morale of the German people and to force a decision on the "battlefield of the war of nerves," just as he did in the First World War. In the West, the efforts of the enemy agitators have been intensified from month to month. I need only mention the increasing number of seditious leaflets in German and the dangerous propaganda broadcast by the provocative enemy station "Soldatensender Calais."

It has become *decisive for the outcome of the war* that we provide officers, non-commissioned officers, and men with convincing counter-arguments well ahead of time and that we promptly parry any propaganda attack by the enemy.

2. There are still occasional cases where unit commanders have not yet been convinced of the importance of this task. We must bear in mind that during the First World War enemy propaganda succeeded in wearing down the morale and fighting spirit of the German people to such an extent as to contribute materially to the economic and military breakdown. *We must always be aware of this precedent as a warning example.*

3. The best means of guiding the morale of the soldier is, in addition to the *example which every officer must set by his conduct,* for the commanders to talk to their men. The purpose of these talks is so to instil the principles of Nationalist Socialist leadership into the individual man that they become part and parcel of him. Therefore *political instruction cannot and*

must not be neglected any more than the cleaning of rifles and guns. It is less important for the subordinate unit commander to deliver a well-prepared elaborate lecture than to discuss with the soldiers current political and military questions, to dispel any doubts, and to look after the well-being of his men. This requires that the unit commander himself shall be so firm in his political belief and so well-versed in National Socialist ideology as to convince the men of the sincerity of the person talking to him about these things. *The commander's heart must be in it.*

4. In those exceptional cases where this type of instruction cannot be carried out regularly or often enough, as in isolated strong-points, it becomes doubly important to insure that officers and men will have an opportunity to read the material reaching them.

5. All commands are regularly supplied with instruction material on the situation, on current political and military events, and on all kinds of problems confronting a soldier, and with material for combating enemy propaganda. We may mention among these, the *Kurznachrichten des O.K.W.* (Brief News from Supreme Headquarters) *Nachrichten des Oberkommandos der Wehrmacht* (News from the Supreme Headquarters), *Mitteilungen für die Truppe* (Communications to the Troops), *Mitteilungen für das Offizierskorps* (Communications to the Officers' Corps), *Armee-Nachrichtenblatt* (Army Journal), newspapers, and periodicals. This material—especially daily papers—can of course be effectively used only if it reaches the lowest units as fast as possible. *The place for newspapers and periodicals in not in offices but with the troops.*

6. The Political Officer [*N.S.-Führungsoffizier*] of the division is available also to individual units for lectures and will call on the units, on my orders, to advise and assist unit commanders.

7. The Führer demands that all commanders down to Com-

pany C.O.'s will do their utmost to utilize fully every opportunity to maintain also the fighting spirit of the troops.

[Sgd.] von SCHLIEBEN

A TRUE COPY
[Signature]
Captain.

"Big Bertha's" intruder operation is referred to in the
weekly report of a certain Party Comrade Steinecke who
was the head of the Nazi area office in Lemgo, Westphalia.
It was found by officers of the advancing United States
9th Army and forwarded to us. The report also refers to
the increased listening to the Soldatensender.

The paragraphs headed "Rumours" and "Propaganda"
contain the references to "Big Bertha." It is interesting
that Herr Steinecke guesses correctly that the intruder
operation was the work of the Soldatensender team.

I reproduce the whole of the document—which gives a
fascinating glimpse of Nazi desperation—in the translation made at the time. The German original in this case,
as in that of the foregoing document, is unfortunately no
longer available.

FROM: Gauamtsleiter [department head in the Party Administration of a Gau] Steinecke.

TO: Gaustabsamtsleiter Detmold, Reichsstatthalterei [Admin-
istrative head of the Gau]

SUBJECT: Short weekly reports.

I am sending you herewith a report on various points for
your information and further exploitation.

Heil Hitler
Sgd. Steinecke

Gauamtsleiter

29 March '45

General:

"Unless something outstanding and positive for Germany occurs within the next few days, we are faced with catastrophe. . . ." This, more or less, is the effect the dramatic war situation in the West has had on the morale of the population.

Rumours, strengthened through enemy radio announcements in German transmissions, do all that remains to finish off the fighting spirit of the Army and the endurance of the people.

The local Volkssturm who have stayed behind are without weapons and form no guarantee for the maintenance of order as the real war zone draws nearer.

The individual feels himself generally deserted, betrayed, and no longer believes in any decisive change. This is increased by the obvious failure of German propaganda in these critical days. The individual is obviously crying out for an unvarnished explanation from the German leadership and for a decision. References to various secret weapons and offensives are no longer accepted and no longer believed.

Radio commentaries "On the situation," etc., echo ineffectively and are bitterly derided, because their content can arouse no hope of any change.

The politically-conscious in the Party and among the people still believe firmly in the historical change announced by the Führer. In the Party itself, the weaker elements are growing restless and beginning to doubt. The argument is then always brought forward "that the eternal favourable colouring of reports and parade-ground displays have darkened the perception of the Führer and cut him off from the people."

The Church is secretly taking great pains to exploit this danger period for its own ends. Never were the churches and prayer hours so well attended as at present. Catholic priests say openly that, "in the event of the unwished for occupation of their Parishes, they would never leave them." They would "as the Shepherd, remain with their sheep." The view is growing increasingly strong in these circles "that the Anglo-Americans are all right and their arrival can be awaited in peace."

This opinion is also spreading to the Home Army, which in many places stands in shameful opposition to the heroic fighting front. Already their bearing on and off duty marks the different units of the Reserve Army—it can also be seen in the carrying out of military greetings and in behaviour on the march.

Rumours:

The creation of rumours takes on ever more grotesque forms. In addition to this, the enemy transmitter West has broken in on the news periods with cleverly disguised orders from the Gauleitung and caused considerable unrest.

The many travellers, who, with the aid of the so-called "resting stations," travel from West and East and vice versa on goods and passenger trains, add to this orgy of rumours.

People say that Germany's last chance lies in a concerted attack by the Air Force and U-boats within the next three weeks. They have this from a reliable source, from the mouth of the Reichsmarshall himself, who is alleged to have said it to a young officer whom he picked up on the Autobahn and gave a lift.

Propaganda:

It must be emphasized again that considerable misunderstandings and great unrest were caused among the population by the intrusion of enemy wireless announcements on the German wireless. The enemy wireless propaganda broadcasts cleverly formulated announcements and orders from the Gauleiter in the Western District, or terrifies whole neighbourhoods by the announcement of the approach of enemy tanks and scouting cars, evacuation orders, etc.—and for only too clear reasons: the creation of chaos in the transport system, targets for terror air attacks, and panic.

It is remarkable that on the German side it took a long time to inform and warn the population. So far absolutely no warning about these false reports has appeared in the press; or if it has, it has not been given sufficient display. On the evening of March 27 the German soldiers' station issued the first warning about these wireless methods of the enemy. Even this announcement was unsophisticated and not convincing. Not until March 28 did the German radio broadcast an official announcement to the German population.

The most effective method would be for the German radio to follow each broadcast of such obvious enemy lies with a correction and explanation. This would be more worth while than the present still-preferred and usually worthless series of musical programmes.

In this eventful period the population is not receiving explanations and encouragement from the responsible men of the German leadership. At this moment words of comfort and support are needed more than ever before. It is to be hoped that the responsible German leadership is clear that morale amongst the workers and the Army is in parts catastrophic. The people are being increasingly broken down by the ever-growing cesspool of rumours in the West and East.

The German radio continues to cause the German citizen great irritation. In these days of German destiny he expects to hear something other than jazz and swing music.

After the announcement of the storming of the German Rhine and the beginning of the decisive battles for it, there was nothing but ordinary records of the most ordinary content—and that at a time when a great number of Germans are waiting anxiously for all news about their lost homeland.

It is not surprising that, with the natural growth of rumours and the worst possible state of morale, many Germans are again listening to the enemy Soldatensender. It is remarkable that the German radio has never taken up the Jewish lies of this enemy transmitter, even when they were obviously false. It is to be expected that attention should be drawn by all possible derogatory means to the German traitor prisoners who have so far forgotten themselves as to sell their voices to the enemy for his radio propaganda.

In Dr. Goebbels' article of last Friday (23/3) one could at last read something other than the only too often heard general statements and the over-excessive use of the comparison between the present with the time of Frederick the Great; one read positive statements of an immediate German decision.

If for any reason it is not possible to prophesy the use of decisive German weapons in the air, on the sea, and on the land, all German propaganda will remain without effect. Up to the present similar prophecies have been made too carelessly and the mass of the people have been disappointed year after year. This failure can only be made good by a really impressive German action. "What's the use of it," the German asks himself, "this late beginning of total participation in the war, total mobilization and organization of service and aid posts [*Dienst- und Hilfsstellen*], if every day German territory shrinks and every life is mercilessly destroyed?" All of it was too late?

There has been too much pleasant talk and pretty colouring and unrealistic organization and not enough concrete thought and action. When the German heavy-worker starves, he lays down his tools. Month after month and year after year we have been consoled for the misery of the enemy air war with "equal reprisals"; our patience has also been exploited endlessly with allusions to a change through the use of decisive German weapons and discoveries.

"So far nothing has been done and no pledge has been kept." This is what people are saying everywhere.

Newspapers in neutral countries were considerably intrigued by the Soldatensender. Here are extracts from two articles which appeared in the Swiss press toward the end of the war.

From *Basler Nachrichten*, February 19, 1945:

THE MYSTERY OF STATION "ATLANTIC"

The "black" station most frequently listened to in Germany is veiled in secrecy. The wildest rumours are current concerning its whereabouts. Is it located in a so-called dead zone of Germany, an area where direction-finding is not possible? Swiss wireless technicians have already made a guess that it might be in the Austrian or Bavarian Alps, but for technical reasons they had at once to discard this conjecture. How could this fantastically strong station get the necessary current and the numerous helpers to work it? Here we can point to a very significant fact which almost certainly excludes the possibility of the station being inside Germany. In one of its most recent transmissions the "Soldatensender West" played records from an army show, which the well-known American composer Irving Berlin wrote in the spring of 1944. That means that the records were placed at the disposal of the station "Atlantic" by the Anglo-Saxons. Do they perhaps know of its whereabouts? A fact which rather points to this is that numerous American dance records have been synchronized with German song texts, a technical process which demands a studio organization, which quite definitely could not exist on German soil. Of course France, the Pyrenees, Belgium, and the Netherlands are also possibilities. Perhaps the transmitter is not on the Atlantic at all. Judging by the reception obtained, it may be surmised that its location is in Western Europe.

The most likely place would be England. But that raises a big "if."

If it did not possess the best news service in the world about German internal conditions. In this respect the station "Atlantic" achieves amazing results. For example, either on the very day of, or in any case within 24 hours of, any heavy raid on a German town, the transmitter is able to give its listeners a complete list of bombed streets. Its news about "Party bosses" is frequently unbelievable. To them it devotes emphasis and attention. During the latest German campaign to get clothes and equipment surrendered by civilians for the Volkssturm, the transmitter gave a daily list of addresses of Party members who had large stores of provisions which could be collected. "In Essen, for instance, the wife of [then follows the name of an influential party man] has hoarded 80 bottles of old Malaga, 34 pairs of silk and woollen stockings, 16 yards of pure wool material, vast quantities of foodstuffs and curtain material which would suffice to redecorate completely the destroyed Reichs-Chancellery."

That is an example which was taken down in shorthand. Every journey abroad of any diplomat or party man is known to "Atlantic." It knows all about secret orders of the day for the Air Force, the Navy, and the Army, about transfers and dismissals. It is informed down to the smallest detail about any resistance in Germany. It gave the news of the attempt on Hitler's life 80 minutes after it happened. In short: it possesses information which both Germany and the rest of the world never hear from official sources, and it receives this information with startling speed. It is for this reason that numerous people guess that the station "Atlantic" is in Germany itself, because—it is argued—how could it be possible for such "inside" internal news to reach the outside world so quickly? Is the "Atlantic" station linked to a secret station inside Germany, or is it perhaps in Berlin itself? This devastated city would be an ideal hideout for a "black" station, but there again the question of obtaining power arises. The mystery as to the whereabouts of the transmitter will, presumably, remain unanswered till the end of the war, but millions of listeners are waiting eagerly for the answer to their questions. . . .

From *"L" Express,* Neuchâtel, April 13, 1945:

> *Every Night a Mysterious Call Echoes over the Air—*
> "HIER, SOLDATENSENDER WEST"
> Is the No. 1 clandestine German transmitter the mouth-piece of internal opposition to the Nazis, or is it the finest instrument of Allied propaganda and the Intelligence Service?

One of the great mysteries of the present war is certainly that surrounding the German-language transmitter which announces itself as "Soldatensender West, angeschlossen Radio Atlantik" [sic]. It started operating more than two years ago, and now one can hear it on three short-wavelengths. Radio technicians are bent upon locating the clandestine transmitter, but in spite of all the progress radio reception has made, the mystery remains practically the same. Is it in Germany, or in one of the last remaining occupied countries, or in France, Belgium, or Luxembourg? Only regular listening and psychological interpretation—if one can call it that—of the transmissions can solve this question. What baffles the listener in the first place is the nature of the broadcasts. They are always addressed to "our" comrades in the Army, Air Force, and Navy. The *Kameradschaftseienste* mention the German High Command communiqués regularly; like the official German stations, the transmitter gives the *Luftlagemeldung.* Acts of bravery by soliders of the Army proper are extolled; but in contrast the activities of S.S. men of the Nazi Party are often stigmatized. The political tendency of the station is to bring out the grave dissension between the Wehrmacht and the

Nazis. Thus it does not miss any chance of showing that it is useless for soldiers to go on shedding their blood for their country, because only the "Party Bonzen" profit. The more the Army resists, the more the prospect of settling accounts fades. "Soldatensender" doggedly pursues its work of demoralizing soldiers of the Third Reich by trying to weaken their confidence in their "Führer." . . .

What finally baffles radio fans is that the announcer has the same tone of voice and the same inflections as the chief announcer on the official German radio.

It is in face of such facts that the curious try to locate this clandestine transmitter. When one analyses certain news items closely, one cannot but believe that "Soldatensender" is certainly in Germany. How would one explain the rapidity with which the news on air raids, the incredible facts on the joys and sorrows of the Party Bonzen and their wives and the losses of the Volkssturm are given? One could deduce that the transmitter was in liaison throughout Germany with a great number of smaller stations continually supplying it with information on the situation. This underground organization would have to comprise hundreds of people, all members of the opposition. To know so precisely what is happening in the very heart of the Party, the informers could only be Nazis of rank, secretly preparing the downfall of Hitler and his regime. It is hardly credible that a station situated abroad could be so well abreast of internal conditions in Germany. Certain of the curious have not hesitated to suppose the No. 1 clandestine transmitter to be right in Berlin, whose ruins offer an excellent hideout. But how can the electric current be obtained? A transmitter would have difficulty concealing itself even in the mountains of Bavaria or the Tyrol.

The most plausible explanation of the mystery is that given by a correspondent of *Basler Nachrichten*—"Soldatensender" is an instrument of Allied propaganda and there is no doubt that it exists in England, because it seems out of the question that a powerful transmitter with its multiple aerials, its conductors of electric current, and its various installations could be set up in the middle of the Third Reich under the noses of the Gestapo. A significant fact is the disappearance from the B.B.C. transmissions of their chief, Sefton Delmer, a specialist in German affairs following long periods in Berlin before the war. He is probably directing the "Soldatensender" news service, because he disappeared from the B.B.C. programmes at the time the so-called clandestine transmitter started its activities.

Continuing his explanation, the above-mentioned correspondent supposes that the announcers are German prisoners from the Army, Air Force, and Navy who, following the example of the Moscow Committee, have rallied round the opposition to Hitler. One psychological factor militates in favour of these arguments—namely, that in London both the press and the B.B.C. simply ignore Soldatensender broadcasts. The other Allied transmitters mentioned its existence at first, and one or two, such as Algiers, quoted its news items. But for a long time silence has reigned and Allied propaganda thereby indicates that it does not consider the station to be a real clandestine one, but very much a child of its own creation. . . .

The Neuchâtel newspaper's correspondent appears to have got hold of some "inside dope." I refuse to believe that the mere fact of my absence from the B.B.C. transmissions made the writer believe I was directing the "Soldatensender"!

Of the "black" leaflets too—we called them "leaflets," although all too often they were anything but that—I have only managed to salvage a small number.

One of my favourites is the "Wanted" poster which the Norwegian underground pasted on notice boards and walls in various districts of Norway, always after stamping it with their local German Kommandantur stamp in addition to the red stamp of the Oslo S.D. chief, with which we had provided it.

It is an exact copy in style of other "Wanted" posters circulated by the German Police in Norway, of which specimens had come into our hands after the British commando raid on the Lofoten Islands. In the normal way, however, the German police did not invite Norwegians to shoot Germans! The story of Bauer revealed on the poster was also a splendid example of police impotence.

Here is a translation of the German text, which appeared alongside the same text in Norwegian:

WANTED

LANCE CORPORAL ERWIN BAUER of Halle on the Saale, described below, is accused of desertion, committed on July 12, 1941, and murder, committed on September 25, 1943. When being arrested he shot dead Field Police Sergeant Franz Vogel.

Everyone has the right to shoot when arresting Bauer. Erwin Bauer is a criminal who shoots at sight. Anyone who recognizes him must shoot.

Erwin Bauer was last seen in the uniform of an S.S. Captain in Oslo, where he spent a night in the Grand Hotel under the name of Heinz Westphal. It is known that Bauer has obtained for himself a variety of officers' uniforms and identity papers. It must be assumed that he appears in the uniform of an S.S. captain, a captain of the Luftwaffe or of the Army, or in the uniform of a Sonderführer [Special Services Officers].

In the course of the many frauds committed by Bauer since 1941 he has used the names Koch, Wendt, Färber, Westphal, and others.

It is requested that Erwin Bauer should be arrested and delivered to the Arrest Institution Oslo, or the nearest Police or Wehrmacht Post. His arrest should be immediately reported to my office under reference J XI 43/41.

Description of the Person

Family name:	BAUER
First name:	ERWIN
Born on:	21.8.1904 in Halle/S
Last place of residence:	OSLO

Characteristics: Height 1.76 meters, thickset, grey-blue eyes, fair hair, parting on the left, straight nose, scar on left forearm.

Clothing: Probably the uniform of the S.S., the Luftwaffe, or the uniform of a Sonderführer.

Oslo. October 4. 1943.   The Commander of the Sipo
Office of Sipo and SD   and SD in Norway
Victoria Terrace 5–7   Fehlis
Standartenführer

To provide "evidence" that the Party feared a peace putsch by the generals, we fabricated a letter from Erich Koch, the Gauleiter of East Prussia, and signed it with a rubber stamp of his signature, copied from another Koch letter.

ERICH KOCH   Königsberg. 20 September 1943
Gauleiter and Super-President

My Dear Comrades,

The Führer is in danger!

The Reactionaries want to do away with the Führer and place the country under a military dictatorship, which against the will of the people, is to begin immediate peace negotiations.

Certain circles, which pay lip service to the sacred name of Prussianism, but show none of the heroic spirit of the Seven Years War, are disseminating rumours to the effect that the Führer, on account of his failing health, is no longer equal to the burden of his office.

With these rumours the Reactionaries are preparing the way for a revolt that is to force the Führer out of his position as Commander-in-Chief of the Armed Forces. His place is to be taken by an oath-breaking general.

In his magnanimity the Führer has so far declined to take drastic steps against the traitors in order not to rob the Army of its leaders in these critical hours. Therefore it is all the more our duty to stand together in the fight against the Reactionaries.

I have recently had the honour to visit the Führer in his H.Q. In his eyes shone the certainty of victory, in the clasp of his hand I could feel the complete healthy strength of the man, who, unbroken by the blows of fate, is and must remain Germany's destiny.

Those who want to rob us of our Führer will plunge Germany into civil war!

We will stand by our leader to whom we have sworn allegiance.

The German people do not want peace—the German people want victory, cost what it may.

Fellow Countrymen—keep your eyes and ears open. Recognize the danger.

Report every suspicious occurrence, every rumour, every hidden lying utterance against the Führer to the nearest service post of the Party, the Police, or the S.S.

LONG LIVE THE FÜHRER

HEIL HITLER,

Your Gauleiter

Erich Koch

This leaflet * purporting to come from fighter pilots of the Luftwaffe, was dropped for us by R.A.F. Bomber Command and by the Special United States Leaflet Squadron.

Comrades of the Army:

On the 31st August 1943 Major General Galland, Inspector of Fighters, sent the following order to Colonel von Maltzahn, Commodore of J.G.53 in southern Italy:

"I was pained to learn that flyers of your J.G. fighter squadron have latterly been showing a deplorable lack of courage and fighting spirit. Not only has the number of enemy planes shot down failed to come up to my expectations, but frequent cases have been reported to me in which fighter pilots of your J.G., despite orders to attack, avoided combat with enemy units or broke off combat prematurely.

"In order that this sort of thing shall cease at once, I order that the enemy shall at all times be attacked without hesitation. Every squadron which is sent to attack must shoot down at least one enemy plane, even if the enemy unit is four times as strong.

"In future, no excuses will be accepted. Court-martial proceedings will be taken against pilots who do not fulfil the following conditions: (1) Returning flyers must provide proof that one enemy plane has been shot down; or (2) the fighter pilot's own plane must show hits, as proof that he did not avoid battle; or (3) his own plane must have been shot down.

"Should the fighting spirit and the number of planes shot down by your J.G. in execution of my order show no con-

* See page 162.

siderable improvement, then you will be relieved of your command and transferred with your flyers to an Air Force infantry battalion on the Eastern Front.

The Inspector of Fighter Pilots
[Signed] GALLAND
Major General"

This order of the party favourite Adolf Galland is typical of the shameless way in which air tycoons from the Reichsmarschall down are now trying to put the blame on us flyers for the lack of air cover you are experiencing in your hard battles, as though we lacked courage.

Comrades, you must know the truth.

It is not our fault. It is not the fault of the men who fly and fight, but that of those who planned the war and the Air Force—and planned both wrong.

Our Air Force was planned for short "blitz" campaigns. It was not designed for a long war over wide areas.

Forced campaigns in Russia, Africa, and Italy in which everything was staked, regardless of the consequences, have wrecked our Air Force.

Lack of fuel has made the training of properly schooled reserve personnel impossible.

The progressive deterioration of our Air Force, and the simultaneous increase in strength of the enemy air forces has caused us to lose our hegemony in the air.

Today our inferiority is such that we are not even in a position to give adequate protection against air attacks to our aircraft industry at home. Although we have withdrawn almost all fighter protection from Russia and the Mediterranean to the home country, with the result that our troops have to fight everywhere without air cover, the factories in which our fresh supplies are being built are being destroyed one after the other.

For all this the blame cannot be given to us flyers. The fault lies clearly with those who planned the war and planned it wrong.

Comrades! If you lack air cover, don't grumble at us flyers, even if the Party propagandists attack our honour as pilots in order to create an alibi for themselves.

This circular, ostensibly from an "Association of Air Raid Victims," was left around by agents. We also dropped it from special leaflet-carrying balloons.

EMERGENCY ASSOCIATION FOR GERMAN AIR RAID VICTIMS

Munich. Aug. 43

A journey into the blue . . . is a journey to death

Dear Fellow Countrymen:

In the last eight weeks over 600,000 air-raid victims have been sent from their shattered home towns to the reception areas in the East.

Every day fresh train-loads of refugees leave air danger zones for the East, because, allegedly, there is no room for them in the home country.

Out of the air-raid shelters they are herded like cattle into freight-trains and, without knowing their journey's end, they are bundled off to Poland and Ruthenia. Only the most primitive arrangements have been made there for their accommodation, often none at all, so that the homeless frequently have to spend the night in the open when they arrive at their destination. Spotted fever, dysentery, trachoma, and other diseases await them. They spread rapidly among the new arrivals, who, as a result of the nights of bombing and the forced journey to the East that followed, often lasting up to 140 hours, are broken down and completely without resistance. There is no hope of combating infection. For every 40,000 inhabitants of the Eastern territories only one doctor is available. Water closets and possibilities of disinfecting and cleaning are as a rule non-existent.

Why can no room be found for air-raid evacuees in the homeland?

In Munich, Potsdam, Berchtesgaden, Schönau, Salzburg, Scheffau, Tegernsee, and many other places in Germany where the Party princes hold their courts there would be room enough.

But all these places have been declared to be focal points of the housing shortage and barred to refugees, so that the bosses won't be disturbed in their equanimity and comfort by the sight of the miserable columns of the homeless from the air-raid areas. As long as these protected areas are kept empty for these over-eating bearers of supreme power, not one bombed-out German should let himself be pushed off to the East.

In the Eastern territories those who do not fall victim to epidemics are exposed to the attacks of the Polish population, who, as a result of the S.S. campaign of extermination, have been driven into a burning hatred of all things German.

On every German evacuated to the Eastern territories waits the thirst for revenge of fourteen million Poles that survive, scarcely one of whom has not had at least one close relative murdered by the S.S.

Their hate breaks out with less and less restraint as the war goes on. One Russian break-through, one landing by the Anglo-Saxons is capable of releasing a blood-bath among all German settler and raid evacuees in the East.

The Party and the S.S. bosses themselves avoid sending their women and children to the Eastern territories. Their families will not reap the hate which they have sown. But the mass of those without pull or connections, they are the ones who shall reap it.

It does not have to be like that.

A bunch of Hamburg refugees brought their train to a stop on a stretch of open country between Schweibus and Bent-

schen and refused to carry on with the journey to the East.
They left the train and marched in a column to Züllichau.
There they were given food by the peasants and estate owners
of the district, and without much ado they were taken on as
harvest helpers on the estates.

And that is where they are today.

If the Nazi bosses, who have provoked the destruction of
our towns while they themselves sit in safety, will not provide
our air-raid victims with accommodation fit for human be-
ings in the homeland, then everyone must get it for himself.
Fellow Countrymen:

Do not wait until you are dragged unconscious out of an
air-raid shelter and sent off to the East.

Go off to the country and stay there while you are still masters of your own destiny. Send your family to the country if
you cannot go yourself.

Everyone can find refuge—it only means making arrangements in time. No German peasant will refuse shelter to a
menaced fellow countryman who has to choose between death
from bombs or death from the Poles.

A journey into the blue—is a journey to death.

      The Self-Help Committee of the E.A.G.A.R.V.
Please copy and pass on.

The next leaflet belongs to a series ostensibly issued by
a German right-wing anti-Nazi Resistance group in the
Army. An unfortunate mishap occurred with the "Soldiers' Wives" leaflet. The balloon which was carrying it,
instead of flying to France and Germany as intended, was
blown back over Britain, and the leaflets spilled out over
Hazelmere Golf-Course. Only with difficulty were socialist M.P.'s restrained from asking awkward questions about
it in the House of Commons.

SOLDIERS' WIVES, WIDOWS, AND MOTHERS

Party [i.e., Nazi] Bolshevism has struck its first blow against one of the most important fundamentals of our German order of life for which we are fighting and dying—the unassailability of your marriage.

By the "executive appendix to the marriage law," which came into force on 1st April 1943, the Party State has assumed the right to decide arbitrarily on the death of a soldier whether the State Attorney shall have the dead soldier's marriage posthumously dissolved and deprive his wife of her legal inheritance, her name, her children, and her pension.

It is clearly stated in the executive appendix:

"A judicial decision granting a decree of divorce to a dead person may also be necessary in such cases where the dead person had not sued for divorce, possibly because he had no knowledge of the grave offence committed by his married partner. In such cases the State Attorney has authority to institute proceedings, provided it is proven or may be assumed as sure, that the dead person would have applied for a divorce had he known the facts, but was prevented from instituting divorce proceedings by his death."

German soldiers' wives:

That is the death blow to your family life.

In the name and allegedly according to the desire of our dead, the Party State arrogates to itself the right to have the last wishes of the dead interpreted and falsified by pettyfogging corrupt State Attorneys in accordance with the materialistic principles of National Socialism hostile to marriage and hostile to family.

If your husband is killed or has already been killed, then, by virtue of this new executive appendix to the divorce law, your rights as a wife become the target of official blackmail and private slander.

The Party boss of your district can hold over you the threat of a posthumous divorce suit in order to make you yield to his wishes. Slanderous neighbours, corrupt and servile block and cell wardens, will provide him with the material for instituting proceedings against you. Legacy robbers and jealous relations have only to put forward a malicious denunciation in order to drive you from your hearth and home and rob you of your heritage. They can smash your family happiness and deprive you of your good name, your children, and your pension.

You are therefore completely in their hands if you don't defend yourself.

But you can defend yourself.

You can prevent the memory of your husband, of his love and understanding, of his comradeship being destroyed at one blow by the murderous intervention of the apostles of Bolshevik utilitarianism.

So long as your husband lives, he can protect you against the event of his death by making out in your favour the following declaration and having it legally witnessed.

Don't wait until your husband next comes home on leave. Write to him now. The Company Commander can witness the deed if necessary instead of a Notary.

DECLARATION
(to be witnessed by the Notary Public or Company Commander)

I, the undersigned member of the Armed Forces, ..., hereby declare that in the event of my death no kind of divorce proceedings shall be instituted against my wife. My happy marriage shall not be broken up after my death. In any event I declare that should I be killed I expressly condone any action by which my wife may have offended against our marriage as a consequence of the circumstances of war.

I further make the following addition to my last will and

testament: in the event of my marriage being annulled after my death by a divorce, I hereby declare my then divorced wife to be my sole heir.

If your marriage is founded on love and mutual trust, as is usual in our people, and is not, as this cynical order of the Home-Bolsheviks presupposes, a shabby business deal between two suspicious marriage partners, then your husband will not for one second hesitate to sign this declaration which will make you and your children secure against the intervention of the State, even should he not return.

GERMANY AWAKE!

The next leaflet, reproduced here in part, is the published text of one of Der Chef's last broadcasts, picked up and printed—allegedly—by the printing section of his patriotic, anti-communist, anti-Nazi and anti-S.S. officers underground. It is designed to spread rumours of an intended S.S. *coup d'état* and cause further jealousy between Regular Army and S.S.

NEWS OF THE GERMAN OFFICERS' ASSOCIATION

On 2.10.43. we picked up a broadcast by G.S.1 which we are publishing here in full, as far as we were able to receive it:

We have proof that the Waffen S.S. are in no case keeping to the munition regulations which have been laid down for all reserve units in the homeland and which allegedly apply to all reserve units, the Waffen S.S. included.

On the contrary, the Waffen-S.S. have not only, contrary to the general order, not emptied the munition dump of their reserve units in the homeland and not delivered up their artillery ammunition to the chief munition arsenals as all the reserve units of the Army have had to do. But it is now a proved fact that Himmler has been hoarding munition and fuel in the local depots of various Waffen-S.S. reserve units in the homeland—for a purpose which is by no means known to Heinrich Himmler alone.

Our Army artillery can no longer be properly trained because the reserve units get as good as no ammunition for practice shooting—our home anti-aircraft batteries are being rationed for the same alleged reason of political unreliability and often do not even get enough ammunition to last through one heavy air raid— In Bochum a whole row of batteries had to cease fire after twelve minutes because they had run out of ammunition—our young flyers have to go to the front with ever fewer flying hours of training behind them because flying schools are not given enough fuel for training—and all this while Heinrich Himmler, this bloody fellow, is quietly building up giant ammunition and fuel stocks in his Waffen-S.S. depots. It will cause me no embarrassment at all to name a few of these S.S. munition hoards.

We have ascertained that, amongst others, in the following Waffen-S.S. depots supplies of munition and fuel have been accumulated which bear not the slightest relation to the present needs of the relative S.S.-reserve units for training and transport.

There are first of all two S.S.-troop-supply depots, that in Berlin-Südende and that in Kassel. Next, the depots of the S.S. Panzer Grenadiero Reserve Battalions in Berlin Lichterfelde, in Buchenwald, near Weimar, and in Rastenburg in East Prussia. In Munich the S.S. artillery reserve division has stored away 15,000 rounds of 7,5; 12,000 rounds of 8,8; 8,000 rounds of 15 am. and a vast amount of two and five cm. Pak anti-tank gun ammunition. Further there is the ammunition store of the S.S. Grenadier Reserve Battalion in Breslau which is full to overflowing with 7.5 Infantry grenades and 5 cm. and 8 cm. mortar shells.

These facts alone suffice—at least they satisfy us—to confirm the suspicion which a few of us formed when the Army Artillery Reserve units first received one after another the ominous order to deliver up immediately all the heavy ammunition in their depots to the chief munition arsenals,—with the result that the Waffen-S.S. now has abundant ammunition in its home depots, and the Army reserve damn all. . . .

And in the meantime Herr Himmler is filling his own munition dumps to the skies—and Himmler's Bolshevist putsch can go ahead.

Himmler has got everything set for the great betrayal. When he thinks the time has come to sell us to the Soviets, he reckons that the Reserve Army will be powerless to do anything against it. The Waffen-S.S. is in possession of all the chief munition establishments and thereby has its hand on the entire artillery ammunition, while the Reserve Army has only a miserable 3000 rounds of rifle ammunition and machine gun ammunition and a few hand grenades per battalion and group.

Himmler calculates that the Field Army will do nothing when faced with having to fight the Russian Bolsheviks at the front and also the Home Bolsheviks within.

Herr Himmler thinks that all is well with his preparations for the founding of the German Soviet Province of the United Soviet States of East Europe, with the noble General von Daniels as C. in C. of the German Red Army, and when the Eastern Front has been pushed back to the German frontier, as Herr Himmler expects it to be and is indeed helping to assure that it shall be, then Herr Himmler will be be all set to make his friendly little gentleman's agreement with the other gentlemen in Moscow.

Comrades, never has our Fatherland been in greater danger than it is today. If we, who see and understand the danger, do not now do our duty, the glorious development of German history will change, everything for which we have been fighting will be lost, and our Fatherland, will be turned into an Eastern sewer.

Himmler's treachery must be prevented—it is we who must prevent it . . .

Finally, I quote the report with which *Nachrichten für die Truppe* announced the first news of the invasion of Europe. My italics show passages in which we were implementing the deception plan.

ATLANTIC WALL BREACHED IN SEVERAL PLACES
ARMOUR PENETRATES DEEP INTO THE INTERIOR:
BITTER FIGHTING WITH PARACHUTE COMMANDOS

The latest reports show that the Atlantic Wall has been breached in several places by Anglo-American Panzer groups. They landed on the Channel coast of France from the sea two hours after dawn this morning. Severe fighting is reported from Normandy *and the mouth of the Seine* [my italics]. Already yesterday evening strong parachute units and airborne commandos in gliders carrying their own artillery and tanks landed behind the Atlantic Wall. They succeeded in seizing and occupying a number of Luftwaffe air fields. In several places they have joined up with the armoured units advancing from the coast.

From the sea, the air, and from land the defenders of the redoubts of the Atlantic Wall are being remorselessly bombarded. The big guns of British and American battleships are covering the works with a ceaseless hail of the heaviest-calibre armour-piercing shells. Port installations along the coast are likewise under fire. The first port to be attacked was Le Havre. In high and low flying attacks troop concentrations and fortifications from *Normandy to well beyond Calais* [my italics] are being bombed by innumerable bomber squadrons. The bombers are protected on all sides by fighters.

For the German command the situation is still unclear. All attempts at air reconnaissance have failed owing to the overwhelming air superiority of the Anglo-Americans.

Communications with several of the coastal sectors are interrupted so that no orders can be passed and no information is being received.

Alarm grade 3 was proclaimed along the whole of the Atlantic Wall shortly after midnight last night when the first airborne landings were reported. The main invasion, however, did not begin until after daybreak. Long rows of assault boats and tank landing craft escorted by innumerable destroyers, gunboats, and escort vessels of all types approached the coast through a thick smoke screen under cover of the gun fire from the battleships and cruisers.

German motor torpedo-boats from Cherbourg, Le Havre, and Ymuiden were sent out in heroic self-sacrifice against the immeasurably superior invasion fleet.

Index